INSURANCE PLANNING

FUNDAMENTALS OF FINANCIAL PLANNING

SECOND EDITION

Michael A. Dalton
Joseph M. Gillice
Thomas P. Langdon

INSURANCE PLANNING

FUNDAMENTALS OF FINANCIAL PLANNING

SECOND EDITION

MONEY EDUCATION
115 JAMES DRIVE WEST
SUITE 140
ST. ROSE, LA 70087
888-295-6023

Copyright© 2011 by ME. All rights reserved.

No part of this publication may be reproduced or transmitted in any form or by any means, electronic or mechanical, including photocopy, recording, or any other information storage and retrieval system, without prior permission in writing from the publisher. Requests for permission to make copies of any part of the work should be mailed to: Permissions Department, ME, 115 James Drive West, Suite 140, St. Rose, LA 70087.

This publication is designed to provide accurate and authoritative information in regard to the subject matter covered. It is sold with the understanding that the publisher, authors, and contributors are not engaged in rendering legal, accounting, tax, financial planning, or other professional services. If legal advice, tax advice, or other professional assistance is required, the services of a competent professional should be sought.

CFP®, CERTIFIED FINANCIAL PLANNER™, and CFP (with flame logo)® are certification marks owned by Certified Financial Planner Board of Standards Inc. These marks are awarded to individuals who successfully complete CFP Board's initial and ongoing certification requirements.

Printed in the U.S.A.

ISBN-13: - 978-1-936602-04-9

Library of Congress Card Number: - 2011933329

ABOUT THE AUTHORS

Michael A. Dalton, Ph.D., JD, CFP®
- Former Chair of the Board of Dalton Publications, L.L.C.
- Associate professor of Accounting and Taxation at Loyola University in New Orleans, Louisiana
- Adjunct faculty in Financial Planning at Georgetown University in Washington, D.C.
- Former Senior Vice President, Education at BISYS Group
- Ph.D. in Accounting from Georgia State University
- J.D. from Louisiana State University in Baton Rouge, Louisiana
- MBA and BBA in Management and Accounting from Georgia State University
- Former board member of the CFP® Board's Board of Examiners, Board of Standards, and Board of Governors
- Former member (and chair) of the CFP® Board's Board of Examiners
- Member of the Financial Planning Association
- Member of the *Journal of Financial Planning* Editorial Advisory Board
- Member of the *Journal of Financial Planning* Editorial Review Board
- Member of the LSU Law School Board of Trustees (2000 - 2006)
- Author of *Dalton Review for the CFP® Certification Examination: Volume I – Outlines and Study Guides, Volume II – Problems and Solutions, Volume III - Case Exam Book, Mock Exams A-1 and A-2 (1st - 8th Editions)*
- Author of *Retirement Planning and Employee Benefits for Financial Planners (1st - 7th Editions)*
- Co-author of *Estate Planning for Financial Planners (1st - 6th Editions)*
- Co-author of *Income Tax Planning for Financial Planners (1st - 4th Editions)*
- Co-author of *Fundamentals of Financial Planning (1st - 2nd editions)*
- Co-author of *Dalton CFA® Study Notes Volumes I and II (1st - 2nd Editions)*
- Co-author of *Dalton's Personal Financial Planning Series – Personal Financial Planning Theory and Practice (1st - 3rd Editions)*
- Co-author of *Dalton's Personal Financial Planning Series – Personal Financial Planning Cases and Applications (1st - 4th Editions)*
- Co-author of *Cost Accounting: Traditions and Innovations* published by West Publishing Company
- Co-author of the *ABCs of Managing Your Money* published by National Endowment for Financial Education

Joseph M. Gillice, MBA, CPA, CFP®
- President, Dalton Education, L.L.C.
- Former Director of University Programs for BISYS Education Services
- Former adjunct instructor in financial planning at Georgetown University in Washington, D.C.
- Former adjunct instructor in financial planning at Duke University in Durham, NC
- Instructor in live online financial planning programs for Rice University, New York University, and Northwestern University
- Author of *Financial Calculator Essentials*
- Co-author of *Fundamentals of Financial Planning (1st - 2nd Editions)*
- Co-author of *Fundamentals of Financial Planning Insurance Supplement (1st Edition)*
- Author of *Financial Calculator Essentials*

- Co-author of *The Dalton Review® Pre-Study Materials in Fundamentals of Financial Planning and Insurance*
- Co-author of *The Dalton Review® Pre-Study Materials in Investment Planning*
- Co-author of *Fundamentals of Financial Planning* (2nd edition)
- Developed the Online Executive Certificate in Financial Planning program for New York University and Northwestern University
- MBA from Georgia State University
- BS in finance from Florida State University

Thomas P. Langdon, JD, LL.M.
- Professor of Business Law, Gabelli School of Business, Roger Williams University, Bristol, RI
- Principal, Langdon & Langdon Financial Services, LLC (Connecticut-based tax planning & preparation firm)
- Former Professor of Taxation at The American College, Bryn Mawr, PA.
- Former Adjunct Professor of Insurance and Economics at The University of Connecticut Center for Professional Development
- Former Member (and Chair) of the CFP Board's Board of Examiners
- Master of Laws (LL.M.) in Taxation from Villanova University School of Law
- Juris Doctor, from Western New England College School of Law
- Master of Science in Financial Services from The American College
- Master of Business Administration from The University of Connecticut
- Bachelor of Science in Finance from The University of Connecticut, Storrs, CT.
- Chartered Financial Analyst (CFA), Certified Financial Planner (CFP), Chartered Life Underwriter (CLU), Chartered Financial Consultant (ChFC), Accredited Estate Planner (AEP), Chartered Advisor in Philanthropy (CAP), Certified Employee Benefits Specialist (CEBS), Chartered Advisor in Senior Living (CASL), Registered Employee Benefits Consultant (REBC), Registered Health Underwriter (RHU), Associate in Life & Health Claims (ALHC), and Fellow of the Life Management Institute (FLMI)
- Associate Editor of the *Journal of Financial Services Professionals*
- Co-author of *Estate Planning for Financial Planners (1st - 6th Editions)*
- Co-author of *Income Tax Planning for Financial Planners (1st - 4th Editions)*
- Contributing author of *Fundamentals of Financial Planning Insurance Supplement (1st Edition)*
- Contributing author of *Fundamentals of Financial Planning (2nd Edition)*
- Faculty member for National Tax Institute

About the Contributing Author

Randal R. Cangelosi, JD, MBA
- Practicing litigator throughout Louisiana, in commercial law and litigation, products liability litigation, wills and trust litigation, environmental law and litigation, medical malpractice defense, and insurance law and litigation
- Has successfully defended numerous corporations, businesses, and doctors in jury and judge trials
- Juris Doctorate from Loyola University New Orleans
- Masters of Business Administration from Loyola University New Orleans
- BS in Finance from Louisiana State University
- Member of the American & Federal Bar Associations
- Member of the New Orleans and Baton Rouge Bar Associations
- Former Chairman of New Orleans Bar Association, Community Service Committee
- Former Chairman of New Orleans Bar Association, Food and Clothing Drives
- Co-author of *Personal Financial Planning: Theory and Practice (1st - 3rd Editions)*
- Co-author of *Professional Ethics for Financial Planners*

About the Reviewers & Contributors

We owe a special thanks to several key professionals for their significant contribution of time and effort with this text. These reviewers provided meticulous editing, detailed calculation reviews, helpful suggestions for additional content, and other valuable comments, all of which have improved this edition.

Dr. James Coleman has over 15 years teaching experience, including undergraduate, graduate, and Executive MBA programs at Troy University, Mercer University, and Dalton State College. In addition, as Vice President of Market Results, a financial planning training and consulting firm, he has helped hundreds of candidates pass the Certified Financial Planner™ exam over the last decade. Prior to his academic career, Jim spent over a decade in public accounting and corporate management, concluding with the position of Managing Director of Public Relations at Federal Express, where he was responsible for the company's global public and investor relations activities. His degrees include a MS and Ph.D. from University of Alabama as well as BBA in accountancy from University of Mississippi.

Donna Dalton made a significant contribution to this textbook by her thoughtful and meticulous editing throughout the book. She provided many valuable improvements to both the textbook and instructor materials. We are extremely grateful for her contributions. This book would not have been possible without her extraordinary dedication, skill, and knowledge.

Phyllis Duhon made a significant contribution to this textbook by her thoughtful and meticulous reading, rewriting, and editing throughout the book. She provided many valuable suggestions and improvements to both the textbook and instructor materials that significantly improved this edition. We are extremely grateful for her contributions. Ms. Duhon is an attorney and received her J.D. from Loyola University New Orleans College of Law and a B.S. in Business Administration/Finance from the University of New Orleans. She is a contributor to *Estate Planning for Financial Planners, Retirement Planning and Employee Benefits for Financial Planners,* and *Income Tax Planning for Financial Planners* by Money Education.

Randy Martinez is a personal financial planner specializing in personal financial planning, estate, and individual income tax planning. He teaches retirement planning, estate planning, and income tax planning through various CFP® Board-Registered Programs as well as comprehensive reviews for the CFP® certification.

Robin Meyer made a significant contribution to this textbook by organizing and directing the entire project. Developing a textbook that is aesthetically pleasing and easy to read is a difficult undertaking. Robin worked diligently with the authors and reviewers to manage the project, performed numerous reviews, and provided invaluable feedback throughout the entire project. This book would not have been possible without her extraordinary dedication, skill, and knowledge.

Dr. Moshe Shmuklarsky has a keen personal interest in the conceptual underpinning and practical knowledge related to business and personal finance as reflected by his Master of Business Administration from the John Hopkins School of Professional Studies and a Certificate in Personal Financial Planning from the Georgetown University. Dr. Shmuklarsky has more than 25 years experience in research and development of drugs and vaccines. Through the application of the Balanced Score Card, Dr. Shmuklarsky has transformed the Department of Clinical Trials at the Walter Reed Army Institute of Research in Washington DC to a center of excellence in clinical research.

Henry Spil is an adjunct faculty member at Oglethorpe University with 25 years of tax experience. He works for a financial planning firm in Atlanta, Georgia, is a CPA and a CFP® certificant. Mr. Spil is a graduate of Emory University with a Bachelor of Business Administration degree. He also has a Master of Science in Taxation from Florida International University.

Kristi Tafalla is an attorney and personal financial planner specializing in income tax and estate planning. She teaches estate planning, income tax planning and comprehensive case courses through various CFP® Board-Registered Programs as well as comprehensive reviews for the CFP® certification. She is a contributor to Money Education's Estate Planning for Financial Planners and Retirement Planning and Employee Benefits for Financial Planners.

Steve Wetzel is the President and founder of a financial planning firm in Pennsylvania. He is both the program director and adjunct professor for the financial planning program at New York University. Mr. Wetzel received his BA in Economics from State University of New York – Stony Brook. He also received his MBA in Finance and International Business from New York University along with his Advanced Professional Certificate in Accounting. Mr. Wetzel is also a CFP® certificant.

Bill Yurkovac has a private practice in Florida focusing on asset management and estate planning considerations for his clientele. Mr. Yurkovac holds a Master's Degree in Education, has more than twenty-five years experience in the financial services arena, and enjoys serving as an instructor for candidates preparing for the CFP® Certification Examination. Current community involvement includes assisting and counseling several nonprofit organizations and a chair on the local Estate Planning Council's Board of Directors.

ACKNOWLEDGEMENTS & SPECIAL THANKS

We are most appreciative for the tremendous support and encouragement we have received throughout this project. We are extremely grateful to the instructors and program directors of CFP® Board-Registered programs who provided valuable comments during the development stages of this text. We are fortunate to have dedicated, careful readers at several institutions who were willing to share their needs, expectations, and time with us.

A special thanks to several of Dr. Dalton's financial planning students at Georgetown University. The students reviewed numerous chapters of this textbook and provided valuable feedback regarding 1st edition improvements.

We would like to pay special thanks to Donna Dalton and Robin Meyer. It takes more than just the writer to produce a finished book and they are an essential element of our team. Thanks also goes out to Desktop Miracles for designing our new cover and chapter title artwork.

PREFACE

Fundamentals of Financial Planning is written for graduate and upperdivision undergraduate level students interested in acquiring an understanding of financial planning from a professional financial planning viewpoint. The text is intended to be used in a Fundamentals course as part of an overall curriculum in financial planning. The text is also intended to serve as a reference for practicing professional financial planners.

This text was designed to meet the educational requirements for a Fundamentals Course in a CFP® Board-Registered Program. Therefore, one of our goals is to assure CFP® Board-Registered Program Directors, instructors, students, and financial planners that we have addressed every relevant topic covered by the CFP® Board Exam Topic List and the most recent model curriculum syllabus for this course. The book will be updated, as needed, to keep current with any changes in the law, exam topic list, or model curriculum.

Special Features

A variety of tools and presentation methods are used throughout this text to assist the reader in the learning process. Some of the features in this text that are designed to enhance your understanding and learning process include:

- **Key Concepts** – At the beginning of each subsection are key concepts, or study objectives, each stated as a question. To be successful in this course, you should be able to answer these questions. So as you read, guide your learning by looking for the answers. When you find the answers, highlight or underline them. It is important that you actually highlight/underline and not just make a mental note, as the action of stopping and writing reinforces your learning. Watch for this symbol:

- **Quick Quizzes** – Following each subsection you will find a Quick Quiz, which checks and reinforces what you read. Circle the answer to each question and then check your answers against the correct answers supplied at the bottom of the quiz. If you missed any questions, flip back to the relevant section and review the material. Watch for this symbol:

- **Examples** – Examples are used frequently to illustrate the concepts being discussed and to help the reader understand and apply the concepts presented. Examples are identified in the margin with the following symbol:

EXAMPLE

- **Exhibits** – The written text is enhanced and simplified by using exhibits where appropriate to promote learning and application. Exhibits are identified with the following symbol:

  EXHIBIT

- **Key Terms** – Key terms appear in **boldfaced type** throughout the text to assist in the identification of important concepts and terminology. A list of key terms with definitions appears at the end of each chapter.

- **End of Chapter Questions** – Each chapter contains a series of discussion and multiple-choice questions that highlight the major topics covered in the chapter. The questions test retention and understanding of important chapter material and can be used for review and classroom discussion.

- **Quick Quiz Explanations** – Each chapter concludes with the answers to the Quick Quizzes contained in that chapter, as well as explanation to the "false" statements in each Quick Quiz.

- **Glossary** – A compilation of the key terms identified throughout the text is located at the end of the book.

Additional Information Available on Money Education's Website (money-education.com)
- Time Value of Money Formulas
- CFP Job Knowledge Requirements
- Resourceful Websites
- Cost of Living Adjustments (COLA) Increases

VISIT OUR WEBSITE AT MONEY-EDUCATION.COM FOR UPDATES TO THE TEXT

Table of Contents

Chapter 1 - Characteristics of Insurance

Introduction 1
Categories of Risk 2
    Pure and Speculative Risk 2
    Subjective and Objective Risk 3
    Fundamental and Particular Risk 3
    Nonfinancial and Financial Risk 4
    Probability of Loss 4
    Law of Large Numbers 4

Risk Management Process 5
    Determining the Objectives of the Risk Management Program 5
    Identifying the Risk to Which the Individual is Exposed 6
    Evaluating the Identified Risks for the Probability and the Severity of the Loss 7
    Determining and Selecting the Best Risk Management Alternative 7
    Implementing the Risk Management Plan Selected 10
    Periodically Evaluating and Reviewing the Risk Management Program 10

Causes of Financial Loss 11
    Perils 11
    Hazards 12
    Large Number of Homogeneous Exposures 14

Requisites for an Insurable Risk 14
    Insured Losses Must be Accidental 15
    Loss Must be Measurable and Determinable 15
    Loss Must Not be Financially Catastrophic to the Insurer 16
    Premium Must be Reasonable 17

Law of Insurance Contracts 18
    Mutual Consent 18
    Offer and Acceptance 18
    Performance or Delivery 19

Lawful Purpose 20
Legal Competence of All Parties 20

Legal Principles of Insurance Contracts 20
Principle of Indemnity 20
Principle of Insurable Interest 21
Principle of Utmost Good Faith 22

Unique Legal Characteristics of Insurance Contracts 24
Adhesion 24
Aleatory 24
Unilateral 25
Conditional 25
Personal 25

Law of Agency 26
Express Authority 26
Implied Authority 26
Apparent Authority 27
Waiver 27
Estoppel 28
Types of Insurance Companies 29
Agents and Brokers 29

Characteristics of Insurance Companies 29
Reinsurance 30
Policy Provisions 31

Important Provisions and Features of Insurance Contracts 31
Riders and Endorsements 33

Underwriting and Managing Adverse Selection 33
Deductibles and Co-payments 34
Coinsurance 35
Actual Cash Value 37
Replacement Cost 37

Valuing Property for Losses 37
Appraised or Agreed Upon Value 38

Regulating the Insurance Industry 38
Legislative 39
Judicial 39
Executive or State Insurance Commissioner 39
National Association of Insurance Commissioners (NAIC) 39
Insurance Rate Regulation 40
Prior Approval Law 40
File and Use Law 40
Use and File Law 40
Open Competition 40

Selecting an Insurance Company 41

Key Terms 42

Discussion Questions	46
Multiple-Choice Problems	48
Quick Quiz Explanations	52

Chapter 2 - Life and Disability Insurance

Introduction	55
Parties to a Life Insurance Contract	**56**
Risk Exposures from Dying Early	58
Life Insurance and Mortality Risk	**58**
Measuring the Life Insurance Need	60
Types and Uses of Life Insurance in Financial Planning	**68**
Term Insurance	68
Universal Life Insurance	73
Whole Life Insurance	75
Variable Life Insurance	80
Modified Endowment Contracts (MECs)	82
Group-Term Insurance	82
Other Types of Group Life Insurance	84
Common Life Insurance Contract Policy Provisions	**84**
Grace Period	84
Incontestability	85
Misstatement of Age or Gender	85
Suicide	86
Reinstatement	86
Policy Loan Provisions	86
Beneficiary Designations	87
Survivorship Clauses	87
Simultaneous Death Provisions	88
Assignment	88
Aviation Exclusion	88
War Exclusion	89
Settlement Options for Life Insurance	**89**
Lump-Sum Payment	89
Interest Only	89
Annuity Payments	89
Taxation of Life Insurance Policies	**91**
Premium Payments	91
Death Benefit Taxation	92
Taxation of Lifetime Benefits	92
Policy Exchanges	94
Transfer for Value	95
Viatical Settlements	95

Accelerated Benefits Provision 96
Annuity Contracts for Life or for Term 96
   Types of Annuities 96
   Timing of Annuity Payments 97
   Taxation of Annuities 98
Disability Insurance 98
   Amount of Coverage 98
   Term of Coverage 99
   Types of Disability Insurance Policies 99
   Typical Provisions in Disability Income Policies 100
   Benefit Period 101
   Partial Disability 101
   Other Disability Policy Provisions 101
   Renewability 102
   Residual Benefit Provision 102
   Group Disability Insurance 103
   Taxation of Disability Insurance Benefits 104

Conclusion 104
Key Terms 105
Discussion Questions 109
Multiple-Choice Problems 111
Quick Quiz Explanations 115

Chapter 3 - Health and Long-Term Care Insurance

Introduction 117
Group Health Insurance 118
   Eligibility 118
   Features of Group Health Insurance 119
Individual Health Insurance 121
   Need for Coverage 121
   Cost of Individual Policies 122
   Eligibility 122
   Types of Individual Policies 122
   Health Insurance Policy Provisions 124
Types of Groups and Individual Plans 127
   Indemnity Health Insurance 127
   Managed Care Insurance 127
Policy Provisions 130
   Preexisting Conditions 130
   Incontestability Clause 131
   Grace Period 131

  Renewability 131

Taxation and Health Insurance 132
Consolidated Omnibus Budget Reconciliation Act of 1985 (COBRA) 133
Health Savings Accounts 135
  Eligibility 136
  High Deductible Health Insurance Plans 137
  Contribution Limitations 137
  Distributions 138

Long-Term Care Insurance 138
  Need for Coverage 140
  Types of Coverage Provided by Long-Term Care Insurance 142
  Long-Term Care Benefit Periods 143
  Tax-Qualified Long-Term Care Contracts 144
  Conditions that Trigger Long-Term Care Coverage 144

Conclusion 145
Key Terms 146
Discussion Questions 148
Multiple-Choice Problems 149
Quick Quiz Explanations 153

Chapter 4 - Property and Liability Insurance

Introduction 155
Personal Property and Liability Insurance 155
  Homeowners (HO) Insurance: Basic Coverages 156
  Summary of General Exclusions (Perils Excluded) 157
  Summary of Section I Coverages 158
  Summary of Section II Coverages 162

Homeowners (HO) Insurance: Basic Forms 166
  HO-2: Broad Form 167
  HO-3: Special Form 167
  HO-4: Contents Broad Form (Designed for Tenants/Renters) 167
  HO-5: Comprehensive Form 168
  HO-6: Unit Owners Form (for Condominium Owners) 168
  HO-8: Modified Form 168

Homeowners (HO) Insurance: Available Endorsements 168
  Replacement Cost for Personal Property 168
  All-Risks Coverage for Personal Property (Open Perils) 168
  Inflation Protection 169
  Earthquake and Sink Hole Collapse Insurance 169
  Refrigerated Property Coverage 169
  Sewer Backup Coverage 169

Personal Injury	170
Business Pursuits	170
Watercraft	170
Other Endorsements	170
Section I Conditions	171

Homeowners Insurance Contractual Conditions ... 171
Section II Conditions ... 173
Sections I and II Conditions ... 174

Automobile Insurance ... 177
The Legal Environment for the Automobile ... 177
Cost of Automobile Insurance ... 178
Summary of Automobile Coverage ... 178

Personal Auto Policy (PAP) Coverages ... 178
Eligible Autos ... 179
Important Policy Definitions ... 179
Part A: Liability Coverage ... 180
Part B: Medical Payments ... 183
Part C: Uninsured Motorists ... 184
Part D: Coverage for Damage to Your Auto ... 185
Part E: Duties after an Accident or Loss ... 186
Part F: General Provisions ... 187

Legal Liability ... 187

Personal Liability Umbrella Policy (PLUP) ... 189
Purpose ... 189
Characteristics ... 189
Exclusions ... 190

Business and Professional Property and Liability Insurance ... 190
The Commercial Package Policy (CPP) ... 190
Inland Marine Policies ... 191
The Business Owner's Policy (BOP) ... 191
Business Liability Insurance ... 191
Workers' Compensation Insurance ... 192
Business Auto Policy (BAP) ... 192
Commercial Liability Umbrella Policy ... 192
Malpractice Insurance ... 192
Errors and Omissions Insurance ... 192
Products Liability Insurance ... 193

Key Terms ... 194

Discussion Questions ... 196

Multiple-Choice Problems ... 197

Quick Quiz Explanations ... 201

Chapter 5 - Social Security

Introduction 203
Social Security Taxes and Contributions 205
    Covered Workers and Insured Status 209
Social Security Benefits – Eligibility and Calculations 209
    Social Security Beneficiaries 210
    Social Security Retirement Benefits – A Closer Look 213
    The Retirement Benefit Calculation 214
Taxation of Social Security Benefits 226
Other Social Security Benefits 232
    Disability Benefits and Disability Insured 232
    Family Benefits 233
    Survivors' Benefits 233
The Maximum Family Benefit 234
Medicare Benefits 236
    Medicare Part D Subsidy 239
    Other Medicare Health Plan Choices 240
Supplemental Security Income Benefits 241
Other Issues 242
    Effect of Marriage or Divorce on Benefits 242
Filing for Social Security Claims 242
    Change of Name 243
    Leaving the United States 243
Key Terms 246
Discussion Questions 248
Multiple-Choice Problems 249
Quick Quiz Explanations 253

Appendix

Appendix A: Glossary 255
Appendix B: Index 271

Characteristics of Insurance

CHAPTER 1

INTRODUCTION

Insurance is a product for individuals and companies to transfer risks and the financial uncertainty regarding those risks to third party insurers. These individuals and companies pay a premium to an insurance company, which determines premiums based upon the expected claims to be paid out during a given time period. The theory behind insurance is that individuals and companies are pooling their premium dollars, so that anyone in the pool of similar risks that suffers a financial loss, will be able to recoup most (if not all) of those financial losses. The third party insurer is providing a convenient way to pool and manage those risks that it insurers.

Insurance coverage is usually a critical component of a personal comprehensive financial plan. As a financial planner, it is important to have an in-depth understanding of various types of risk exposures, appropriate types of insurance and dollar amounts of appropriate coverage for a client. The most important types of risk most individuals need insurance coverage for include:
- Life insurance to protect against premature death of the primary wage earner of a family;
- Health insurance to protect against injury or sickness for all family members;
- Disability insurance to protect against the loss of income from the inability to work due to sickness or accident;
- Property insurance to protect a home, personal property and the personal auto;
- Long-term care insurance to provide benefits for custodial care; and
- Personal liability insurance to protect personal assets and earnings from potential liability judgments.

One of the financial planner's responsibility is to assist the client in avoiding catastrophic financial consequences in the event of a loss. This chapter will explore types of insurable risks, elements of an insurance contract, legal characteristics of an insurance contract, the risk management process, and risk management techniques.

CATEGORIES OF RISK

Insurance is simply a legal contract between the insured and the insurance company (insurer), by which the insured transfers risks to the insurer and the insured pays a premium to the insurer. In return, the insured receives a promise from the insurer to pay in the event the insured experiences a covered financial loss. There are certain types of risks than can be transferred to an insurance company, while other risks are uninsurable. These uninsurable risks are discussed later in this chapter. Risk is defined as the chance of loss, uncertainty associated with loss, or the possibility of a loss. Risk can be divided into four categories:

- Pure and Speculative Risk
- Subjective and Objective Risk
- Fundamental and Particular Risk
- Nonfinancial and Financial Risk

Key Concepts

Underline/highlight the answers to these questions as you read:

1. Distinguish between pure risk and speculative risk.

2. Identify the differences between subjective and objective risks.

3. Determine why the law of large numbers is useful for insurance companies.

PURE AND SPECULATIVE RISK

Pure risk is the chance of a loss or no loss occurring. With pure risks, there is no chance of experiencing a gain. An example of a pure risk is, either your car is in an accident and damaged or it's not. Pure risks are insurable, since an insurance company is only going to pay when the insured actually suffers a financial loss. Pure risks include many of the same risks all individuals are exposed to and the types of risk a planner must evaluate and plan for each client. Examples of pure risks include:

- Premature death of a primary wage earner.
- A prolonged illness or injury of client or family member.
- The inability of the client to work because of sickness or accident.
- Wind damage to personal residence.
- The inability of the client to take care of himself in old age.
- A legal judgment against the client due as the result of negligence.

Speculative risk is the chance of loss, no loss, or a profit. Speculative risk is the risk that an investor takes when buying a stock or an entrepreneur takes when starting a business. The investor or entrepreneur makes an investment and takes the risk in the hopes of experiencing a profit. Insurance is not available for speculative risks because most speculative risks are willingly entered into for the purpose of earning a profit.

SUBJECTIVE AND OBJECTIVE RISK

Subjective risk is the risk that an individual perceives based on their prior experiences and the severity of those experiences. Individuals perceive risks differently and their behavior in addressing that risk depends upon how they perceive the risk. If an individual perceives the subjective risk to be high, then the individual will take appropriate steps to reduce the subjective risk.

> **EXAMPLE 1.1**
>
> Every Friday night, Brandon and Ivan go to their local bar to celebrate the start of a new weekend. They typically have multiple shots of whisky and wash them down with a few mojitos. One Friday night, while driving home, Brandon is pulled over and arrested for DUI. Brandon serves six months in jail, pays a $10,000 fine, and serves 200 hours of community service. Ivan on the other hand, manages to drive home each Friday night without being stopped. The next time Brandon and Ivan go out, Brandon currently has one drink and calls a cab to drive him home. Ivan on the other hand, has multiple drinks, gets in his car and drives home. Brandon currently has higher subjective risk than Ivan, because Brandon perceives severe negative consequences of another DUI. Objective risk in this case is measured by blood alcohol level.

Objective risk is the variation of the actual frequency and amount of losses that occur over a period of time compared to the expected frequency and amount of losses. As the number of loss exposures (or the pool of insureds) increases, objective risk is reduced because the actual results are more likely to approximate expected claims. Objective risk varies indirectly with the number of loss exposures in an insured pool. The better an insurer is able to manage its objective risk, the more efficiently they can determine premiums.

> **EXAMPLE 1.2**
>
> An insurance company has 50,000 auto policies and expects to pay claims on 10% or 5,000 policies during the year. The actual claims for the year are 4,900 which are 100 less claims than the insurance company expected. The variation between expected claims of 5,000 and actual claims of 4,900 is objective risk. Objective risk is generally measurable while subjective risk is a feeling.

FUNDAMENTAL AND PARTICULAR RISK

Fundamental risk is a risk that can impact a large number of individuals at one time, such as an earthquake or flood. Fundamental risks are difficult for insurers to insure, because they can lead to severe financial consequences for the insurance company. Some fundamental risks are uninsurable such as war or a nuclear hazard. Other fundamental risks are insurable such as an earthquake or flood, but a separate earthquake or flood insurance policy is necessary. Some fundamental risks, such as flood insurance or unemployment insurance, require government support or social insurance programs.

A **particular risk** is a risk that can impact a particular individual, such as death or the inability to work because of a sickness or accident. An important difference between fundamental risk and particular risk is that fundamental risk will impact a large group of individuals simultaneously, whereas a particular risk only impacts an individual.

NONFINANCIAL AND FINANCIAL RISK

Nonfinancial risk is a risk that would result in a loss, other than a monetary loss. An example of nonfinancial risk is the emotional distress a family experiences when a loved one dies. **Financial risk** is a loss of financial value, such as the premature death of a family's primary wage earner. Life insurance can protect against this financial risk, help the family achieve financial goals and provide a lump-sum amount to pay expenses for the family during the grieving process; however no insurance can help the family with the emotional distress from losing a loved one.

PROBABILITY OF LOSS

The probability of loss is the chance that a loss will occur. For example, suppose historical data establishes that 1 in 10 males (10%) age 50 are going to become disabled in a year. It's possible with a sample size of 10 that all 10 could become disabled or that none of the sample become disabled. As the pool of insureds increases to 100,000, it's more likely that the actual number of disability claims for the pool will be 10 percent as expected. The larger the sample size the more likely that the actual losses will approach the expected losses.

LAW OF LARGE NUMBERS

The **law of large numbers** is a principle that states that actual outcomes will approach the mean probability as the sample size increases. So, if a coin is flipped 10 times, we would expect five heads and five tails. However, with only ten flips, it is more likely that the actual results will be different than a 50/50 distribution between heads and tails. Here is a computer simulation of a coin being flipped 10 times. This exercise was conducted five times, with the following results for each.

Quick Quiz 1.1

Highlight the answer to these questions:

1. Pure risks include many of the same risks all individuals are exposed to and the types of risk a planner must evaluate and plan for each client.
   a. True
   b. False

2. Subjective risk is the variation of actual amount of losses that occur over a period of time compared to the expected amount of losses.
   a. True
   b. False

3. The law of large numbers is useful for insurance companies because the larger the insured pool, the more likely actual losses will approach the probability of losses.
   a. True
   b. False

True, False, True.

Round	Heads vs. Tails	Result
Round 1	2 vs. 8	20/80
Round 2	3 vs. 7	30/70
Round 3	6 vs. 4	60/40
Round 4	4 vs. 6	40/60
Round 5	7 vs. 3	70/30
Total	22 vs. 28	44/56

With a small sample size the average result was 44 percent heads and 56 percent tails. When the computer simulation determines the outcome of 100 coin flips, the percentage of heads versus tails is 48.5 percent heads and 51.5 percent tails; however at 1,000 flips the percentage is 49.4 percent heads and 50.6 percent tails. As sample size increases, the actual results of the coin flips approach the expected probability of 50/50. The law of large numbers is useful for insurance companies because the larger the insured pool, the more likely actual losses will approach the expected losses, therefore reducing forecasting error and objective risk. This results in insurance premiums that are more efficient and thus lower in terms of cost to the insured.

RISK MANAGEMENT PROCESS

Part of the "analyze and evaluate" step in the financial planning process requires that a planner perform the risk management process. The risk management process includes the financial planner reviewing all of the client's risk exposures and determining the appropriate risk management technique for each risk. The risk management process includes:

- Determining the objectives of the risk management program.
- Identifying the risk to which the individual is exposed.
- Evaluating the identified risks for the probability and severity of the loss.
- Determining the alternatives for managing the risks.
- Selecting the most appropriate alternative for each risk.
- Implementing the risk management plan selected.
- Periodically evaluating and reviewing the risk management program.

Key Concepts

Underline/highlight the answers to these questions as you read:

1. Explain the risk management process.

2. Describe the four responses to pure risks.

3. Identify the most appropriate risks to insure based on loss severity and loss frequency.

DETERMINING THE OBJECTIVES OF THE RISK MANAGEMENT PROGRAM

The first step in the risk management process is to determine the objectives of the risk management program. Risk management objectives can range from obtaining the most cost-effective protection against risk to protection for continuing income after a loss. An example of a client's stated objective may be to insure only those risks that have the potential for causing catastrophic financial loss to the client and to do so at the minimum premium.

IDENTIFYING THE RISK TO WHICH THE INDIVIDUAL IS EXPOSED

The next step is to identify all possible pure risk exposures of the client. *Identifying the potential risk* is primarily a function of the client's lifecycle position. The risk exposures for an individual may be subdivided into: (1) personal risks that may cause the loss of income (untimely death, disability, health issues), or alternatively cause an increase in the cost of living (disability, health issues), (2) property risks that may cause the loss of property (automobile, home, or other asset), and (3) liability risks that may cause financial loss (injury to another or to property for which the client is determined to be financially responsible).

The client's lifecycle position will help to determine if the client needs to protect against premature death, disability, and long-term care. The following chart identifies the likely potential risks for a specific client based on the client's lifecycle position.

EXAMPLE 1.3

Frank (age 33) and Stephanie (age 31) are married with one child, Frankie (age 10). Frank and Stephanie both work, each earning $60,000 per year. They have a 30 year mortgage, with 25 years remaining, and two car loans. They want to retire at age 62 and they plan to pay for Frankie's college education.

Potential Risks	Relevant	Reason
Life (Premature Death)	✓	They will need a lump-sum amount to retire their debt, provide for their retirement and education goals.
Health	✓	They need health insurance to cover major medical expenses.
Disability	✓	During their working years, disability coverage provides protection if one of them is unable to work because of sickness or accident.
Property	✓	The residence and personal autos should be insured because any loss could have catastrophic financial consequences.
Long-Term Care		They are too young to need long-term care which is more relevant in their 50's.
Personal Liability	✓	The risk of a lawsuit due to their negligence should be insured.

EXAMPLE 1.4

Matt (age 66) and Elma (age 65) are married with four adult children and ten grandchildren. Matt and Elma are both retired, on Social Security, and have significant retirement savings. They own their primary residence and two autos that are debt free. They do not believe they will be subject to estate taxes. Their risks are identified below:

Potential Risks	Relevant	Reason
Life (Premature Death)		They have already reached retirement, have zero debt and do not need insurance to pay estate taxes.
Health	✓	Health insurance is important, although they qualify for Medicare at age 65. They may consider supplemental insurance to pay for gaps in Medicare (discussed later in the Social Security chapter).
Disability		They are already collecting retirement benefits, so they are not concerned about not being able to work for income.
Property	✓	The residence and personal autos should be insured because any loss could have catastrophic financial consequences.
Long-Term Care	✓	The risk of needing adult day care based on their age is relevant.
Personal Liability	✓	The risk of a lawsuit due to their negligence should be insured.

EVALUATING THE IDENTIFIED RISKS FOR THE PROBABILITY AND THE SEVERITY OF THE LOSS

Once the potential risks are identified, the planner must analyze each of the risks based on expected loss frequency and loss severity. When evaluating risks based on their expected loss frequency we are attempting to determine how often the event is likely to occur. Loss severity measures the dollar magnitude or the absolute dollar amount of the expected financial loss were it to occur. Based on the relationship between expected loss frequency and loss severity, an appropriate risk management response to the risk can be identified and implemented. Only those risks that have severe financial consequences but occur infrequently are appropriate to transfer or insure. Insurance is most appropriate for those risks that have severe financial consequences but occur infrequently. Examples include the inability to work because of sickness or accident, premature death, an auto accident or a house fire.

DETERMINING AND SELECTING THE BEST RISK MANAGEMENT ALTERNATIVE

Selecting the appropriate risk management technique is the most critical component of the risk management process. A risk that is not properly managed may have severe financial consequences for the client. To determine the appropriate response to a pure risk, we must understand the techniques for risk management, which include:
- Risk Reduction
- Risk Transfer
- Risk Avoidance
- Risk Retention

A planner may use a matrix to analyze each risk, such as:

Severity / Frequency	Low Frequency of Occurrence	High Frequency of Occurrence
High Severity (catastrophic financial loss) (e.g., long-term disability)	Transfer and/or Share Risk Using Insurance	Avoid Risk
Low Severity (non-catastrophic financial loss) (e.g., car gets dented in parking lot)	Retain Risk	Retain/Reduce Risk

Risk Reduction

Risk reduction is the process of reducing the likelihood of a pure risk that is high in frequency and low in severity. Examples of risks that are high in frequency and low in severity are: car door dings, the common cold, and damage to inexpensive personal property. Risks that are high in frequency and low in severity are risks that should be reduced by taking steps to reduce the likelihood of a loss occurring.

Risk	Risk Reduction Implementation
Car Door Dings	Do not park a car next to other cars.
The Common Cold	Exercise, take vitamins, eat healthy foods, and wash hands frequently.
Damage to Household Property	Do not let children play with a ball in the house.

EXAMPLE 1.5

Joe and Holly are married with two children, ages 8 and 4. They have a two-car garage where Holly parks her SUV next to Joe's car. Every time Holly parks her SUV next to Joe's car in the garage, the 4 year old opens the door of the SUV and a new ding is put in the side of Joe's car. After six months, there are multiple door dings in the side of Joe's car. The frequency of the door dings is high, but the severity of having the door dings fixed is relatively low, just a couple hundred dollars.

The appropriate steps for Joe and Holly would be to help the 4-year old to open the door of the SUV, or for Joe to park his car in the driveway.

Risk Transfer

Risk transfer involves transferring a low frequency and high severity risk to a third party, such as an insurance company. Examples of risks that are low in frequency but high in severity include disability (or the inability to work), premature death, or damage to a personal residence. These risks don't occur very often, but when they do, there are severe financial consequences that should be transferred and insured.

EXAMPLE 1.6

Erica (age 33) and Daniel (age 35) are married with two young children, ages 2 and 4. Erica works as a vice-president of marketing earning $125,000 per year and Daniel works in the home taking care of the children. Erica and Daniel own a house with an outstanding mortgage of $400,000, they have saved $75,000 for retirement and anticipate needing $1.25 million. They have not started saving for their children's college education but they anticipate needing $80,000. Erica and Daniel are concerned about Erica becoming disabled or her premature death, and the family not having the financial resources to payoff the mortgage or fund their retirement and education goals. Disability and premature death are risks that are low in frequency but high in financial severity. Both disability and premature death are risks that should be transferred.

Risk Retention or Accepting the Risk

Risk retention is accepting some or all of the potential loss exposure for risk that are low in frequency and low in severity. Examples of risks that are low in frequency and severity include minor property damage to a personal residence or personal auto. Deductibles and co-payment are a form of risk retention where the insured is sharing in the first dollar of a financial loss. Risk retention is an appropriate risk management strategy for risks that are low in frequency and low in severity.

EXAMPLE 1.7

Liz has a young daughter Ashley (age 16). Liz just purchased a car for Ashley, which is a 1977 VW Bug, for $500. Liz decided not to purchase collision insurance on the car, since the severity of a loss would be $500. Liz is retaining the risk of the car being totaled and suffering a financial loss of 100% or $500.

However, Liz would need liability insurance in the event Ashley was in an accident and sued. A judgment against Ashley (and Liz) could potentially have severe financial consequences and the liability portion of the risk should be transferred/insured.

Risk Avoidance

Risk avoidance is a risk management technique used for any risks that are high in frequency and high in severity. Activities that will very frequently result in severe financial consequences should be avoided.

EXAMPLE 1.8

Dave is an avid smoker and smokes about 3 packs of cigarettes per day. As a matter of fact, just before he falls asleep at night, he smokes one last cigarette in bed.

EXAMPLE 1.9 Brandon likes to drink heavily while tailgating before a football game. During the football game, Brandon drinks heavily and then after the football game, has a few more drinks before driving home.

Both examples, smoking in bed and drunk driving, are risks that will frequently lead to a loss (house fire or DUI accident) and result in high severity or a large financial loss. High frequency and high severity risks should be avoided. Avoidance can be applied to many pure risks, such as:

- The risk of being injured on a construction site – avoid the construction site.
- The risk of dying in a private plane crash – avoid flying in private planes.
- The risk of getting a DUI – avoid drunk driving.
- The risk of getting into an accident while talking or texting on a cell phone – avoid cell phone use while driving.

IMPLEMENTING THE RISK MANAGEMENT PLAN SELECTED

The planner should work closely with the client to insure implementation of appropriate risk management techniques. Simply identifying and selecting the risk management technique is insufficient without implementation. The risk management plan should reflect the chosen response to a risk scenario. If risk reduction is the appropriate response to a given risk, the proper risk reduction program must be designed and implemented. If a decision is made to retain a risk, the individual must determine whether an emergency fund will be used (e.g., pet needs medical care). If the response to a given risk is to transfer the risk through insurance, an assessment and selection of an insurer usually follows.

PERIODICALLY EVALUATING AND REVIEWING THE RISK MANAGEMENT PROGRAM

The purpose for periodic evaluation and review is twofold. First, the risk management process does not take place independently from external influences. Things change over time, and risk exposures can change as well. The risk management response that was suitable last year may not be the most appropriate this year, and adjustments may need to be a made.

Quick Quiz 1.2

Highlight the answer to these questions:

1. Selecting the appropriate risk management technique is the most critical component of the risk management process.
   a. True
   b. False

2. Risk reduction is the process of avoiding the likelihood of a pure risk that is high in frequency and low in severity.
   a. True
   b. False

3. Risk transfer involves transferring a high frequency and high severity risk to a third party, such as an insurance company.
   a. True
   b. False

True, False, False.

> **EXAMPLE 1.10**
>
> The first time Kathy met with her financial planner was three years ago. At that time, Kathy was single, age 30, earning $80,000 per year and renting a home. Today, Kathy is married, age 33, and has two young children, John age 1.5 years old and Bob 3 months old. Kathy's salary is now $125,000 per year and her husband works from home and takes care of the children. Three years ago, her financial planner would have recommended disability insurance, renter's insurance, and possibly a small life insurance policy. Now that Kathy is married, with children and a homeowner, the planner would continue to recommend disability insurance, but also homeowner's insurance and significant life insurance. Without periodic monitoring of a client's risks, it is possible to have new risks that are not properly managed or inappropriate amounts of coverage. In Kathy's example, she likely needed a small amount of life insurance while single; but after getting married, having children, and purchasing a home, she needs significantly more life insurance.

Errors in judgment regarding the selected alternatives may occur, and periodic reviews allow the planner and client to discover such errors and revise the risk management plan as appropriate.

CAUSES OF FINANCIAL LOSS

PERILS

Perils are the immediate cause and reason for a loss occurring. Perils can be the result of an accident or sickness. Common perils include accidental death, disability caused by sickness or accident, and property losses caused by fire, windstorm, tornado, earthquake, burglary, and, collision of an automobile.

Perils can be specifically insured (named) in an insurance policy on a "named peril" basis where only specific perils listed in the policy are covered. Alternatively, a policy can cover perils on an "open perils" basis, which covers all perils, unless specifically identified and excluded.

EXHIBIT 1.1 — TYPICAL COVERED PERILS FOR AUTO AND HOME

Personal Auto Policy (PAP)	Homeowners Insurance Policy (HO)
Fire	Fire
Storm	Lightning
Theft	Windstorm
Collision	Hail
Hail	Riot
Flood	Falling Objects
Contact with a Bird or Animal	Weight of Ice, Snow, and Sleet
Falling Objects	Smoke
Earthquake	Explosion
Windstorm	Theft

The above list is not complete, but is an example of some of the perils covered by each policy.

HAZARDS

Hazards are a specific condition that increases the likelihood of a loss occurring. A hazard does not cause the actual loss, but simply increases the probability of a loss. There are three types of hazards:
- Moral
- Morale
- Physical

The underwriter of the insurer must be aware of and be able to identify and manage these hazards.

> **Key Concepts**
>
> Underline/highlight the answers to these questions as you read:
>
> 1. Identify typical perils covered under a personal auto policy.
>
> 2. Identify typical perils covered under a homeowner's insurance policy.
>
> 3. Differentiate between moral, morale, and physical hazards.

Moral Hazard

Moral hazard is that potential loss because of the moral character of the insured such as the filing of a false claim with the insurance company. Burning down your own house or claiming a theft occurred when it did not are all types of moral hazard. Insurance companies cannot insure false claims because insurance is only meant to provide coverage in the event of an actual financial loss not intentionally caused or fraudulently claimed by the insured.

EXAMPLE 1.11 — Maurice, a famous college football player for State University, filed a false police report that he had $10,000 worth of clothing, cash, and CDs stolen from a borrowed car. There actually was no theft. The football player was hoping to collect a $10,000 check from the insurance company for the alleged stolen items, however he found himself in jail charged with filing a false police report.

The filing of a false insurance claim is an example of a moral hazard and cannot be insured. If false claims were paid by insurers, it would results in increased premiums and people that actually need insurance would be unable to afford the insurance products.

Morale Hazard

Morale hazard is defined as indifference to risk created because the insured has insurance. Consider the person that drives to a convenience store to purchase a gallon of milk. They pull into the parking spot, leave the keys in the ignition, the car running and doors unlocked, while they enter the convenience store. This person is not concerned about their car being stolen perhaps because they have auto insurance.

From an insurer's perspective, they want to incentivize an insured to prevent morale hazard. The way an insurer accomplishes this is through the use of deductibles. With a deductible, the insured pays the first dollars of loss until the deductible is satisfied. Thus, when an insured is considering leaving the keys in the ignition and the car running while they are in a convenience store, the insured may stop and think "do I want to risk paying a $500 or $1,000 deductible if my car is stolen?" Deductibles help to align the best interest of the insurer and the insured to reduce the risk of morale hazard.

Quick Quiz 1.3

Highlight the answer to these questions:

1. Perils can be specifically covered in an insurance policy on a "named peril" basis where only specific perils listed in the policy are covered.
   a. True
   b. False

2. Physical hazard is indifference to a loss created because the insured has insurance.
   a. True
   b. False

True, False.

Physical Hazard

Physical hazard is a physical condition that increases the likelihood of a loss occurring. Examples of physical hazards include wet floors, icy roads or roads with poor lighting. A physical hazard doesn't actually cause the accident or the loss, it's just a condition that increases the probability of a loss occurring.

EXAMPLE 1.12

Peter is walking down the sidewalk to the local hardware store. While looking across the street he doesn't notice the banana peel on the sidewalk, steps on it, slips and falls breaking his arm. The banana peel was a physical hazard that increased the likelihood of someone falling.

REQUISITES FOR AN INSURABLE RISK

Not all risks are created equally, and not all risks are insurable. A risk that is ideally situated to be an insured risk meets the following requirements:
1. It has a large number of homogeneous exposures.
2. The insured losses must be accidental, from the insured's point of view.
3. The insured losses must be measurable and determinable.
4. The loss must not be financially catastrophic to the insurer.
5. The loss probability must be determinable.
6. The premium for such as risk coverage must be reasonable and affordable.

Items 1 – 5 are required from the insurer's perspective for the insurer to be willing to provide insurance for a particular risk. Item 6 is a requirement of consumers and represents the likely willingness to purchase an insurance product to cover a pure risk.

LARGE NUMBER OF HOMOGENEOUS EXPOSURES

There are two important requirement of "A Large Number of Homogeneous Exposures." The first requirement is that there are a large number of exposures and the second requirement is that the large number of exposures is homogeneous. Both of these requirements are important for a risk to be insurable so that an insurance company can accurately predict future losses and charge affordable premiums based on forecasted claims.

Key Concepts

Underline/highlight the answers to these questions as you read:

1. Identify the requisites for an insurable risk.

2. Identify why the law of large numbers is important to insurance companies.

Law of Large Numbers

The law of large numbers tells us that the more similar the events or exposures, the more likely the actual results will equal the expected probability. This is important for an insurance company so that the actual claims they pay, are very close to the probability of total losses. If the pool of insureds is small, the actual losses could vary significantly from the expected losses, which could lead to financial insolvency of the insurer.

EXAMPLE 1.13

Assume the probability of males, ages 55-64, dying this year, is 1 out of 1,000, and that each insured owns a $1 million death benefit policy. For every pool of 1,000 males, the insurance company is going to charge premiums based upon paying 1 death benefit (or $1 million) claim this year. If the insurance company experienced two, three or four deaths this year from this pool, their actual death benefit claims would be $2, $3 or $4 million, which is significantly greater than the expected total losses of $1 million per 1,000 male pool. The premiums charged for a probability of 1 out of 1,000 may not offset two or more deaths if such variance continued for many years.

EXAMPLE 1.14

Now, assume the probability of males dying this year, between the ages of 55-64 is 890 out of 100,000. Now the insurance company is able to base premiums on 890 claims out of 100,000 insureds. If 900 - 910 of the age 55 - 64 group insureds die this year, the deviation from the expected results is much smaller, since the population of insureds is 100,000 rather than 1,000.

Large Number of Homogeneous Exposure Units

The second requirement for an insurable risk is that the large number of exposures is homogeneous. An insurance company needs the pool of loss exposures to be homogeneous (alike). This allows the insurance company to more accurately predict the loss probability and charge an appropriate premium. For example, when determining the premium for an auto policy, the type of car driven is a risk factor. The insurance company pools all male drivers of sports cars, with turbo v-8 engines into one group of homogeneous risks and charges a risk premium. Other drivers who drive a four dour, four-cylinder Honda Accord are classified into a different homogenous risk pool and charged a lower premium because the risk exposure is greater for a sports car than for a four-door sedan. Also, consider an Alaska King Crab fisherman working on the Bering Sea with 60-foot waves in the freezing cold versus a stand up comedian. The probability of the insurance company paying a disability or life insurance claim on an Alaska crab fisherman is much greater than paying a disability or life insurance claim on a stand-up comedian that gets hit by a tomato for a bad joke.

INSURED LOSSES MUST BE ACCIDENTAL

Actual losses must be accidental from the insurer's perspective because premiums are based on the probability of a loss occurring based on historical information and claims. A tree falling on a house during a bad storm is an accidental loss and covered because the insurer can estimate the probability of losses based on historical information and claims for trees falling on a house. However, intentionally burning down a house that you own and insure to collect the insurance proceeds is an intentional act and is not a covered loss. If insurance companies covered intentional acts of insureds, premiums would increase and may become unaffordable by most individuals.

LOSS MUST BE MEASURABLE AND DETERMINABLE

Since most losses covered by an insurance contract result in a financial payment to the insured, the actual timing of the loss and amount of the loss must be known. A typical insurance contract is going to offer the promise to pay in the event of a loss, but that promise to pay is only good for a period of time. Consider insurance on a primary residence. The premium is paid for the year, so the insurance company agrees to pay in the event of a loss, if the loss occurs during that one-year period. Once that time expires, the insured must pay a new premium to receive the promise for the insurer to pay for a loss over the next one year period of time.

Losses must also be measurable in terms of the amount of loss. If the loss probability is too uncertain, the risk will be considered uninsurable. Back in the mid 1950s, it was determined that the loss caused by a nuclear power plant melt down was too uncertain and potentially so severe that the insurance industry excluded nuclear power plant failures from insurance policies.

When considering insurance on a primary residence, it's fairly easy to determine the amount to rebuild the house in the event it burns to the ground. However, it's more difficult to determine the amount of cash or jewelry kept in the house, in the event of theft or fire. For hard to value items and those that have moral hazard associated, the insurer may place specific limits on such items.

Typical limits placed on items include:
- Money / Cash = $200
- Jewelry, Furs, and Watches = $1,000
- Firearms = $2,000
- Silverware and Goldware = $2,500

If an insured owns items that exceed these limits, it will be necessary to provide the insurance company with documentation regarding the value and then increase the underlying limits of the policy. Riders and endorsements enable an insured to increase these underlying limits for an increased premium and are discussed later in this text.

Loss Must Not be Financially Catastrophic to the Insurer

Some loss exposures are so financially devastating because the loss would impact too big an area or segment of the population, that an insurance company cannot afford to pay all the claims if the event occurs. The amount that an insurance company receives for any loss is relatively small in comparison to the total possible. For example, a war or nuclear hazard could affect such a large area, such as multiple cities and states, and the financial loss so severe, that an insurance company could not afford to pay all of the claims. A loss exposure that would be financially catastrophic to the insurer is an uninsurable risk which is why an insurer excludes perils such as flood, earthquake, nuclear hazard and acts of war.

EXAMPLE 1.15

Hurricane Katrina hit Louisiana and Mississippi in September of 2005 causing over $100 billion in damages. Much of the damage shown on the news was the result of massive flooding when the levees surrounding New Orleans and the local parishes were breached. Approximately ½ of all residents affected by the flooding did not have flood insurance. Flood is excluded from homeowners' insurance policies; and must be purchased from the National Flood Insurance Program administered by the

Federal Emergency Management Agency.[1] One of the issues raised in the aftermath of Hurricane Katrina was whether the property damage and losses were the result of windstorm or flood. Homeowners that did not have flood insurance argued that the damage from a hurricane is due to windstorm, which is a covered peril under a homeowner's policy. However, the insurance industry argued that the damage was caused by flooding when the levees were breached.

Also, recall the terrorist acts on September 11th, 2001 which in addition to the loss of over 3,000 lives, caused almost $10 billion in losses for the insurance industry. The insurance companies did not call the events of 9/11 an "Act of War," which is an exclusion on property insurance policies. However, shortly after 9/11, insurance companies began to exclude "Acts of Terrorism" from insurance policies. As a result, The Terrorism Reform Act of 2002 was passed to provide a federal government "backstop" for losses arising out of acts of terrorism. Private insurers are now able to offer coverage for acts of terrorism, with the federal government paying 90 percent of losses above a threshold.[2]

PREMIUM MUST BE REASONABLE

Premiums must be reasonable and affordable for the insured. Before an individual transfers a risk to an insurer, the individual will conduct a cost benefit analysis of the premium relative to the risk and severity being covered.

EXAMPLE 1.16

Sydney, age 17, drives a 15-year-old Honda Accord with 175,000 miles on the car. The fair market value of the car is $800. To insure the car in the event of a collision, the premium is $900. The benefit Sydney would receive if she totals her car would be $800, less

---

Quick Quiz 1.4

Highlight the answer to these questions:

1. The law of large numbers tells us that the more similar events or exposures, the more likely the actual results will equal the probability expected.
   a. True
   b. False

2. Actual losses must be accidental from the insurer's perspective because premiums are based on the probability of a loss occurring based on historical information and claims.
   a. True
   b. False

3. A loss exposure that would be financially catastrophic to the insured is an uninsurable risk.
   a. True
   b. False

True, True, False.

---

1. FEMA http://www.fema.gov
2. http://www.thefreelibrary.com/Understanding+the+benefits+of+the+Terrorism+Risk+Insurance+Act.+...-a096554237

EXAMPLE 1.17

any deductible. Sydney would be better off self-insuring against the risk of property damage to her car.

William, age 33, drives a new Mercedes Benz, with a fair market value of $50,000. To insure the car for collision, the premium is $900 per year. The benefit William would receive if he totals his new Mercedes would be $50,000 less his deductible. William is better off transferring the risk of property damage to his $50,000 Mercedes, for the $900 premium, rather than self-insuring.

The insurance company must also do their own cost-benefit analysis. The costs of filing and settling small claims, like minor fender benders, causes auto policy premiums to increase. As a result, insurers use deductibles, which require the insured to cover the first dollar in losses, typically $250 to $500 to dissuade small claims. Deductibles prevent the filing of small severity claims, which helps to keep the premiums of auto policies down. Deductibles also reduce morale hazard.

LAW OF INSURANCE CONTRACTS

A contract is a legal agreement that binds two parties to each other to perform certain obligations. The following elements must be present for a contract to be valid:
- Mutual Consent
- Offer and Acceptance
- Performance or Delivery
- Lawful Purpose
- Legal Competency of all Parties

MUTUAL CONSENT

Mutual consent implies that both parties to the contract have a mutual understanding regarding what the contract covers and they are in agreement as to the terms of the contract. Typically contracts may be terminated by mutual consent of both parties.

OFFER AND ACCEPTANCE

Offer and acceptance consists of one party making an offer to purchase a good or service and the acceptance is when consideration is received. Consideration can be in the form of a cash payment or providing a service.

Key Concepts

Underline/highlight the answers to these questions as you read:

1. Identify the elements of a valid contract.

2. Define conditional acceptance.

3. Identify the two categories of legal competence.

4. Define the parol evidence rule.

EXAMPLE 1.18

Mike is selling his Mercedes and is asking $50,000. Joe offers Mike $45,000 for the car. Mike agrees to accept $45,000 and Joe hands Mike a check for $45,000. The original offer was $50,000, Joe made a counter-offer of $45,000 and the acceptance was when Mike agreed to the price of $45,000.

EXAMPLE 1.19

Joe went to his insurance agent to apply for auto insurance for his new Mercedes. Joe completes the auto insurance application, however completing the application is not an offer. The insurance company presenting Joe with a policy and requiring a premium of $1,000 is the offer. Joe writing a check for $1,000 would be acceptance of the offer.

With insurance there is also "conditional acceptance." Conditional acceptance is if Joe had completed the auto insurance application and attached a check for the premium of $1,000. The insurance agent conditionally accepted the policy, upon final review by the underwriter. If Joe leaves the insurance agent's office, gets hit by a bus in his new Mercedes, and the insurance company would typically have accepted his application, he would be covered. As long as Joe would have met the typical underwriting standards of the insurance company, he will have coverage. Coverage would not exist if the premium was returned and Joe was notified that the policy was not accepted.

PERFORMANCE OR DELIVERY

In order for a contract to be enforceable, the party to a contract must perform a duty under the contract. So, using the previous example, if Joe is buying a car from Mike and gives Mike a check for $45,000, Joe has performed under the contract. He would expect Mike to hand him the keys and title to the car. If Joe asked Mike to deliver the car to his front door before Joe pays, then Mike cannot enforce payment from Joe until the car is delivered to Joe's front door.

Quick Quiz 1.5

Highlight the answer to these questions:

1. Typically contracts may be terminated by consent of at least one party.
   a. True
   b. False

2. If the subject matter of the contract is illegal, then the contract is not enforceable.
   a. True
   b. False

3. If a minor enters into a contract, the minor may only void the contract within 30 days of entering the agreement.
   a. True
   b. False

False, True, False.

LAWFUL PURPOSE

Another element of a valid contract is that the subject of the contract cannot be contrary to public policy or be in violation of any laws. If the subject matter of the contract is illegal, then the contract is not enforceable. If Joe enters into a contract to pay Mike $10,000, if Mike steals his neighbor's Mercedes, neither Joe nor Mike will not be able to enforce the contract, as the contract is not valid since to steal the neighbor's Mercedes is a violation of the law.

LEGAL COMPETENCE OF ALL PARTIES

When entering into a contract, both parties must be legally competent, otherwise the contract is unenforceable. Legal competence includes the following situations:

- **Minors** - In most states, a minor is under the age of 18. If a minor enters into a contract, the minor can void the contract at any time. If one party can void a contract at any time, there really isn't an enforceable contract.
- **Lacking Sound Mind** - A person lacking a sound mind does not have the capacity to understand the purpose and terms of the contract, therefore the contract lacks a meeting of the minds or mutual consent. Examples of persons lacking sound mind would include a person who is drunk, mentally handicapped, or under the influence of drugs.

Other important considerations of a contract include the **parol evidence rule** which states that "what is written prevails." Any oral agreements prior to writing the contract have been incorporated into the written contract. Oral agreements that are not reflected in the written contract are not valid.

LEGAL PRINCIPLES OF INSURANCE CONTRACTS

PRINCIPLE OF INDEMNITY

The **principle of indemnity** asserts that an insurer will only compensate the insured to the extent the insured has suffered an actual financial loss. In other words, the insured cannot make a profit from insurance. The principle of indemnity does not assert that an insured will recoup 100 percent of any loss, as most policies have deductibles and limits on the amount of losses covered.

A **subrogation clause** in an insurance policy requires that the insured relinquish a claim against a negligent third party, if the insurer has already indemnified the insured. A subrogation clause entitles the insurer to seek a claim against a negligent third party, for any claims paid to the insured. The principle

Key Concepts

Underline/highlight the answers to these questions as you read:

1. Distinguish between the principal of indemnity and subrogation.

2. Identify the difference in insurable interest between property and liability and life insurance.

3. Identify the difference between a representation, warranty, and concealment.

20   CHAPTER 1: CHARACTERISTICS OF INSURANCE

of indemnity and the subrogation clause are closely aligned to accomplish the goal of preventing an insured from profiting from insurance.

PRINCIPLE OF INSURABLE INTEREST

The **principle of insurable interest** asserts that an insured must suffer a financial loss if a covered peril occurs, otherwise no insurance can be offered. The principle of insurable interest is closely aligned with the principle of indemnity, which both limit the insured from experiencing a gain using insurance.

Property and Liability Insurance

An insurable interest for property and liability insurance must exist both at the inception of the policy and at the time of loss. If no insurable interest exists at the inception of the policy, then there would be an incentive on the insured's behalf to damage the property. If there is no insurable interest at the time of loss, then the insured that received a monetary settlement would experience a profit from the insurance claim, which would violate the principle of indemnity.

EXAMPLE 1.20

Mike purchases a property insurance policy on a wine warehouse, in the amount of one million dollars. Mike does not have any financial interest in the wine warehouse. Mysteriously the wine warehouse burns to the ground and Mike collects the face value of the policy. This would be a violation of the principles of insurable interest and indemnity, as Mike would have experienced a profit from this insurance policy when he had no insurable interest.

For the past ten years, Mike has owned a wine warehouse, and has property insurance on the warehouse in the amount of one million dollars. Mike decided to sell the wine warehouse, but keep the property insurance policy. Shortly after selling the warehouse, it mysteriously burned to the ground. If Mike collected under the property policy, it would be a violation of the principles of insurable interest and of indemnity.

Life Insurance

An insurable interest for life insurance need only exist at the inception of the policy. A life insurance policy is not an indemnity policy but instead pays the face value of the policy based on the "value" of the amount of insurance purchased. Some people refer to this as a "modified" indemnity policy or an "agreed to value" policy.

EXAMPLE 1.21

When Karen and Joe were married, Karen purchased a life insurance policy on Joe, and named herself as the beneficiary. After being married for two years, they divorced but Karen continued to pay the premiums on the life insurance policy. Ten years after their divorce, Joe died. Karen will be able to collect the death benefit from the life insurance policy, because Karen only needed to have an insurable interest at the inception of the life insurance policy.

To purchase life insurance, the owner of the policy must have an insurable interest in that person's life. An insurable interest exists for a person to purchase life insurance on their own life and name either themselves or someone else as the beneficiary. An insurable interest also typically exists for close family relationships but may also exist in a business relationship.

EXAMPLE 1.22

Brian and Kevin started a pilot training school together and they each own 50% of the business. Brian and Kevin decide to take out a life insurance policy on each other's life, so that in the event one business partner dies, the proceeds from the life insurance policy can be used to buy the deceased partner's share of the business from the decedent's heirs. Since Brian and Kevin are business partners, they each have an insurable interest in the life of the other.

PRINCIPLE OF UTMOST GOOD FAITH

The principle of utmost good faith requires that the insurer and insured act in a manner that is forthcoming with all information about the risks being considered during the underwriting process. The insured and the insurer follow three legal doctrines during the application and throughout the life of the policy:
- Representation
- Warranty
- Concealment

Representation

A **representation** is a statement made by the applicant during the insurance application process. A representation can be an oral statement or information disclosed on an insurance application such as age, gender, occupation, marital status and family medical history. A misrepresentation during the application process can lead to the insurer voiding the insurance contract. In order for the contract to be voidable, the misrepresentations must be material and the insurer must have relied on the

Quick Quiz 1.6

Highlight the answer to these questions:

1. The subrogation clause asserts that an insurer will only compensate the insured to the extent the insured has suffered an actual financial loss.
   a. True
   b. False

2. An insurable interest for life insurance must exist both at the inception of the policy and at the time of loss.
   a. True
   b. False

3. A representation is a statement made by the applicant during the insurance application process.
   a. True
   b. False

False, False, True.

misrepresentation to issue the policy. A misrepresentation is considered "material," if during the application process the insured knew the statement was false, and the insurer would not have issued the insurance contract but for the false misrepresentation. Misrepresentations about age and gender for a life insurance policy are not considered material. The insurance company will simply determine the benefit based upon the actual age or gender of the insured and the amount of premium actually paid.

Barbara, age 40, has always been told that she has looks ten years younger than her actual age. Barbara recently completed a life insurance application and stated her age as 30, rather than 40. Based on a female age 30, the premiums for a one million dollar policy was $400. A few months later, Barbara was hit by a bus and died. Upon reviewing the death certificate, the insurer realized that Barbara was 40 and not 30. The insurer calculated a death benefit of $600,000 based on the amount of coverage a $400 premium would have purchased for a 40-year-old female.	**EXAMPLE 1.23**

Warranty

A **warranty** is a promise made by the insured that is part of the insurance contract. The warranty can be a promise to perform or take a certain action. Alternatively, a warranty can be a promise by the insured to not do something. A breach in warranty may allow the insurer to void the insurance contract and not pay any claims.

Joe and Barbara own a retail hardware store and are constructing a new addition to their building. In an effort to reduce their insurance premiums and as a requirement of the policy, they agree to install a fire sprinkler system throughout the store. They then warrant in the application that they have installed the sprinkler system. During construction, they decide to not have the sprinkler system installed, as it would cost more than they anticipated. If a fire causes a loss, the insurer will likely avoid paying the claim, as Joe and Barbara would have breached a warranty.	**EXAMPLE 1.24**

Concealment

Concealment is when the insured is intentionally silent regarding a material fact during the application process. The insurer has the right to void an insurance contract based on material concealments by the insured. In order for the insurer to void a contract or avoid paying a claim because of concealment, the insurer must prove that the insured knew the concealed fact was material.

EXAMPLE 1.25

Rey is completing a life insurance application and answers questions such as:
- What is your age, marital status, height, and weight?
- Are you a smoker?
- Do you pilot small planes?
- Do you scuba dive?
- Do you have any other dangerous hobbies?

Rey answers "no" to all of the questions on the insurance application. Rey does not disclose that he likes to "base jump" which is jumping off tall building and bridges with a parachute in his hand and releasing the parachute at the last possible moment. Rey's insurance company would void paying a claim if Rey dies as a result of a base-jump accident.

UNIQUE LEGAL CHARACTERISTICS OF INSURANCE CONTRACTS

ADHESION

Insurance contracts are contracts of **adhesion**, which is a take it or leave it contract. The insured has no opportunity to negotiate the terms of the contract. Before an insurance product can be sold in a state, the state insurance commissioner must approve the product. The product is then sold "as is" and the insured must accept the policy as written. Since the insured has no ability to negotiate the terms of the insurance policy, the courts will rule in favor of the insured if there are ambiguities found in the contract. The insurer had the opportunity to draft the contract clearly and therefore will be charged for any ambiguities.

Key Concepts

Underline/highlight the answers to these questions as you read:

1. Identify the distinguishing characteristics of insurance contracts.

2. Determine if property and life insurance policies are assignable.

ALEATORY

Insurance contracts are **aleatory** in nature, which means the dollar amounts exchanged between the insured and the insurer are unequal. The insured may pay a lifetime of premiums for a disability insurance policy and never collect a benefit under the policy. Alternatively, an insured may pay a small premium for a life insurance policy, and his heirs collect a large face value after only one premium payment if the insured dies while covered by the policy.

UNILATERAL

Insurance contracts are **unilateral** in that there is only one promise made, and it's made by the insurer to pay the beneficiary in the event of a covered loss. The insured in not legally obligated to make premium payments. As long as the insured makes the required premium payments, the insured is legally obligated to provide coverage under the terms of the policy.

Quick Quiz 1.7

Highlight the answer to these questions:

1. Insurance contracts are aleatory in nature, which means the dollar amounts exchanged are even.
   a. True
   b. False

2. The insured is not legally obligated to make a premium payment.
   a. True
   b. False

3. Property insurance policies cannot be assigned to a third party without the consent of the insurer.
   a. True
   b. False

False, True, True.

CONDITIONAL

Insurance contracts are **conditional** in that the insured must abide by all the terms and conditions of the contract if the insured intends to collect under the policy. If the insured has violated any of the terms or conditions under the policy, the insurer may not pay a claim. One of the conditions of a policy is that the insured take steps to mitigate and reduce any additional damage to property after a covered loss. Another is that the insured timely pay the premiums.

EXAMPLE 1.26

During a severe storm, a tree falls on the roof of Jill's home causing a large hole. Jill discovers the hole immediately but does nothing. The storm continues to rain on Jill's house for the next three days and the rain causes additional damage to the interior of Jill's house. Jill did not take any steps to cover the hole in her roof and the rain causes extensive damage to her walls and floors. The insurance company will pay for the damage to Jill's roof but will not pay for the interior rain damage because Jill did not take the appropriate precautions to prevent (mitigate) further damage after the tree fell on Jill's roof.

PERSONAL

Property insurance polices are personal contracts between the insurer and the insured, therefore the policy cannot be assigned to a third party without the consent of the insurer. When applying for property insurance, the insurer evaluates the riskiness of the applicant based on their credit score, work history and other personal factors. When the property is sold, the new buyer needs to apply for their own property insurance to give the insurance company an opportunity to evaluate the riskiness of the new owner.

Life insurance contracts, unlike property insurance contracts, can be assigned without the consent of the insurer because the contract continues to cover the insured regardless of who owns the policy. Assigning ownership rights to someone else even one who has no insurable interest under the life insurance contract does not change the underlying insurer's risk associated with the insurance contract.

LAW OF AGENCY

The law of agency describes the relationship and authority an agent possesses when acting on behalf of a principal. A principal, such as an insurance company, hires an agent (insurance agent) to act on the principal's behalf and enter into agreements on behalf of the principal. The authority that an agent possesses is the result of express, implied and/or apparent authority. In the case of an insurance agent, the statements or actions of the agent that are in the course and scope of the agency agreement, will bind the insurance company to the insured.

EXPRESS AUTHORITY

Express authority is given to an agent through a formal written document. In the case of an insurer and insurance agent, the express authority is an agency agreement. The agency agreement specifically outlines the duties, responsibilities, and scope of authority that the agent can act upon and thus bind the principal. The agency agreement stipulates the terms, conditions, and length of period the agent is allowed to sell insurance policies and bind the insurer to the insured.

Key Concepts

Underline/highlight the answers to these questions as you read:

1. Differentiate between express, implied, and apparent authority.

2. Identify how a waiver may impact the insurer's ability to deny a claim.

3. Identify how estoppel pertains to insurance contracts.

IMPLIED AUTHORITY

Implied authority is that authority that an agent relies on to do their job when the expressed authority is insufficiently precise or that a third party relies upon when dealing with an agent, based upon the position held by the agent. When a customer walks into an insurance agent's office, the customer will see the company logo on the front door, signs on the wall of the agent's office with the company's logo, and business cards on the agent's desk. All of these signs would indicate and lead the customer to believe that the agent sitting behind the desk has the implied authority to bind the insurance company, if the customer purchases an insurance policy.

APPARENT AUTHORITY

Apparent authority is when the third party believes implied or express authority exists, but no authority actually exists. If an insurance company and agent had an agency agreement but that agreement expired, it is the responsibility of the insurance company to lock the door to the office, take down any signs, and remove the business cards and company letterhead. The insurance company must take the necessary steps to remove any indications of implied authority. If a customer reasonably relies on apparent authority and is issued an insurance policy by an agent who no longer has either express or implied authority, the insurance company is bound by the policy.

EXAMPLE 1.27

Randy walks into his insurance agents office to purchase an auto policy for his new convertible sports car. Randy notices the business cards on the desk with both the insurance company's logo and his agent's name. There is company letterhead on the agent's desk along with policy applications. Randy completes the auto policy application and pays the first year premium. Upon leaving his agent's office, he gets into an accident and totals his new sports car. Little does Randy realize that his agent's agency agreement expired last week and that the agent was not really licensed, however Randy will still have coverage from the insurer due to apparent authority.

WAIVER

A **waiver** is relinquishing a known legal right. If an insurer waives a legal right, they may not deny paying a claim based on the insured violating or breaching that right.

EXAMPLE 1.28

David is applying for a health insurance policy. Before the policy can be issued, David must complete an application and take a physical exam. David completes the exam but never takes the physical exam. The insurer issues David the health insurance policy. The insurer cannot later deny paying claims on the policy because David did not take a physical exam.

ESTOPPEL

Through the legal doctrine of "**estoppel**" the principal will not be able to deny the insured an insurance contract. Estoppel is where through a legal process, you are denied a right you might otherwise be entitled to under the law. Estoppel applies when one party relies on information from another party and that information causes harm to the party that relied on the information. The party that made the statements can be estopped from denying the statements.

Quick Quiz 1.8

Highlight the answer to these questions:

1. Express authority is the agency agreement, which specifically outlines the duties, responsibilities and scope of authority that the agent can act upon.
   a. True
   b. False

2. Apparent authority is when the third party believes implied or express authority exists, but no authority actually exists.
   a. True
   b. False

3. Waiver is where through a legal process, you are denied a right you might otherwise be entitled to under the law.
   a. True
   b. False

True, True, False.

EXAMPLE 1.29

Walter and his wife walk into an insurance agent's office and take out a $10 million life insurance policy on Walter's life, with his wife as the beneficiary. Walter's wife asks the insurance agent if the policy will pay a death benefit if Walter commits suicide and the agent responds "yes." Two days later, Walter is found dead from an apparent suicide. Walter's wife then attempts to collect the $10M death benefit under the policy. However, the policy has a "Suicide Clause" that stipulates that if the insured commits suicide within two years of the policy being issued, then the premiums will be returned and no death benefit will be paid. Although the insurer will attempt to produce the policy and suicide provision, the insurer may be estopped from denying paying of the claim based on information the agent expressed to Walter's wife presuming she can prove the agent's statements.

CHARACTERISTICS OF INSURANCE COMPANIES

TYPES OF INSURANCE COMPANIES

Stock Insurers
A stock insurer is an insurance company that issues stock, and is owned by shareholders with the intent of earning a profit. A stock insurer collects premiums, pays operating expenses and may return dividends to shareholders based on the performance of the company. The Board of Directors for a stock insurer is responsible for making a decision to pay dividends to the shareholders and shareholders elect the Board of Directors.

Mutual Company Insurers
A mutual company is an insurance company that is owned by the policyholders, not shareholders. The policyholders elect the Board of Directors for a mutual company. Profits earned by a mutual company are returned to policyholders in the form of a dividend. The dividend is not treated as taxable income but is instead a return of premiums paid.

Key Concepts

Underline/highlight the answers to these questions as you read:

1. Identify the difference between stock insurers and mutual company insurers.

2. Identify the differences between agents and brokers.

3. Determine the underwriting process.

4. Understand the term adverse selection.

5. Explain why insurance companies are reinsured.

AGENTS AND BROKERS

Agents
Agents are legal representatives of an insurer and act on behalf of an insurer. Agents are only permitted to sell the policies written by their company. Agents have the authority to bind the insurer to an individual. There is typically a difference between the authority an agent has when selling a property and casualty policy versus a life insurance policy. An agent may immediately issue a temporary binder on an auto policy over the telephone. A temporary binder is temporary insurance coverage until the insurance company issues the permanent policy. However, an insurance agent may not immediately bind an insurer when selling a life insurance policy. The insurer must approve the life insurance application before coverage is issued.

Brokers
Brokers are legal representatives of an insured and act in the best interest of the insured. A broker may sell insurance polices from any one of a number of different insurance companies. Since the broker does not represent the insurer, they may not bind an insurer.

Insurance brokers typically help individuals obtain property and casualty, life, and health insurance. Some brokers assist in surplus lines market, which are markets where there is a need for a particular type of insurance but no insurance product exists in that state. A broker may use an insurer that is licensed in another state to provide the insurance product.

REINSURANCE

Reinsurance is a means by which an insurance company transfers some or all of its risks to another insurance company. The company that transfers the risk is the ceding company, while the company accepting the risk transfer is the reinsurer. The primary reason an insurance company may transfer risk is to reduce their exposure in their portfolio of insured risks to catastrophic financial risk that may result in the company becoming insolvent. A company may decide to transfer some of their risks to create additional portfolio capacity to underwrite new policies.

Quick Quiz 1.9

Highlight the answer to these questions:

1. Agents are legal representatives of an insured and act in the best interest of the insured.
   a. True
   b. False

2. Underwriting is the process of classifying applicants into risk pools, selecting insureds, and assigning a premium.
   a. True
   b. False

False, True.

EXAMPLE 1.30

Hurricane Katrina made landfall over Louisiana and Mississippi on August 29, 2005. Hurricane Katrina caused $81 billion in property damage,[3] with approximately $40 billion in losses covered by reinsurance companies. Some of the largest reinsurance companies in the world shared in the losses as a result of hurricane Katrina.

Reinsurance Company	Dollar Amount of Loss from Katrina
Berkshire Hathaway	$3 billion
Munich Re	$1.5 billion
Swiss Re	$1 billion

Market Info Briefing October 21, 2005, Guy Carpenter

---

3. http://www.nadmat.org/hurricane-katrina/what-was-the-impact-of-hurricane-katrina

IMPORTANT PROVISIONS AND FEATURES OF INSURANCE CONTRACTS

POLICY PROVISIONS

Most insurance contracts are generally designed with similar provisions, including:
- Definitions of terms used in the contract
- Declarations
- Description of what is insured
- Perils covered
- Exclusions
- Conditions

Key Concepts

Underline/highlight the answers to these questions as you read:

1. Identify the typical sections of an insurance contract.

2. Identify examples included in each section of an insurance contract.

Definitions

The **definition section** of an insurance policy defines key words, phrases or terms used throughout the insurance contract. The purpose of the definitions is to clarify the contract the parties and the coverages provided throughout the policy.

- Insured: Upon the insured's death a death benefit is payable to the beneficiary.
- You, Your: Refers to the owner of the policy.
- We, Us, Our: Refers to the insurance company (insurer).

Declarations

The **declarations section** describes exactly what property or person is being covered. For property insurance, the declaration page will describe the property, address, owner of the property, name of the insured, amount of coverage, deductible and premium. For life insurance, the declaration page will contain the insured's name, face value of the policy, term or length of the policy and the issue date.

- End of Initial Term Period: This identifies the last date the policy is effective.
- Amount of Insurance: This is the amount of the death benefit or policy limit that is payable to the beneficiary of the policy.
- Premiums: Depending on the type of the policy, this section may identify the amount of the current premium and perhaps any renewable premium.

Description of What is Being Insured

The **description section** describes exactly what is being insured. For a life or health insurance policy, the name of the insured is included in this section. For a property and casualty policy, the address of the property is in the description.
- Insured: Name of the insured.
- Effective Date: The start date of when the policy is effective.
- Age and Sex of the Insured: Used to determine the insured class and premium due for life, health, and disability policies.

Perils Covered

The perils covered section may cover perils on a named peril basis where specific perils are listed as covered in the policy. Alternatively, the policy may cover perils on an open peril basis, which covers all risks of loss that are not specifically identified and excluded in the exclusions section of the policy. For a term life insurance the peril covered is death of the insured within the term period.

Exclusions

The **exclusions section** of an insurance policy will exclude certain perils, losses and property. Perils are excluded because they may be uninsurable perils, there is a moral hazard, or the coverage is potentially financially catastrophic to the insurer. Examples of excluded perils for a property insurance policy include:
- War or nuclear hazard
- Flood
- Power failure
- Intentional acts
- Neglect
- Movement of ground

Losses that are excluded from a policy are due to the insured not taking steps to prevent further losses after a covered loss has occurred. Some property is not covered such as damaged or stolen business property in the home.

Quick Quiz 1.10

Highlight the answer to these questions:

1. For a life or health insurance policy, the name of the insured is included in the declarations section.
   a. True
   b. False

2. The exclusion section of an insurance policy will exclude certain perils, losses, and property.
   a. True
   b. False

False, True.

Conditions

Conditions are provisions in an insurance policy that require an insured to perform certain duties. If the policy conditions are violated, the insurer may refuse to pay the full amount of the claim. Examples of conditions include:
- Notifying the insured in the event of a loss.
- Filing of a police report in the event of a theft.
- Cooperating with the insurer after a loss.
- Taking appropriate steps to reduce further damage after a loss.

Miscellaneous Provisions

Miscellaneous provisions in an insurance policy cover topics not addressed within other areas of the policy. Examples of miscellaneous provisions include:

- Errors in Age or Sex: In the event of a misstatement of age or sex, the death benefit payable under a life insurance policy will be based upon the actual age or sex at death.
- Suicide Exclusion: A typical exclusion under a life insurance policy is if the insured commits suicide within the first two years of the policy. Premiums will be returned in the event of the insured committing suicide.
- Payment of Benefits: This section will outline where and how the death benefit will be payable to the beneficiary.
- Grace Period: The grace period will identify the amount of time after the due date of the premium that the policy will stay in force. If the premium is not paid within the grace period, the policy will lapse. The typical grade period is 31-60 days.

Key Concepts

Underline/highlight the answers to these questions as you read:

1. Differentiate between a rider and an endorsement.
2. Identify the purpose of a deductible.
3. Identify the purpose of coinsurance.

RIDERS AND ENDORSEMENTS

An **endorsement** is a modification or change to the existing property insurance policy. A **rider** is a modification or change to a life or health insurance policy. Riders and endorsements are a way for an insured to customize a policy. Since insurance policies are contracts of adhesion and the insured has no opportunity to negotiate the terms of the contract, riders and endorsements are a method of customizing an insurance policy. If there are conflicting terms between the policy and a rider or endorsement, then the rider or endorsement language prevails.

A property insurance policy is typically endorsed when the insured owns property in excess of the coverage limits within the policy. If a policy only provides coverage of up to $2,000 in jewelry, an endorsement can be used to increase the jewelry limit to an amount appropriate for the value of the client's jewelry.

A rider can be added to a disability policy that waives the premium if the insured becomes disabled for a short period of time.

UNDERWRITING AND MANAGING ADVERSE SELECTION

Underwriting is the process of classifying applicants into a risk pools, selecting insureds, and determining a premium. An underwriter is responsible for evaluating risks and determining whether the risk is insurable or non-insurable. The underwriter is also responsible for managing adverse selection. **Adverse selection** is the tendency of those that most need insurance to seek it while those with the least perceived risk avoid paying the premiums by not buying insurance. In an ideal world the insurer would only insure those persons least likely to have a claim. However, that would not lead the insurer to profitability as those who are least likely to have a claim are also most likely to self insure. An underwriter wants to maintain an appropriate mix of those that need insurance and are likely to file a claim versus those that are unlikely file a claim. The underwriter follows underwriting principles that are established by the company which outline acceptable risks, borderline risks, and risks that are unacceptable.

An underwriter groups risks into similar classes and assign a premium or class rate to all members of the class, such that the premium is expected to cover all claims, operating expenses, and produce a profit.

The underwriter attempts to manage adverse selections with the use of deductibles, co-payments, and coinsurance.

DEDUCTIBLES AND CO-PAYMENTS

Deductibles are the first dollar in loss, which the insured is responsible to pay. Deductibles may be a flat dollar amount such as $250, $500 or $1,000. A deductible may also be a percentage of the covered loss, which is typical for flood insurance or homeowner's insurance in states like Florida. The purpose of such a deductible is to reduce the filing of small claims, reduce premiums, and eliminate moral and morale hazard. Without deductibles, the paperwork, time, and resources needed to process claims of $50 or $100 would make insurance premiums unaffordable. Deductibles also serve as motivation for an insured to take precautions to avoid losses or to prevent the filing of false claims since an insured with a deductible will not receive 100 percent of the value of loss.

EXAMPLE 1.31

Holly has a two-year-old car that she purchased for $40,000 that is now worth $30,000. Her car recently caught on fire and was a complete loss. Her insurance company paid her $29,500, which is the actual value of her car, less her $500 deductible.

Co-payments are paid in addition to deductibles or as a substitute for deductibles and are commonly used in health insurance policies. **Co-payments** are loss-sharing arrangements whereby the insured pays a flat dollar amount or percentage of the loss in excess of the deductible. An example of a deductible is when a person must pay the first $1,000 of medical expenses each year, and then 20 percent of all expenses over that amount. The insurer pays 80 percent of covered medical expenses that exceed the $1,000 deductible. An example of a co-payment is when a person is covered for health insurance by a HMO, PPO, or POS and pays $25 each time they go to the doctor.

Quick Quiz 1.11

Highlight the answer to these questions:

1. Actual cash value is the method used to value damage to a personal residence under a property insurance policy.
   a. True
   b. False

2. Replacement cost is how a PAP values property or personal auto.
   a. True
   b. False

False, False.

COINSURANCE

Coinsurance defines the percentage of financial responsibility that the insured and the insurer must uphold in order to achieve equity in rating. Coinsurance exists primarily in property insurance and encourages insureds to cover their property to at least a stated percentage of the property's value, or else suffer a financial penalty. Because the vast majority of property losses are partial, without coinsurance clauses many insureds would attempt to save money on insurance by purchasing less insurance than the full value of their property. While underinsuring is not illegal, it presents a problem for the underwriter and actuary who base expected loss estimates, and thus premiums, on the full value of the properties in the insured pool.

The amount paid for a property insurance claim with a policy with a coinsurance clause is determined by comparing several values. If the insured purchases coverage that meets or exceeds the coinsurance requirement (usually 80 percent of replacement value for homeowners insurance), then payment on a claim for a loss will be the lesser of the face value of the policy, replacement cost, or actual expenditures. However, if the insured purchases coverage that is less than the coinsurance requirement (say, 60 percent of the replacement value), then payment on a claim for such a loss will be the greater of the actual cash value (ACV) or the result of the following formula subject to the limit of the face value of the policy:

The purpose of coinsurance in a property insurance policy is to encourage the insured to maintain a stated percentage of minimum coverage, otherwise the insured will become a coinsurer and proportionately share in any loss.

The coinsurance formula is:

$$\frac{\text{Amount of Insurance Carried}}{\text{Amount of Insurance Required}} \times \text{Covered Loss} = \text{Amount Insurer Pays}$$

EXAMPLE 1.32

Jerry owns a home with a replacement cost of $500,000. A tree falls on Jerry's house, causing $100,000 in damage. Jerry has a policy with an 80% coinsurance amount and a $500 deductible.

How much will the insurer pay if Jerry carries $300,000 of coverage?

$$\frac{\$300,000}{0.80 \times \$500,000} \times \$100,000$$

= $75,000 - $500 = $74,500 (paid by insurer)

EXAMPLE 1.33

How much would the insurer pay if Jerry had $400,000 of coverage?

$$\frac{\$400,000}{0.80 \times \$500,000} \times \$100,000$$

= $100,000 - $500 = $99,500 (paid by insurer)

EXAMPLE 1.34

How much would the insurer pay if Jerry had $600,000 of coverage?

$$\frac{\$600,000}{0.80 \times \$500,000} \times \$100,000$$

= $150,000* ($99,500 paid by insurer)

* The insurer payment is limited to the loss of $100,000 less the deductible of $500, therefore $99,500. The insured has over insured but is subject to the principle of indemnity.

The maximum amount the insurer will pay is up to the covered loss or the face value of the policy or policy limits, less any deductible, even though the coinsurance formula may result in a percentage greater than 100 percent.

Coinsurance is also a term used in medical insurance indemnity policies. In these policies, coinsurance refers to the percentages paid by the insurer and the insured for claims after a deductible has been met and before the stop-loss limit is reached. For example, in a plan with an 80/20 coinsurance, a $1,000 deductible, and a $2,000 stop-loss limit, the insured will pay 100 percent of all covered costs until the $1,000 deductible is reached. After the first $1,000 in claims, the insured pays 20 percent of covered costs until claims reached $6,000 ($2,000 stop-loss / 20% + $1,000 deductible) and then 0 percent. The insurance company is responsible for 100 percent of all covered claims in excess of $2,000 during the policy period.

VALUING PROPERTY FOR LOSSES

Insurance policies must not only specify what perils are covered and what is excluded, but must also explain how losses are to be valued. Without valuation provisions in the policy, the insured and the insurer would not have clarity over how much a particular claim is worth.

Insurance policies generally value and pay losses based on one of three valuation methods:
- Actual cash value
- Replacement cost
- Appraised or agreed upon value

Key Concepts

Underline/highlight the answers to these questions as you read:

1. Differentiate between actual cash value, replacement cost, and appraised value.

ACTUAL CASH VALUE

Actual cash value represents the replacement cost less the depreciated value of the property. Actual cash value is used to value the amount of coverage for a personal auto or personal property in a homeowners policy or business property policy.

> Three years ago Karen purchased a new car for $30,000. Yesterday, she was in an accident and her car was totaled. Her car had depreciated by $12,000 over the three years she owned the car. The actual cash value of the car was $18,000 ($30,000 - $12,000), which is how much the insurer will pay Karen for her loss, less any deductible.

EXAMPLE 1.35

For personal property in a homeowner's policy actual cash value (ACV) means replacement cost less depreciation.

REPLACEMENT COST

Replacement cost represents the amount to repair or replace property, without any deduction for depreciation. Replacement cost is the method used to value damage to a personal residence (dwelling) under a property insurance policy.

> A windstorm blows off a portion of a room on Sylvia's house. The cost to replace the damaged roof is $75,000. Under the replacement cost method of valuing a loss, the insurer will pay the full $75,000 less any deductible to repair the damaged roof.

EXAMPLE 1.36

Personal property can be valued using actual cash value (ACV) or replacement cost (RC). Replacement cost is more preferable to the insured because the insured will receive replacement for damaged property rather than the depreciated value under actual cash value.

EXAMPLE 1.37

A tree falls on Joe's house damaging his room and crushing his refrigerator. The roof damage is valued at $15,000. He purchased the refrigerator 10 years ago for $2,000. The actual cash value of the refrigerator is now $200. If Joe has replacement cost for the roof but actual cash value for the refrigerator, his insurance company will pay $15,000 for the roof and $200 for the refrigerator less any applicable deductible. However, if Joe has replacement cost for both the roof and refrigerator, Joe will receive $15,000 to repair the roof and $2,000 to purchase a new refrigerator less any deductible.

APPRAISED OR AGREED UPON VALUE

Appraised or agreed upon value is used for hard to value items and where the insured may own property that exceeds standard limits of a property insurance policy. Typically jewelry, art, furs, and collectibles are covered using appraised or agreed upon value; such that any underlying limits in the property insurance policy are increased.

REGULATING THE INSURANCE INDUSTRY

The insurance industry is regulated primarily at the state level, but federal law also overlaps state insurance regulation. At the federal level, The Gramm-Leach-Bliley Act of 1999 repealed the Glass-Steagal Act, which prevented banks, investment firms, and insurers from competing outside of their core business. As a result of the Gramm-Leach-Bliley Act, banks and investment firms can sell insurance, and insurance companies can provide banking and investment services. Now that firms in financial services provide insurance, banking, and investment services, the regulatory environment has become more complex with firms now subject to regulation by the Federal Reserve for banking, the Securities and Exchange Commission on investments, and state regulation for insurance products.

Key Concepts

Underline/highlight the answers to these questions as you read:

1. Identify the three levels of state regulation of the insurance industry.

2. Determine if the NAIC has regulatory power.

3. Identify the goals of the NAIC.

4. Differentiate between various methods to regulate insurance rates.

The insurance industry is highly regulated by three levels of state government, which are:
- legislative,
- judicial, and
- executive or State Insurance Commissioner.

LEGISLATIVE

The legislative branch of state government passes laws and regulations that regulate how insurance companies conduct business in their state. The legislature defines how insurance products are sold, insurance agents are licensed and protects consumer rights by passing consumer protection laws.

JUDICIAL

The judicial branch of state government rules on the constitutionality of laws passed by the legislative branch. The judicial branch also rules on decisions and actions taken by the executive branch. The judicial branch provides oversight of the legislative and executive branch, along with the insurance industry.

EXECUTIVE OR STATE INSURANCE COMMISSIONER

All states have a state insurance commissioner, which is an elected or appointed position. The state insurance commissioner is responsible for enforcing the legislature's laws and regulations, licensing of insurance agents, reviewing rate increases, and auditing insurance companies.

NATIONAL ASSOCIATION OF INSURANCE COMMISSIONERS (NAIC)

The National Association of Insurance Commissioners (NAIC) is a voluntary organization of insurance regulators from the 50 states, the District of Columbia and the five U.S. territories (Guam, Puerto Rico, Virgin Islands, American Samoa, and Commonwealth of the Northern Mariana Islands).[4] The mission of the NAIC is to "assist state insurance regulators" in serving the public. The goals of the NAIC is to:
- Protect the public,
- Promote competition,
- Promote fair treatment of insurance consumers,
- Promote the solvency of insurance companies, and
- Support and improve state regulation of insurance.

The NAIC does not have regulatory power, but it does issue model legislation to address problems within the insurance industry. States may or may not adopt the model legislation.

The NAIC also provides a watch list of insurance companies based upon financial ratio analysis. The ratio analysis measures the financial health of an insurance company. To promote solvency and avoid insurers from being unable to pay claims, life and health insurance companies are subject to a Risk-Based Capital test (RBC) that was developed by the NAIC. Risk-based capital measures how much capital is invested and the riskiness of the investments. The more risky the investments, the more capital the insurer is required to maintain. If the insured does not maintain adequate capital, then regulatory action may be required. Regulatory action includes the state seizing the company, rehabilitating, or liquidating the company.

---

4. http://www.naic.org/index_about.htm

INSURANCE RATE REGULATION

The rates that insurance companies use when determining premiums is regulated at the state level. The regulation varies by state and rate laws may also differ based upon the insurance product. Some of the insurance rate regulation laws include:
- Prior Approval Law
- File and Use Law
- Use and File Law
- Open Competition

PRIOR APPROVAL LAW

Under prior approval law, an insurance company must file the rate increase request with the State's Insurance Commissioner's office. The rate increase will either be approved, disapproved, or modified. During 2009 and 2010, many states denied health insurance rate increases due to the increasing unemployment rate and potential political fallout arising from 10 to 20 percent health insurance rate increases.

FILE AND USE LAW

States that allow a "file and use" law permit an insurance company to file the rate increase with the State Insurance Commissioner's office but immediately implement the rate increase. The state insurance commissioner may later deny the rate increase in which case the insurance company must rebate the premium denied.

USE AND FILE LAW

A "use and file" state permits an insurer to increase rates, but they must file the rate increase within a specific time period, as determined by state law. Both the "file and use" and "use and file" laws avoid any delays associated with the rate increases being approved, as they allow the insurer to implement rate increases quickly.

OPEN COMPETITION

Open competition laws allow insurers to set their own rates, and the State presumes that supply and demand will determine the appropriate rates for various insurance products. The open competition approach assumes that fair competition among insurers will result in efficient premium prices.

Quick Quiz 1.12

Highlight the answer to these questions:

1. The insurance industry is regulated primarily at the state level.
   a. True
   b. False

2. The NAIC does not have regulatory power, but it does issue model legislation to address problems within the insurance industry.
   a. True
   b. False

3. States that allow a "use and file" law permit an insurance company to file the rate increase with the state insurance commissioner's office but immediately implement the rate increase.
   a. True
   b. False

True, True, False.

SELECTING AN INSURANCE COMPANY

The financial stability of an insurance company is a primary determinant for selecting an insurer. Rating agencies analyze and evaluate the financial health and ability of an insurer to pay claims. The better the insurer's rating, the more likely they are to sell policies, as consumers will have confidence in the insurer's ability to pay claims, should the insurer experience a loss.

Rating Agency	Highest Ratings		Lowest Ratings	
A.M. Best	A++	A/A-	C/C-	D
Fitch	AAA	AA -	B+	CCC -
Moody's	Aaa	Aa2	B1	Caa
Standard and Poor's	AAA	AA-	B+	CCC
Weiss	A+	B -	F	U

A consumer should compare insurer ratings across several rating agencies. An insurer with consistently high ratings across multiple rating agencies is a low risk and acceptable provider. However, an insurer with consistently low ratings from multiple rating agencies is a high risk and should be avoided.

Key Terms

Actual Cash Value - Represents the depreciated value of the property.

Adhesion - A take it or leave it contract.

Adverse Selection - The tendency of those that most need insurance to seek it out.

Agents - Legal representatives of an insurer and act on behalf of an insurer.

Aleatory - A type of insurance contract in which the dollar amounts exchanged are uneven.

Apparent Authority - When the third party believes implied or express authority exists, but no authority actually exists.

Appraised or Agreed Upon Value - Used for hard to value items and where the insured may own property that exceeds standard limits of property insurance policy.

Brokers - Legal representatives of an insured and act in the best interest of the insured.

Coinsurance - The percentage of financial responsibility that the insured and the insurer must uphold in order to achieve equity in rating.

Concealment - When the insured is intentionally silent regarding a material fact during the application process.

Conditional - The insured must abide by all the terms and conditions of the contract, if the insured intends to collect under the policy.

Co-payment - A loss-sharing arrangement whereby the insured pays a percentage of the loss in excess of the deductible.

Declarations Section - The section of an insurance policy that describes exactly what property is being covered.

Deductible - A specified amount of money the insured is required to pay on a loss before the insurer will make any payments under the policy.

Definition Section - The section of an insurance policy that defines key words, phrases, or terms used throughout the insurance contract.

Description Section - The section of an insurance policy that describes exactly what is being insured.

Key Terms

Endorsement - A modification or change to the existing property insurance policy.

Estoppel - The legal process of denying a right you might otherwise be entitled to under the law.

Exclusion Section - The section of an insurance policy that will exclude certain perils, losses and property.

Express Authority - Authority given to an agent through a formal written document.

Financial Risk - A loss of financial value, such as the premature death of a family's primary wage earner.

Fundamental Risk - A risk that can impact a large number of individuals at one time (earthquake or flood).

Hazards - A specific condition that increases the potential or likelihood of a loss occurring.

Implied Authority - The authority that a third party relies upon when dealing with an agent based upon the position held by the agent.

Lacking Sound Mind - The state of not having the capacity to understand the purpose and terms of the contract, therefore the contract lacks a meeting of the minds or mutual consent.

Law of Large Numbers - A principle that states the more similar events or exposures, the more likely the actual results will equal the probability expected.

Minors - In most states, a minor is under the age of 18. If a minor enters into a contract, the minor can void the contract at any time.

Moral Hazard - The potential loss occurring because of the moral character of the insured, and the filing of a false claim with their insurance company.

Morale Hazard - The indifference to a loss created because the insured has insurance.

Mutual Consent - Common understanding and agreement between parties to a contract regarding what the contract covers and the terms of the contract.

Nonfinancial Risk - A risk that would result in a loss, other than a monetary loss.

Key Terms

Objective Risk - The variation of actual amount of losses that occur over a period of time compared to the expected amount of losses.

Offer and Acceptance - Consists of one party making an offer to purchase a good or service, and the acceptance is when consideration is received.

Parol Evidence Rule - States that "what is written prevails." Oral agreements that are not reflected in the written contract are not valid.

Particular Risk - A risk that can impact a particular individual, such as death or the inability to work because of a sickness or accident.

Perils - The immediate cause and reason for a loss occurring.

Physical Hazard - A physical condition that increases the likelihood of a loss occurring.

Principle of Indemnity - Asserts that an insurer will only compensate the insured to the extent the insured has suffered an actual financial loss.

Principle of Insurable Interest - Asserts that an insured must suffer a financial loss if a covered peril occurs, otherwise no insurance can be offered.

Pure Risk - The chance of loss or no loss occurring.

Reinsurance - A means by which an insurance company transfers some or all of its risk to another insurance company.

Replacement Cost - Represents the amount to repair or replace property, without any deduction for depreciation.

Representation - A statement made by the applicant during the insurance application process.

Rider - A modification or change to a life or health insurance policy.

Risk Avoidance - A risk management technique used for any risks that are high in frequency and high in severity.

Risk Reduction - The process of reducing the likelihood of a pure risk that is high in frequency and low in severity.

Risk Retention - Accepting some or all of the potential loss exposure for risk that are low in frequency and low in severity.

Key Terms

Risk Transfer - The process of transferring a low frequency and high severity risk to a third party, such as an insurance company.

Speculative Risk - The chance of loss, no loss, or a profit.

Subjective Risk - The risk an individual perceives based on their prior experiences and the severity of those experiences.

Subrogation Clause - A clause in an insurance policy that requires that the insured relinquish a claim against a negligent third party, if the insurer has already indemnified the insured.

Underwriting - The process of classifying applicants into a risk pools, selecting insureds, and assigning a premium.

Unilateral - There is only one promise made; and in the case of an insurance contract, it's made by the insurer to pay in the event of a loss.

Waiver - The relinquishment a known legal right.

Warranty - A promise made by the insured that is part of the insurance contract.

DISCUSSION QUESTIONS

1. Describe the personal risk management process.

2. List the four responses to managing risk.

3. Define a peril.

4. Define the three main types of hazard.

5. List some unique characteristics of an insurance contract.

6. Explain the differences between pure risk and speculative risk.

7. Explain the four differences between subjective and objective risks.

8. Describe the law of large numbers and why it is useful for insurance companies.

9. List typical perils covered under a personal auto policy.

10. List typical perils covered under a homeowner's insurance policy.

11. What are the requisites for an insurable risk?

12. Describe the elements of a valid contract.

13. Define conditional acceptance.

14. Define the parol evidence rule.

15. Explain the differences between the principal of indemnity and a subrogation clause.

16. When must an insurable interest exist for property, liability, and life insurance?

17. Define representation, warranty, and concealment.

18. List unique characteristics of insurance contracts.

19. Describe the differences between express, implied, and apparent authority.

20. Identify the differences between agents and brokers.

21. List the responsibilities of an underwriter.

22. Identify why insurance companies are reinsured.

23. List and define typical sections of an insurance contract.

24. Differentiate between a rider and an endorsement.

25. Describe the purpose of a deductible.

26. Describe the purpose of coinsurance.

27. Describe the differences between actual cash value, replacement cost, and appraised value.

28. Identify the three levels of state regulation of the insurance industry.

29. Identify the goals of the NAIC.

30. Describe the differences between various methods to regulate insurance rates.

MULTIPLE-CHOICE PROBLEMS

1. The risk that individuals of higher than average risk will seek out or purchase insurance policies is called?

    a. Peril.
    b. Hazard.
    c. Law of Large Numbers.
    d. Adverse Selection.

2. What type of hazard results from the indifference that a person has to the potential loss because he or she has insurance?

    a. Peril.
    b. Physical Hazard.
    c. Moral Hazard.
    d. Morale Hazard.

3. Which of the following is correct regarding a peril and hazard?

    a. A hazard is the proximate or actual cause of a loss.
    b. A peril is the proximate or actual cause of a loss.
    c. A peril is the condition that creates or increases the likelihood of a loss occurring.
    d. None of the above.

4. Which of the following is not a requisite for an insurable risk?

    a. A large number of homogeneous exposure units must exist.
    b. Insured losses must be accidental from the insured's standpoint.
    c. Insured losses must be measurable and determinable.
    d. The loss must not pose a catastrophic risk for the insured.

5. The principle of indemnity requires that:

    a. A person is entitled to compensation only to the extent that financial loss has been suffered.
    b. Insured cannot indemnify himself from both the insurance company and a negligent third party for the same claim.
    c. The insured must be subject to emotional or financial hardship resulting from the loss.
    d. The insured and insurer must both be forthcoming with all relevant facts about the insured risk and coverage provided for that risk.

6. A subrogation clause means that:
    a. A person is entitled to compensation only to the extent that financial loss has been suffered.
    b. Insured cannot indemnify himself from both the insurance company and a negligent third party for the same claim.
    c. The insured must be subject to emotional or financial hardship resulting from the loss.
    d. The insured and insurer must both be forthcoming with all relevant facts about the insured risk and coverage provided for that risk.

7. When must an insurable interest exist for a property insurance claim?
    a. At the policy inception and time of loss.
    b. At the policy inception only.
    c. At the time of the loss.
    d. Either at the policy inception or at the time of the loss.

8. When must an insurable interest exist for a life insurance claim?
    a. At the policy inception and time of loss.
    b. At the policy inception only.
    c. At the time of the loss.
    d. Either at the policy inception or at the time of the loss.

9. When the insured is silent to a fact that is material to the risk being insured, what has occurred?
    a. Breach of Warranty.
    b. Misrepresentation.
    c. Concealment.
    d. Breach of Indemnity.

10. Jennifer is applying for life insurance, with her two children as the beneficiary. Jennifer has always been told she looks young for her age and although she is 58, she stated that she is 28 on her life insurance application. What would the insurer be most likely to do if Jennifer's beneficiaries attempt to collect on the life insurance policy?
    a. Void the policy.
    b. Require payment on premiums for a 58 year old insured.
    c. Recalculate the face value of the policy based on actual premiums paid.
    d. Bring a lawsuit against the estate.

11. Which of the following statements regarding the characteristics of an insurance contract is false?

    a. They are a contract of adhesion, which means the insured must accept it or leave it.
    b. They are aleatory contracts, which means amounts exchanged may be unequal.
    c. They are unilateral, meaning there is only one promise, which is a promise by the insured to pay the premium.
    d. The contracts are conditional, which means the terms are under the condition that premiums are paid.

12. Joe walks into his insurance agent's office and notices his agent's name on a business card and the insurer's name on letterhead. If an agency agreement exists, what type of authority does Joe believe his agent has to enter into an insurance contract?

    a. Express Authority.
    b. Implied Authority.
    c. Apparent Authority.
    d. None of the Above.

13. Donna owns a house with a replacement cost of $500,000. She purchases $300,000 of insurance with a coinsurance requirement of 80% and a $500 deductible. If Donna's house is hit by a hurricane and she suffers a $150,000 loss, what will the insurer pay?

    a. $74,500.
    b. $112,000.
    c. $119,500.
    d. $149,500.

14. Insurance regulation is primarily conducted by?

    a. The Securities and Exchange Commission.
    b. The State Insurance Commissioner.
    c. The Federal Insurance Commission.
    d. The FDIC.

15. Which of the following statements regarding loss frequency is true?

    1. Loss frequency is the expected number of losses that will occur within a given period.
    2. Loss frequency is the potential size or damage of a loss.

    a. 1 only.
    b. 2 only.
    c. Both 1 and 2.
    d. Neither 1 nor 2.

16. Which of the following statements regarding loss severity is true?
    1. Loss severity is the expected number of losses that will occur within a given period.
    2. Loss severity is the potential size or damage of a loss.
        a. 1 only.
        b. 2 only.
        c. Both 1 and 2.
        d. Neither 1 nor 2.

Quick Quiz Explanations

Quick Quiz 1.1

1. True.
2. False. Objective risk is the variation of actual amount of losses that occur over a period of time compared to the expected amount of losses.
3. True.

Quick Quiz 1.2

1. True.
2. False. Risk reduction is the process of reducing the likelihood of a pure risk that is high in frequency and low in severity.
3. False. Risk transfer involves transferring a low frequency and high severity risk to a third party, such as an insurance company.

Quick Quiz 1.3

1. True.
2. False. Morale hazard is indifference to a loss created because the insured has insurance. A physical hazard is a physical condition that increases the likelihood of a loss occurring.

Quick Quiz 1.4

1. True.
2. True.
3. False. A loss exposure that would be financially catastrophic to the insurer is an uninsurable risk.

Quick Quiz 1.5

1. False. Typically contracts may be terminated by mutual consent of both parties.
2. True.
3. False. If a minor enters into a contract, the minor can void the contract at any time.

Quick Quiz 1.6

1. False. The principle of indemnity asserts that an insurer will only compensate the insured to the extent the insured has suffered an actual financial loss. A subrogation clause in an insurance policy requires that the insured relinquish a claim against a negligent third party, if the insurer has already indemnified the insured.
2. False. An insurable interest for property and liability insurance must exist both at the inception of the policy and at the time of loss.
3. True.

Quick Quiz Explanations

Quick Quiz 1.7

1. False. Insurance contracts are aleatory in nature, which means the dollar amounts exchanged are uneven.
2. True.
3. True.

Quick Quiz 1.8

1. True.
2. True.
3. False. A waiver is relinquishing a known legal right. Estoppel is where through a legal process, you are denied a right you might otherwise be entitled to under the law.

Quick Quiz 1.9

1. False. Agents are legal representatives of an insurer and act on behalf of an insurer. Brokers are legal representatives of an insured and act in the best interest of the insured.
2. True.

Quick Quiz 1.10

1. False. For a life or health insurance policy, the name of the insured is included in the description section.
2. True.

Quick Quiz 1.11

1. False. Replacement cost is the method used to value damage to a personal residence under a property insurance policy. Actual cash value is used to value the amount of coverage for a personal auto or personal property.
2. False. A PAP uses actual cash value when providing coverage for a personal auto.

Quick Quiz 1.12

1. True.
2. True.
3. False. States that allow a "file and use" law permit an insurance company to file the rate increase with the state insurance commissioner's office but immediately implement the rate increase. A "use and file" state permits an insurer to increase rates, but they must file the rate increase within a specific time period, as determined by state law.

CHAPTER 2

Life Insurance, Annuities, & Disability Insurance

INTRODUCTION

When managing the personal risk exposures of individuals, life insurance, disability insurance, health insurance, and long-term care insurance are frequently purchased as a hedge to ensure that a client can meet his or her financial goals. This chapter covers life insurance, annuities, disability insurance, and the planning associated with each of them. Chapter 3 covers health risks and the use of health insurance and long-term care insurance.

It is often said that two things in life are certain: death and taxes. Many individuals tend to ignore these eventualities, particularly those who do their own financial planning without the benefit of a professional financial planner providing them with objective advice. The prospect of paying taxes, and certainly the prospect of one's own death, are not thoughts that people prefer to harbor. The inevitability of death, however, is a very real issue when addressing financial goals. Younger clients tend to ignore this risk as something too remote. While they will eventually have to face the inevitability of death, young people tend to believe that they won't have to worry about that for a long time. From a financial planning perspective, however, the younger the client, the more important the management of mortality risk (the risk of dying within the year) becomes. After reading this chapter you should be able to identify situations where the use of life insurance is an appropriate hedge against the client's mortality risk exposures, should be able to recommend the most appropriate form of life insurance for the client, and should understand common provisions found in life insurance policies.

After considering mortality risk, we shift our focus to morbidity, the risk of becoming disabled and being unable to work. The prospect of disability, like the prospect of death, is not a pleasant one for a client to consider, but is very real nevertheless. In fact, at any age up to retirement, the risk of becoming disabled is at least 1.5 times greater than the risk of death. Disability insurance can be used to protect the income stream of a client in the event of disability, and, in doing so, can protect the client's ability to achieve his or her financial goals in the event the client becomes disabled. Disability insurance should be considered as part of a client's comprehensive financial plan.

PARTIES TO A LIFE INSURANCE CONTRACT

Up to three parties may have an interest in any life insurance contract that is issued – the owner, the insured, and any beneficiary. Sometimes, the same person is the owner, the insured, and the beneficiary (if the proceeds are payable to his or her estate). In other cases, different individuals, groups, or legal structures may be the owners and/or beneficiaries of a life insurance policy.

The **insured** is the individual whose life is covered by the life insurance policy. When the insured dies, the life insurance company will pay the death benefit to the beneficiary named on the policy.

The **owner** of the policy is the person who can exercise the economic rights in the policy, and typically pays the premiums on the life insurance policy. For example, if permanent life insurance is purchased, the owner can borrow from the cash value, pledge the cash value as collateral for a loan, and receive policy dividends (all of these situations will be discussed later). When a client wishes to have access to the savings element of permanent life insurance policies, he or she needs to be the owner of those policies. The owner and insured are often the same person. In some cases it may make sense to have the life insurance policy owned by someone other than the insured (for example, the policy might be owned by the insured's spouse, by a beneficiary, or by a trust created to hold the policy). Typically, when a person other than the insured is the owner of the policy, the insured is attempting to save taxes (in particular, estate taxes), or is attempting to achieve greater asset-protection of policy values that might otherwise occur. These life insurance applications are beyond the scope of this text, but are covered in both Income Tax and Estate Planning courses.

If the owner and insured are different parties, the owner will have to possess an insurable interest in the life of the insured to obtain life insurance coverage, or the insured must consent to the owner purchasing coverage on his or her life. If the insured was the original owner, and transfers the policy to a third party, the insured is deemed to have given consent to that third party to hold insurance on his life. As discussed in prior chapters, insurable interest rules are designed to limit exposure to moral hazards (i.e., creating an incentive for the insured to die early as a means of collecting the death benefit).

The **beneficiary** is the person entitled to receive the death benefit. The owner of the policy can name the beneficiary, which may include him/herself. If the owner does not name a beneficiary, the policy death benefit is typically paid to the owner, or, if the owner is also the insured, to the owner/insured's estate.

EXAMPLE 2.1

Randy purchased a $1 million life insurance policy on his life to protect his family in the event of his early death. Randy decided to retain ownership of the policy so that he could access the cash value of the policy if needed. Randy never named a beneficiary, so if he dies, the life insurance death benefit will be payable to his estate. The situation would be the same if Randy named his estate as the beneficiary of the policy.

As the example above illustrates, the insured, owner, and beneficiary may be the same person. Typically, when the insured is different from the owner, the owner is also listed as the beneficiary on the policy.

EXAMPLE 2.2

John is the insured on a $1 million life insurance policy. His wife, Patty, is the owner, and she has named herself as the primary beneficiary, and their son, Ryan as the secondary or contingent beneficiary. If John dies, the policy will pay the death benefit to Patty (who is also the owner), or if Patty predeceases John, the proceeds will be paid to Ryan.

EXAMPLE 2.3

Bertie is independently wealthy, and when he dies he expects to pay estate tax. Bertie created a trust, and made cash gifts to the trust over time, which the trustee used to pay the premiums on a life insurance policy on Bertie's life that was owned by the trust. The trust is listed as the beneficiary on the life insurance policy, and after Bertie dies the Trustee will use the death benefit in accordance with the instructions set forth in the trust document.

As noted earlier, it is also possible for the owner, insured, and beneficiary to all be different parties. This is commonly referred to as the "unholy trinity" and when this occurs, planners need to be very careful about potential gift and estate tax consequences (these issues are discussed more fully in estate and gift tax courses).

EXAMPLE 2.4

Wally is the insured on a life insurance policy owned by his wife, Hilda. Hilda doesn't need the money, so she named Wally, Jr., their son, as the beneficiary. Wally is the insured, Hilda is the owner, and Wally Jr. is the beneficiary. During Wally's life, Hilda can access the cash value of the policy and receive policy dividends. When Wally dies, the death benefit is paid to Wally, Jr., which is considered a taxable gift from Hilda to Wally, Jr., and may cause a gift tax liability.

When clients purchase life insurance, planners should be aware of the identity of the insured, the owner, and the beneficiary. Without this knowledge, the planner will not be able to make appropriate recommendations for managing the client's risk and tax-planning needs.

LIFE INSURANCE AND MORTALITY RISK

RISK EXPOSURES FROM DYING EARLY

To understand the risk exposure of early death, it is important to have a general understanding of the life-cycle model of financial planning. Individuals typically progress through three stages from the beginning of their career to their death. These stages include:
1. the asset accumulation phase;
2. the conservation/risk management phase; and
3. the distribution/gifting phase.

EXHIBIT 2.1 LIFE CYCLE STAGES

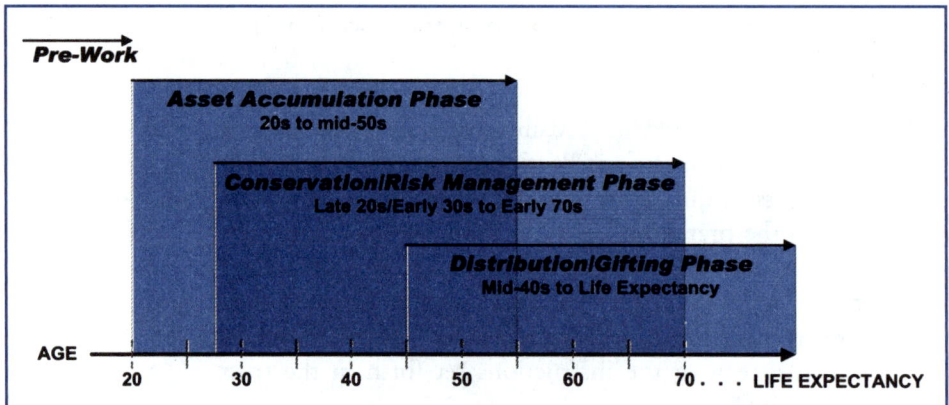

The **asset accumulation phase** of the lifecycle begins after a person completes his or her schooling and enters the workforce, and typically last through age 45-50. The early period of this phase is characterized by relatively high debt and low savings. In the early years of the accumulation phase, individuals often marry, begin to have children, purchase houses and cars, and make further investments in their human capital by pursuing professional or graduate education. In the later years of the accumulation phase, debt is declining, savings and investments are increasing, and earnings from work or self employment are increasing.

During the **conservation/risk management phase** of the life-cycle model, which typically lasts from age 45-50 until retirement (at about age 65), earnings from employment have reached their peak, children enter and exit college, the outstanding balance on the client's mortgage shrinks substantially, and savings increase to support retirement. It is common for individuals in this phase of the life cycle to take a more conservative approach to investing, since retirement is on the horizon. During the early part of this phase, clients become acutely aware of their insurance needs.

The **distribution/gifting phase** of the life-cycle begins near retirement and ends at death. During this phase, the client begins to spend down his or her accumulated assets, and may begin to transfer excess assets to family members and loved ones as gifts. After the client dies, any remaining assets will be transferred to intended beneficiaries by bequest, either through a validly executed will, the probate process, or a non-probate transfer vehicle.

Key Concepts

Underline/highlight the answers to these questions as you read:

1. Identify the three stages in the life-cycle model.

2. Highlight / identify the reasons for life insurance.

3. Identify the three methods used to determine life insurance needs.

As individuals age, their **mortality risk** (the risk that they will die within the year) increases. While it is unlikely that a healthy 25 year old person will die this year, some 25 year olds will pass away. Actuaries measure the likelihood of death at each age by observing the actual incidence of death by age for the population as a whole, and publish these probabilities in mortality tables. Not surprisingly, the risk of dying (mortality risk) increases as a person ages.

If a person dies prior to accumulating sufficient financial assets to meet his or her financial planning goals, the person's family (not the deceased individual) will feel the financial impact. Life insurance can be used as a hedge against the risk of early death so that if the client dies before making the money necessary to satisfy his financial objectives, the life insurance death benefit received by the family will cover the cost of unfunded financial goals.

As a person moves through the life cycle, from the asset accumulation phase to the distribution/gifting phase, his needs for life insurance as a hedge against early death change. In the accumulation phase of the life cycle, life insurance is often used to provide an income stream for the family if the breadwinner dies, to pay off existing debts (such as outstanding mortgages, car loans, personal loans, and consumer credit accounts), to fund financial objectives (such as education for the children), and to provide a retirement income for the surviving spouse.

Moving from the asset accumulation phase of the life cycle to the conservation/risk management phase, the need for life insurance to fund financial goals and income streams declines, but very slowly (a reverse exponential curve). All else equal, if a person dies at an older age compared to a younger age, the need for income replacement declines (assuming that the surviving spouse is roughly the same age). Many of the client's financial objectives will already have been partially met, such as paying down the mortgage on the principal residence, and helping the children obtain a college education. Once the mortgage is paid off, and the children are out of school, those objectives may be fully satisfied, and life insurance to fund these objectives may no longer be needed. If the surviving spouse needs supplemental income during retirement, however, life insurance may still be needed to fund this objective.

The conservation/risk management phase may result in increased needs for life insurance as well. If the client started a business, additional life insurance may be needed to: (1) fund buy-sell agreements between the owners of the business when one of the owners dies; or (2) provide liquidity for the estate of the business owner so that taxes and administration expenses can be paid without reducing the family's inheritance. High income individuals, or those who have accumulated significant assets during the accumulation phase, may also be interested in acquiring life insurance as a way of maintaining and enhancing family wealth. The tax benefits of life insurance make it an attractive tool to help to achieve these objectives.

As the client enters the distribution/gifting phase of the life cycle income needs are generally no longer an issue and the retirement income needs of the client and spouse should already be fully funded. Ideally, when the client retires most if not all of the client's financial goals should have been met:
- typically, there is no outstanding mortgage on the house;
- the children have completed school and are independent; and
- other client objectives have been fully funded.

The need for life insurance in the distribution phase of the life cycle often focuses on estate liquidity needs, and a desire to create and sustain family wealth. Death benefits paid on a life insurance policy can be used to cover medical expenses prior to death (to the extent that those expenses were not covered by health insurance), funeral expenses, probate and estate administration costs, and estate and inheritance taxes, which allows the full value of decedent's assets to be transferred to the surviving family. Properly constructed planning arrangements combined with life insurance coverage can also create a pool of capital for the family, allowing a client to achieve financial goals that extend beyond his or her death.

MEASURING THE LIFE INSURANCE NEED

Over time, different approaches to calculating life insurance needs have been developed. Most practitioners use one of three models to determine the life insurance needs of their clients:
1. The human life value approach;
2. The needs approach; and
3. The capitalized earnings approach.

EXHIBIT 2.2   METHODS TO DETERMINE LIFE INSURANCE NEEDS

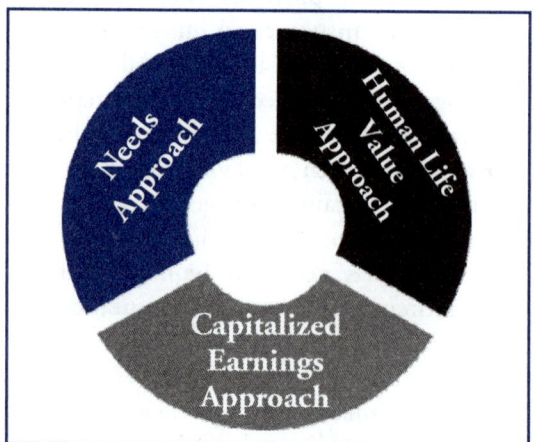

Some planners routinely use one of these approaches when advising clients. Given client needs and objectives, however, a better approach is to fit the projection model to the client's circumstances instead of using only one approach. Some planners use all three models and then consider other issues such as cash flows and bend points to determine how much life insurance to purchase.

Human Life Value Approach

The **human life value approach** suggests that the death benefit of a client's life insurance should equal the economic value of the client's future earnings stream discounted to its present value while considering the client's tax and consumption patterns. While religious scholars and philosophers teach us that we cannot place a monetary value on human life itself, it is possible to calculate the economic value of a person's expected future earnings. When an individual dies before reaching retirement, the loss of that person's earnings could create a hardship on the family, but with appropriate planning that income stream can be replaced with the life insurance death benefit. Assuming that a client's income stream will be sufficient to achieve all of his or her financial goals, replacing the lost income stream for the family should permit the family to meet their financial objectives. The human life value approach was one of the earliest techniques used to estimate life insurance needs, and was espoused by Dr. Solomon Heubner, a professor at The Wharton School of The University of Pennsylvania and founder of the American College of Life Underwriters, who is widely regarded as the "father of insurance education."

The steps in calculating a human life value include:
1. Determine the client's annual earnings.
2. Subtract personal expenses and taxes that the client would have incurred (consumption and taxes).
3. Determine the client's work life expectancy (WLE), or the number of years he or she would have continued to earn income (alternatively stated, the number of years before retirement).
4. Calculate the future value of the lost earnings for the family (sometimes referred to as the family's share of earnings, or FSE) taking into consideration the expected growth rate in earnings.
5. Calculate the present value of the family's share of earnings at the inflation rate to determine the human life value.

> **EXAMPLE 2.5**
>
> Chelsea is a 30 year old marketing executive who earns $100,000 per year. She is married to Louis and has 2 children. She expects her salary to increase at an annual rate of 4% until her retirement at age 65, and anticipates that inflation will average 3%. Chelsea and Louis's income places them in the 25% average tax bracket (including both state and federal taxes) and she uses 15% of her after tax income for personal consumption. Based on the Human Life Value approach, how much life insurance should Chelsea purchase?
>
> Using the approach outlined above, we begin by taking Chelsea's income of $100,000 and subtracting the personal expenses that she will incur. The first 25% of her income goes to the payment of taxes, making her after-

tax income $75,000. Of this amount, Chelsea uses $11,250 (15% x $75,000) for her own personal consumption and contributes $63,750 (85% x $75,000) of her income toward the achievement of family goals and objectives.

Since Chelsea is 30 years old and will retire at age 65, her Work Life Expectancy (WLE) is 35 years. The family share of earnings (FSE) can be calculated by determining the future value of $63,750 per year growing at 4% per year (the expected increase in Chelsea's income) for 35 years (her WLE). Using a financial calculator, the inputs would be:

>PMT = -63,750 (Chelsea's annual FSE)
>
>N = 35 (Chelsea's Work Life Expectancy)
>
>i = 4% (Expected growth rate in Chelsea's salary)
>
>Solve for FV = $4,695,329

If Chelsea died today, her family would lose, in nominal terms, $4,695,329 in future income based on these assumptions. To determine Chelsea's Human Life Value, and the amount of life insurance she should have on her life, we need to calculate the present value of her lifetime FSE (of $4,695,329) at the inflation rate over her work life expectancy. Using a financial calculator, the inputs would be:

>FV = $4,695,329 (Chelsea's lifetime FSE)
>
>N = 35 (Chelsea's WLE)
>
>i = 3% (Anticipated Inflation Rate)
>
>Solve for Present Value = $1,668,642
>
>Note: This is about 16 times her gross pay!

Using the Human Life Value approach to calculating life insurance needs, Chelsea should purchase a life insurance policy with a death benefit of approximately $1,700,000. If she had a life insurance policy with this death benefit and she died today, that amount, growing at the assumed annual increase in salary, will provide Chelsea's family with a full replacement of that portion of her income that she contributed toward the attainment of the family's financial goals.

When considering the use of the Human Life Value approach, a few relationships are worth considering. First, younger clients have a higher human life value (all else equal) than older clients because they will earn income for a longer period of time. As a client ages, the human life value, and the need for life insurance protection, will decline. Second, as the income of the client rises (all else equal) so will the client's human life value. As income increases, a greater amount will have to be replaced in the event that the client dies prior to the planned retirement date. Third, higher inflation expectations will lead to a lower human life value, since the lifetime FSE is discounted at a higher rate. If a planner would like to make a conservative projection of human life value, therefore, lower expected inflation rates should be used.

For many clients, use of the Human Life Value approach to determining life insurance needs may be appropriate. If the client will have funded all of his or her financial objectives for the family by retirement, will not have liquidity needs at death, does not have a need to use life insurance for business succession planning purposes, and does not wish to use life insurance to fund family legacies, the Human Life Value approach to determining life insurance needs will provide an insurance amount that will closely estimate the family's actual financial needs.

The Needs Approach

The second approach to estimating life insurance requirements is the **Needs Approach**. Instead of determining the present value of a future income stream, the planner will estimate the cash needs that the family will require at and after the death of the insured. Some of the financial needs that are typically considered when calculating a life insurance amount under the needs approach include:
1. payment of final expenses, medical care, and adjustment period expenses,
2. eliminating debt,
3. funding specific goals, such as education for the children,
4. income needs of the surviving spouse and the family, and
5. retirement needs of the surviving spouse.

Final expenses typically include funeral costs, administration expenses, taxes (income, estate, inheritance, and generation-skipping taxes) and medical care provided shortly before death. Depending upon the level of service selected, funeral costs can be significant, and must typically be paid before services are provided. Many people incur most of their lifetime medical expenses within the last few months before their death, and these expenses usually have to be paid before beneficiaries can receive their inheritances. For clients with tight cash-flow and few liquid assets, including estimated funeral and medical expenses in the life insurance need calculation is appropriate. Clients with higher net worth and sufficient liquid assets may not have to include funeral expenses and medical costs when calculating the insurance need since other resources are available to pay the expenses, but are likely to have higher costs of estate administration and, possibly, higher transfer taxes that will be due within nine months of death. As an alternative to self-funding or using insurance to fund these costs, the client can prepay funeral expenses, and maintain adequate health insurance during lifetime to ensure that medical expenses are covered.

One way to ease the burden on survivors is to pay off all outstanding debt at death. For example, if a client's principal residence is mortgaged, and at death the client leaves the principal residence to the surviving spouse subject to the outstanding mortgage, the surviving spouse will have an increased need for cashflow after the decedent's death to service the mortgage. Paying off the loan will simplify matters for the survivors (there are no monthly payments to make) and will reduce the survivor's need for cashflow (since they will no longer have to make principal and interest payments on the loan). Clients may also wish to pay off other forms of debt, such as car loans, personal loans, student loans, and revolving charge accounts, and these amounts should be included in the life insurance needs estimate.

Aside from retirement, perhaps the largest funding objective many families will face is the (partial or full) payment of their children's higher education costs. Education is expensive and recently has grown at a rate greater than inflation. The early death of the family's breadwinner could result in limited or no funding to cover college education expenses. If education funding is a client goal the planner should calculate the lump sum (present value) needed to pay for the tuition costs at the target college, and include that in the life insurance needs analysis.

If the client has been well advised by the planner, an emergency fund should have been established to cover unexpected major expenses, and possibly, the loss of employment. If a young person dies prior to establishing an adequate emergency fund, however, it may be wise to include a lump sum in the retirement need calculation that can be set aside by the survivors to pay for emergencies so that the other portion of the policy death benefit can be used for its intended purpose.

Finally, when calculating life insurance requirements under the needs approach, the income needs of the surviving spouse and dependents of the client must be considered. Income needs will vary depending upon the circumstances facing the family, the age of the family members, and the availability of public and private benefit payments. These changes to the income needs of the survivors are often broken down into various periods, identified below.

The Readjustment Period
After the death of a family's breadwinner, the family will need time to adjust to their new reality – a life without an important member of the family. For a period of six months to two years the family should have access to the same amount of income that was available when the breadwinner was alive. Often, non-recurring expenses will be incurred as a result of the family members death and having the cashflow to cover these expenses without affecting the family's lifestyle may be important.

The Dependency Period
The length of the dependency period will depend on the number and the ages of the client's dependents. Traditionally this period lasted from the end of the readjustment period to the time when all of the children reached the age of majority. As members of the sandwich generation will suggest, another factor that can extend the dependency period occurs when the decedent's parents are dependents. If parents rely on the client's income to make ends meet, the present value of the anticipated support over the parent's lifetime should also be included in the life insurance need calculation.

If the surviving spouse has an independent source of income that is sufficient to meet the needs of him/herself and the family, additional life insurance funding may not be necessary. In some cases, however, the dependency period may have to be extended to provide supplemental income for the decedent's spouse in the event the spouse cannot work or cannot replace the income lost when the decedent died.

If the surviving spouse is caring for minor children at the time of the decedent's death, both the surviving spouse and the children will qualify for Social Security survivors benefits. When the youngest child reaches the age of 16 survivor benefit payments to the surviving spouse will cease and the surviving spouse will typically need additional income to act as a substitute for those lost payments. When Social security payments resume in the form of retirement benefits as early as age 60 for a surviving spouse, those supplemental income payments can be reduced. The period between the cessation of survivor benefits and the receipt of retirement benefits is sometimes referred to the "blackout period" by planners. When forecasting the amount of income the surviving spouse will need, be sure to consider the impact of the blackout period on the income needs of the surviving spouse.

Quick Quiz 2.1

Highlight the answer to these questions:

1. Generally, people accumulate wealth throughout their lives.
   a. True
   b. False

2. Life insurance can be an effective tool for enhancing a family's wealth.
   a. True
   b. False

3. Death benefits paid from a life insurance cannot be used to pay the decedent's hospital bills.
   a. True
   b. False

4. Generally, as clients age, the human life value and the need for life insurance protection will increase.
   a. True
   b. False

False, True, False, False.

After calculating the amount of each of the family's financial needs, these amounts can be added together to determine the appropriate life insurance death benefit for the client. Of course, if the client already has some life insurance coverage or has existing assets that could be used to fund these needs in the event of an early death, those amounts can be subtracted from the total to determine the net amount of life insurance protection that should be obtained on the client's life. Example 2.6 provides an analysis of a needs approach to life insurance needs and a graphical presentation of the component parts.

EXAMPLE 2.6

Assume the following information:

Husband	Age 30	$100,000 income
Wife	Age 30	
Child A	Age 4	
Child B	Age 2	

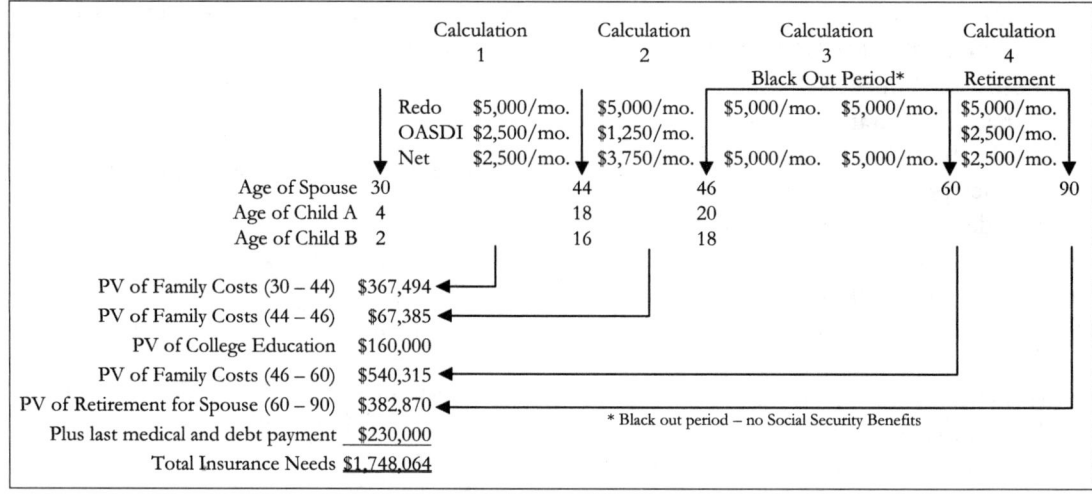

- Social Security OASDI benefit until Child B becomes age 16, $2,500 per month.
- Social Security OASDI benefit until Child B becomes age 18, $1,250 per month.
- Social Security OASDI widow's benefit from age 60 to life expectancy age 90, $2,500 per month.
- College education costs $20,000 per year per child in today's dollars at age 18 for four years.
- Total income needs of spouse for dependency period until Child B is age 22 = $5,000 per month in today's dollars.
- Inflation is expected to be 3%.
- Investment rate of return expected to be the riskless rate of 5%.
- Funeral, last medical, and adjustment period expense equal lump-sum of $30,000.
- Mortgage and debt repayment lump sum of $200,000.
- Education inflation rate is 5%.

Present Value Calculations

1			2		
N	=	14 x 12	N	=	2 x 12
i	=	(1.05÷1.03-1)÷12	i	=	(1.05÷1.03-1)÷12
PMT	=	$2,500	PMT	=	$3,750
PV	=	$367,494	PV$_{@44}$	=	$88,205
			PV$_{@30}$	=	$67,385*

3			4		
N	=	14 x 12	N	=	30 x 12
i	=	(1.05÷1.03-1)÷12	i	=	(1.05÷1.03-1)÷12
PMT	=	$5,000	PMT	=	$2,500
PV$_{@46}$	=	$734,987	PV$_{@60}$	=	$681,732
PV$_{@30}$		$540,315*	PV$_{@30}$	=	$382,870*

* Note: The second present value calculation in calculations 2, 3, and 4 use whole years instead of months (e.g., 14 for 2, 16 for 3, and 30 for 4) and use an i of (1.05/1.03 - 1) x 100 and are rounded to whole dollars.

The Capitalized Earnings Approach

The **capitalized earnings approach** is a modification of the human life value approach. The modifications include that there is no need to determine the work life expectancy, and the investment returns on the life insurance are presumed to be at the long-term riskless rate. This is a very efficient method to determine the approximate amount of life insurance needed for one who has dependents and life insurance needs.

EXAMPLE 2.7

Assume the following:

Earnings	$100,000
Raise Rate	3%
Inflation Rate	3%
Riskless Rate	6%
Consumption by Insured	25%
Federal and State Taxes	25%

The numerator: Earnings - Consumption - Taxes

The denominator: $\dfrac{1 + \text{Riskless Rate}}{1 + \text{Inflation Rate}} - 1$

Calculation:

$$\frac{\$100,000 - \$25,000 - \$25,000}{(1.06 \div 1.03) - 1} = \frac{\$50,000}{0.0291262} = \$1,716,667$$

The reason the riskless rate is used as the investment rate of return is because dependents cannot be assumed to have knowledge in investments. The method may be modified for more sophisticated investors with higher expected rates of return.

Summary of the Three Methods		
Human Value Approach	=	$1,668,642
Needs Approach	=	$1,748,064
Capitalized Earnings Approach	=	$1,716,667

The three methods coalesce in this case but not always. From numerous applications of the three methods we have developed a benchmark metric of 10-18 times gross pay as the general guide for life insurance needed.

TYPES AND USES OF LIFE INSURANCE IN FINANCIAL PLANNING

Life insurance is a product that transfers the risk of losses associated with early death to an insurance company in return for a fee (the premium on the policy). If the insured party dies, the insurance company pays the specified death benefit to a designated beneficiary. Several types of life insurance policies exist in the market today. The type of policy that is appropriate for one client may not be appropriate for another. Planners need to understand the client's purpose for buying and holding life insurance and select the policy that most closely matches the client's needs.

The two most common types of life insurance are term and permanent. Permanent life insurance includes universal, whole, variable, and modified endowment contracts, all of which are discussed in this section.

TERM INSURANCE

A **term insurance** policy, like all other life insurance policies, is a contract. If the insured dies during the term of the policy the insurance company will pay the specified death benefit. The term of the policy is typically one year or longer, although many term policies are designed to permit the insured to renew the policy for a longer period of time than the initial term.

When a term insurance policy is purchased the owner pays a premium equal to the risk the insurance company is undertaking. Term insurance policies do not have cash accumulation features and do not provide for continuing insurance after premium payments cease. Quite literally, the owner of a term policy is shifting the financial risk of death for the current year to the insurance company in return for the annual premium. If the owner wishes to shift the financial risk of death to the insurance company in future years, additional premiums must be paid.

As individuals advance in age, the actuarial risk that they will die within the year increases. This means that every year the mortality cost of the term insurance policy increases to reflect the increased risk of death. The term insurance premium for a young person tends to be very low due to the decreased risk of death, but term insurance policies can get very expensive for older individuals. In fact, at age 99, the premium for a term insurance policy approximates the death benefit of the policy (discounted for a few months of time value) since the risk of death within the year is substantial. For this reason, term insurance policies tend to be used by younger individuals and for those who need life insurance protection for shorter periods of time to ensure that, in the event of their early death, their financial goals can be met. When the need for life insurance is permanent, some form of cash-value policy will generally be used since the premiums on term insurance at advanced ages becomes prohibitive.

Key Concepts

Underline/highlight the answers to these questions as you read:

1. Describe the differences between annual renewable term (ART) life insurance, level-term life insurance, decreasing term life insurance, convertible annual renewable term life insurance, and group term insurance.

2. Describe some of the benefits and negatives of universal life insurance.

3. Describe the differences between straight whole life insurance, limited pay whole life insurance, modified whole life insurance, and variable whole life insurance.

4. Describe the income tax benefits that can be arranged with life insurance planning.

EXAMPLE 2.8

Aside from funding her retirement, Maggie's primary financial goal is to pay for the college education costs of her son, Dylan. She is currently 32 years old. Maggie has met with a financial planner and has developed a savings plan that will, over time, meet both her retirement and educational funding needs. If Maggie dies before she can earn the money to fund these objectives, Dylan's education may not be fully funded. To hedge against this risk Maggie purchases a term insurance policy with a death benefit of $500,000 so that Dylan will be able to attend the college of his choice. If Maggie lives, she will meet the educational funding goal through savings and investments and will no longer need to pay for the insurance.

Since Maggie's life insurance need is temporary and she is relatively young, term insurance is a good option for her.

EXAMPLE 2.9

Bertie (grantor) recently created a Grantor Retained Annuity Trust. He funded the trust with stock of Wooster Enterprises, Ltd. The trust states that Bertie will receive an income stream equal to 20% of the value of the stock he transferred to the trust for 5 years (thus the retained annuity). After the 5 year period expires, the trust terminates, and whatever is left in the trust at that time will be transferred to his cousin, Claude. If Bertie dies while he is receiving the income stream from the trust, the value of the trust assets will be taxable in his gross estate.[1] If Bertie purchases a term insurance policy for the five year duration of the trust, and dies during that term, the policy will provide sufficient money to pay any estate taxes. Since Bertie's need for life insurance is temporary (in this case, 5 years), term insurance is an appropriate product.

EXAMPLE 2.10

Clarence is the president and CEO of Empress of Blandings Holdings Company, Inc. He owns approximately 30% of the shares of the company and the remaining ownership interest is held by members of his extended family. Since Empress of Blandings is a family-owned company and the owners wish to keep it that way, they have entered into a buy-sell agreement so that if any of the current owners dies, the surviving owners must purchase the deceased owner's interest from his or her estate. The company is a large one and neither Clarence nor the other owners expect to have sufficient cash on hand to purchase the stock as required by the buy-sell agreement. Instead, they fund the buy-sell agreement using life insurance policies purchased on all of the owners lives. Since the need for life insurance is permanent in this case, term insurance would <u>not</u> be an appropriate type of insurance to purchase.

There are several variations of term insurance in the market today. Perhaps the most common type of term insurance is **Annual Renewable Term (ART)**. An Annual Renewable Term policy permits the policyholder to purchase term insurance in subsequent years without evidence of insurability, but premiums on the policy increase each year to reflect the increasing mortality risk being undertaken by the insurer. Many insurance companies will limit the renewal period to a specified number of years, or to a specific age, at which time the

---

1. IRC Section 2036.

insured would have to then provide further evidence of insurability in order to obtain a new policy. The limitation on renewal protects the insurer against possible adverse selection risk (the risk that only unhealthy insureds will renew their term life insurance coverage).

RENEWABLE TERM PREMIUM AND YEARLY RENEWABLE TERM PREMIUM (ISSUED AT AGE 25)

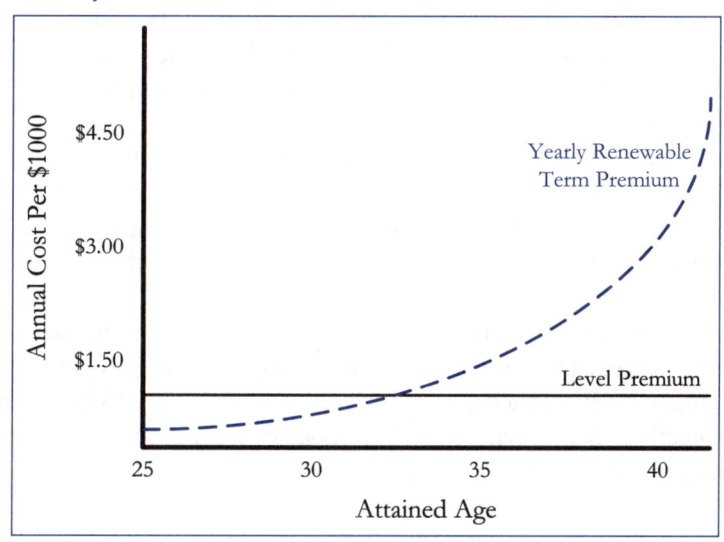

For some individuals the increasing premium on annual renewable term insurance may be unattractive and they would prefer to commit to a specific premium amount that will not change over a specific period of time (the term). **Level premium term insurance** charges a fixed premium each year over a specified period of years (often 5, 10, 15, 20, or 30 years), so the premium does not increase over that period. When a level-term insurance policy is purchased, the premiums paid by the owner will be larger than the premiums on an annual renewable term policy in the earlier years but will be less than the premiums on an annual renewable term policy in later years. All else equal, the total premium outlay on an annual renewable term policy will be less than that on a level term policy since time value of money principles are used to discount the premiums over the leveling period. For clients who prefer simplicity in budgeting, however, level premium term may be appropriate since their insurance costs will be "fixed" over the leveling period.

For individuals who do not anticipate having a permanent need for insurance, the life-cycle theory of financial planning suggests that their need for life insurance protection will decrease as they get older. As each year passes and income is earned that income can be employed to meet their financial goals, thereby allowing them to rely less on life insurance to satisfy those goals in the event of an untimely death. **Decreasing-term insurance** allows the owner to pay the same premium for the insurance protection each year. The death benefit on the policy will, however, decrease each year to offset the increasing mortality cost due to the passage of time.

EXAMPLE 2.11

Randy is married to Kelly and they have three children. Five years ago, Randy and Kelly purchased a house subject to a 30 year mortgage. Since the children have arrived, Kelly stopped working, and Randy is the sole breadwinner for the family. He has expressed a concern to his financial planner that if he died before the mortgage was paid off, Kelly and the children would not be able to afford to live in the house. Randy purchases a decreasing term insurance policy that he plans to keep in force for the remaining term of the mortgage. As each year passes by, the death benefit on the policy will decline, but so will the outstanding balance on the mortgage as monthly mortgage payments are made. The decreasing term policy allows Randy to budget a fixed dollar amount for insurance protection while ensuring that the balance of the mortgage can be paid off in the event of his untimely death.

A common problem faced by young individuals who have a permanent need for life insurance protection is that they often cannot afford to purchase permanent life insurance. In cases such as this, term insurance can be used as an interim step to obtaining permanent life insurance protection. Many term insurance policies permit the insured to convert the term policy into a permanent policy during the renewability period.

EXAMPLE 2.12

Roderick is the 22 year old heir to Spode Enterprises, Inc. He anticipates receiving large inheritances when his grandparents and parents pass away, and would like to use permanent life insurance policies to pay for estate taxes and administration expenses when he dies. Since he just graduated from college, and his salary is relatively modest, he does not currently have the funds to purchase a large amount of permanent life insurance protection. Instead, Roderick can purchase a convertible annual renewable term life insurance policy. Given his young age, the term-insurance premiums will be manageable now, and he can convert the policy to a permanent policy when his income increases.

Term insurance provides low cost life-insurance protection that can be particularly valuable for younger clients and for clients that have temporary insurance needs. As the client's age increases, so will the premium on the term insurance policy. Clients with a permanent need for death benefit protection should consider the use of permanent life insurance policies (such as whole life or universal policies).

The premiums for term-life insurance are very inexpensive and the term of death benefit coverage can be extended well into one's 80s. Below is a table of level premiums for various age clients for various term policies and for universal insurance.

LIFE INSURANCE PREMIUM COSTS COMPARISON FOR TERM AND UNIVERSAL (PER $1,000 OF COVERAGE)

EXHIBIT 2.4

Age	Term* (10 year)	Term* (25 year)	Term* (30 year)	Universal Life
25	$0.25	$0.52	$0.60	$2.31
30	$0.25	$0.56	$0.64	$2.92
35	$0.26	$0.65	$0.72	$3.77
40	$0.31	$0.96	$1.04	$4.74
45	$0.51	$1.52	$1.68	$5.99
50	$0.83	N/A	N/A	$7.45
55	$1.40	N/A	N/A	$9.05
60	$2.39	N/A	N/A	$11.74
65	$4.08	N/A	N/A	$15.40

Price is per $1,000 of coverage ($ per 000).
For very healthy non-tobacco using male insured.
* Usually available to terminate at or before age 75.

LEVEL-TERM INSURANCE SAMPLE FOR MALE, AGE 67

EXHIBIT 2.5

Amount	10-Year Term*	15-Year Term**
$1,000,000	$6,659	$10,454
$2,000,000	$13,249	$20,838

* MetLife Insurance
** Genworth Life Insurance

UNIVERSAL LIFE INSURANCE

Universal life insurance is similar to a term life insurance product with several additional features or options, including a cash value accumulation pot. Universal life insurance allows individuals to make premium contributions in excess of the term insurance premium or not make them at all. If premiums are not paid, ultimately the policy will lapse. Any excess premiums made are deposited into an investment account. The owner of the policy can make contributions to the policy at any time, and each year the insurance company will take enough out of the cash value accumulation pot to pay the equivalent of the term life mortality premium. As long as there is sufficient money in the policy to pay the premium, the policy will remain in force. If there is not enough money in the policy to cover the current premium payment, and the owner does not make additional premium contributions at least sufficient to pay for the mortality costs, the policy will lapse.

One of the advantages of universal life insurance is that the owner of the policy can make contributions to the policy when he or she has the cash-flow to do so, and the policy will remain in force as long as the term insurance premium can be paid from the cash value. The cash value is invested by the insurance company, and interest is credited to the accumulation. To the extent that the earnings on the cash accumulation are used to pay for life insurance protection, the growth in investment value is not subject to tax. Over time, this creates the potential for the owner of the policy to pay for the term insurance protection with pre-tax dollars (from earnings on the cash invested in the policy) as opposed to after-tax dollars (premium payments paid directly by the policy owner).

Universal life policies typically offer two death benefit options, referred to as Option A and Option B. If the client chooses Option A for the death benefit, the policy provides a level death benefit. This means that as the cash value accumulation in the policy increases, the amount of death benefit protection decreases. Once the cash accumulation gets to a specified level, however, the death benefit will have to increase to ensure that the policy continues to meet the definition of life insurance. A life insurance policy must have an amount "at risk" (net amount at risk) if the cash value equals the death benefit, there is no longer an actuarial amount at risk.

EXAMPLE 2.13

Edward purchased a universal life insurance policy several years ago, and has been making contributions in excess of the term insurance cost. The death benefit for the policy is $100,000 and the death benefit option selected was option A. The cash value in the policy is $20,000 after the current year's term insurance premium was paid. If Edward dies this year, his beneficiary will receive a $100,000 death benefit from the insurance company. Since $20,000 of the death benefit is covered by the cash value of the policy, the amount at risk under the policy is only $80,000 ($100,000-20,000). Edward's term insurance premium for the year will be based on an $80,000 death benefit, which will reduce the annual cost he will incur compared to the term insurance premium on a $100,000 death benefit.

If the client chooses Option B for the death benefit, the policy provides an increasing death benefit. If the insured dies, the policy death benefit will equal the specified death benefit in the policy plus the cash value of the policy.

EXAMPLE 2.14

Refer to the facts in the prior example. If Edward chose Option B coverage instead of Option A, and he died this year, his beneficiary would receive a death benefit of $120,000 (equal to the policy death benefit of $100,000 plus the policy cash value of $20,000). The term insurance premium that Edward will pay will be based on $100,000 of insurance protection, which is the amount that the insurance company must pay upon Edward's death. Compared with an Option A death benefit, the annual costs of the policy will be greater (because there is a greater amount at risk) but the death benefit received by the beneficiary will be greater as well.

Universal life insurance is attractive for clients who have temporary needs for life insurance protection and who would like to pre-fund the costs of the term insurance protection by making contributions to the cash value accumulation pot attached to the policy. Clients with a permanent need for insurance protection should consider other types of policy alternatives. Since the term insurance costs (mortality costs) increase each year and must be paid to keep the policy in force. A standard universal policy does not guarantee a death benefit but it can. If it does, it requires maintaining the premiums. However, flexibility in premium payments is one of the attractions of universal life insurance, but that same flexibility may cause the death benefit to be reduced or, in the extreme, cause the policy to lapse.

WHOLE LIFE INSURANCE

Whole life insurance provides guarantees from the insurer that are not found in term insurance and universal life insurance policies. As long as the premium specified in the insurance contract is paid, whole life insurance will remain in force during the life of the insured even if there is no longer cash in the cash value accumulation pot to pay term insurance premiums (as is the case with Universal Life Insurance). In arriving at the premium payment amount, the insurer considers the cost of insurance protection over the lifetime of the insured (usually to age 100), and prices the premium amount accordingly. As a consequence, the premiums on whole life insurance policies are larger than the premiums on term life or universal life policies because the insured is pre-funding the cost of insurance protection. The premium payments over the term insurance cost of protection are invested by the life insurance company, which typically guarantees a minimum investment return. Unlike the situation with a universal life insurance policy, which transfers investment risk to the insured, the insurer retains the investment risk on a whole life policy and, even if the invested excess premium payments are not sufficient to pay the future pure cost of insurance protection (term insurance cost) each year, the insurer promises to keep the policy in force.

Whole life policies are useful when the client wants to ensure that life insurance protection will be available on a permanent basis. Whole life policies are also useful for middle-age and older clients who need death benefit protection but do not wish to retain investment risk (as would be the case in a Universal Life Insurance Policy).

The most common form of whole life policy, referred to as an **ordinary (or straight) life** policy requires the owner to pay a specified level premium every year until death (or age 100). The premium can be paid on a monthly, quarterly, semi-annual, or annual basis, and the policy will remain in force as long as the premium is paid. Older straight life policies provided that if the insured lived to age 100, the face amount (the death benefit) on the policy would be paid to the policyowner as a living benefit. If this occurs, the amount received in excess of the owner's basis in the policy would be subject to income tax, so many policies now provide for the insurance policy to remain in force until death even if the insured lives to or past age 100 to lock in the income-tax-free character of the death benefit.

| EXHIBIT 2.6 | **THE SAVINGS ELEMENT OF A LEVEL-PREMIUM, WHOLE LIFE INSURANCE POLICY** |

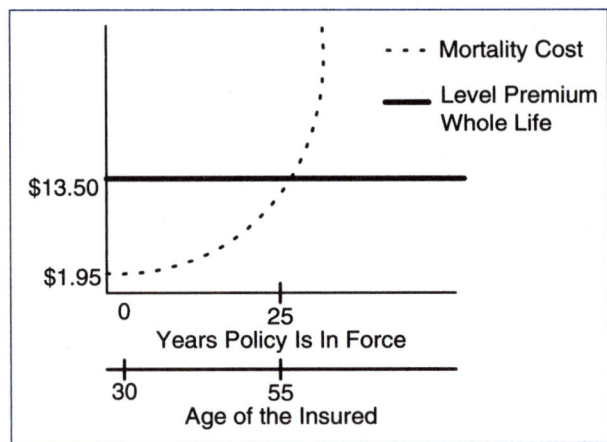

One of the problems with an ordinary (straight) life policy is that premium payments must be made throughout the lifetime of the insured. Many individuals would prefer to make premium payments over a shorter period of time (perhaps their work-life-expectancy) that will be sufficient to keep the policy in force for their lifetime. Insurance companies will often provide quotes for whole life policies on a 10 or 20-year payment schedule. At the end of the payment period the policy is considered to be paid-up, at which time no additional premium payments are due. These policies are referred to as **limited-pay policies**. Of course, the premium on a limited pay policy will be greater than the premium on an ordinary (straight) life policy since the lifetime premium payments are being front-loaded over the payment period.

While some clients have a need for permanent life insurance protection, the normal premiums on a whole life policy may not be affordable based on current income, but as income rises in the future, however, the client may anticipate being able to pay the premium. When a client finds him/herself in this situation, and would like to lock in the insurance protection now (to ensure insurability), a **modified whole life policy** should be considered. Modified Whole Life Policies have lower premiums than a regular policy for an initial policy period (often three to five years), and increase to a higher level premium at the end of the initial period. This allows a client who is currently insurable the opportunity to purchase a whole life policy with lower payments now that increase when income increases in the future, and is an alternative to convertible term insurance.

Whole life insurance policies can also be purchased on a single-premium basis. A **single premium policy** requires the owner to pay a lump sum in return for insurance protection that will extend throughout the insured's lifetime. These policies require a substantial initial cash outlay, and are typically used for estate and generation-skipping transfer tax purposes. One downside to using a single premium policy is that if the owner receives lifetime benefits from the life insurance policy (by borrowing money from the cash value), income tax must be paid on the cash received to the extent of the growth on policy cash value. A single premium policy is a form of **Modified Endowment Contract (MEC)**, which has different tax attributes than regular life insurance policies.

Some clients object to whole life policies on the grounds that the rates credited (earned) to the cash value accumulation within the policy are often low, increasing the premium that must be paid for insurance protection. **Variable whole life policies** provide for a fixed premium payment and permit the cash value of the policy to be professionally managed by the insurance company or an outside investment manager. The policy owner can choose among various investment options and will receive the investment returns earned by the funds purchased with the cash value inside the life insurance policy. This type of policy transfers investment risk to the owner and the amount of the death benefit available on the policy will fluctuate with the investment performance of the underlying investments. Younger clients (who have a long-term investment horizon) and clients with moderate to high risk tolerance may find variable whole life policies appealing since they hope to capture some of the upside benefits of allocating their cash value to equities instead of fixed-income investments. Unlike universal life insurance policies, variable whole life policies have a minimum death benefit that will be paid regardless of the investment performance of the underlying investments and the owner of the policy will be guaranteed the minimum death benefit as long as the scheduled premium specified in the contract is paid.

Whole life policies can also be tailored to meet specific financial needs. **Second-to-die** policies are often used in estate planning to provide liquidity at the death of the second spouse to die (since this is typically when estate taxes for the couple will be due). A second-to-die policy names two insureds and pays the death benefit only when the second insured dies. Since two lives are covered by the policy, a second-to-die policy is a type of joint life insurance policy.

Another type of joint life policy is a **first-to-die** policy. Like the second-to-die policy, the first-to-die policy covers two individuals but the death benefit is paid upon the death of the first individual. First-to-die policies are sometimes used to provide funding to pay off a mortgage at the death of the first spouse, to provide a fund for children's educational costs when one spouse dies early, or to provide a supplemental pool of capital for the surviving spouse to provide additional retirement income.

Policy Dividends
Policy dividends represent cost savings realized by the life insurance company that were not anticipated when the life insurance policy was originally priced.

Whole Life Insurance policies are permanent policies that are priced using current actuarial mortality assumptions. Over the past century life expectancies have been increasing and that trend is expected to continue into the future. Life insurance policies that were priced using actuarial tables that assumed the group of covered insureds, as a whole, would die at a younger age that current mortality tables would suggest resulted in higher premium payment requirements when compared to premiums calculated using current mortality assumptions. In addition to favorable mortality experience (which occurs when the group of insureds lives longer than they were anticipated to live based on mortality assumptions), the insurance company may realize expense savings, and greater than anticipated returns on investments than it assumed when it originally priced a life insurance policy. Insurance companies return these excess premium payments to policyholders by issuing dividends on participating, or permanent, insurance policies. Unlike a dividend on a stock investment, which is a distribution of corporate earnings and profits and is therefore subject to income tax in the hands of the stockholder, dividends on life insurance policies are treated as a nontaxable return of part of the owner's premium payment.

Policy owners can choose to receive the dividend payments in cash, or may choose one of several other options provided by the insurance company. Insurance companies commonly offer options to use dividends to purchase paid-up additional life insurance protection, to purchase one-year term insurance, to accumulate interest, or to reduce premium payments.

If the policy owner chooses the paid-up additions option, an additional amount of paid up life insurance protection is purchased, which increases the death benefit on the policy. The paid-up additions option is often attractive to individuals who are uninsurable and would like to receive additional death benefit protection.

Instead of purchasing a paid-up addition to the death benefit, the policy owner could also enhance the death benefit by using the dividend to purchase one-year term insurance. This option will provide a greater death benefit if the insured dies during the year when compared to the paid-up additions option, but, like all other term insurance contracts, the coverage will expire at the end of the year unless another dividend distribution is received and is again used to purchase term insurance. Recall that if the dividend stays the same, the amount of one-year term insurance that can be purchased each year will decline due to the increasing mortality risk (and premium cost) as a result of increasing age.

Quick Quiz 2.2

Highlight the answer to these questions:

1. All else being equal, the total premium outlay on an ART policy will be less than a level-term policy.
   a. True
   b. False

2. Universal life insurance is a breed of term life insurance.
   a. True
   b. False

3. Universal life insurance option A provides for increasing death benefits.
   a. True
   b. False

4. Two ways to receive tax-free benefits from a whole life policy during one's life are: taking a loan against the death benefit amount and not withdrawing an amount in excess of the basis.
   a. True
   b. False

True, True, False, True.

If the insured does not need additional death benefit protection, the dividends can be left on deposit with the life insurance company, which will pay interest on the dividends. The owner of the policy can access these amounts at any time, and if the dividends and the accumulated interest payments are left with the insurer until the insured's death, they are added to and paid out with the death benefit of the policy. While the policy dividends themselves are not taxable, interest earned on policy dividends is subject to income tax. Each year that interest is credited to dividends deposited with the insurance company, the insurance company will send the policy owner a Form 1099-INT which will specify the interest payments that are subject to tax.

One final way to use policy dividends is to use them to offset (decrease) the premium payments due on the policy for the current year. This permits the life insurance premium payments to decline over time if dividends are regularly declared on a life insurance policy.

Taxation of Whole Life Insurance Policies
Both the growth in the cash value of the policy and the policy death benefit are exempt from Federal Income Tax under current law.

Policyowners who wish to receive lifetime benefits from a whole life insurance policy without triggering an income tax consequence can achieve this in two ways:
1. they can withdraw their tax basis in the policy; and
2. they can take loans against the cash value of the policy. Provided that the policy is in force at the date of the insured's death, loans outstanding against the policy cash value will be free of federal income tax but will reduce the death benefit on the policy by the amount of the outstanding loan.

IRC Section 101(a) exempts the death benefit on any life insurance policy from income tax provided that the policy has not been exchanged for valuable consideration. A detailed discussion of the Transfer-for-Value Rule is covered later.

Surrender Charges
The insurer incurs several costs when issuing a whole life insurance policy that often exceed the first premium payment made by the insured. To prevent incurring losses when policyowners purchase and then quickly cancel their insurance contracts, insurance companies typically enforce a **surrender charge** that is designed to compensate them for the up-front costs they incur when issuing the policy. The amount of the surrender charge and the length of the surrender-charge period are regulated by state law. Typically, surrender charges decrease over a period of time and, after a period of seven to ten years, cancellation of a life insurance policy will not result in the imposition of a surrender charge. In most cases where careful planning is conducted, this should not be a major concern, since most people who choose to purchase permanent life insurance typically want that coverage to stay in force until the death of the insured.

Nonforfeiture Options for Life Insurance
Nonforfeiture options protect the cash values of a policyowner who chooses to discontinue coverage under a whole life policy. This provision states that the insured, by lapsing or surrendering the policy, does not automatically forfeit the cash value accumulation. The nonforfeiture options give the policyowner some choice in how to receive the cash value of the policy. The most common nonforfeiture options include:
- Cash Surrender Value.
- Reduced Paid-Up Insurance.
- Extended Term Insurance.

Cash Surrender Value

This option gives the owner immediate access to a certain amount of cash specified in the policy, in exchange for termination of the policy. This option should be exercised with care because the same amount of cash may be obtained through one of the other options, which provide for a continuing amount of coverage. Where an insured is retired or elderly with no surviving dependents, the need for a large amount of life insurance is reduced, so the cash surrender option could be a suitable choice. In any other situation where the need for death protection has ceased or where alternative death protection has been purchased, this is a viable option. Consumers who surrender policies may incur an income tax liability on part of the cash value accumulation, so a complete policy surrender should be thoroughly evaluated from a tax perspective. Note that surrender value is usually less than cash value for the first 10-15 years of the policy.

Reduced Paid-Up Insurance

This option allows the policyowner to purchase a fully paid-up whole life insurance policy using the cash value of the policy. The face amount of the policy will be dependent upon the amount of cash value accumulation, less surrender charges. Reduced paid-up insurance is essentially an option to purchase a single premium whole life insurance policy. It is suitable for someone who wants to maintain some level of permanent death protection but does not want to pay any future premiums.

Extended Term Insurance

Extended term insurance uses net cash surrender value as a net single premium to purchase a paid-up term insurance policy equal to the original face amount for a limited period of time, usually a certain number of years and days. The length of the term protection is dependent upon the insured's age at the time he or she chooses to exercise the option. The net single premium will also be determined by the company's current premium rates. This option is most suitable for someone who wants to preserve, for only a limited time, death protection equal to the forfeited policy's face value.

VARIABLE LIFE INSURANCE

The structure of a **variable life insurance** policy is much like a universal life insurance policy with one major exception – variable insurance policies permits the owner of the life insurance policy to direct the investment of the policy's cash value. In the case of whole life insurance, or a regular Universal life insurance policy, the insurance company invests the cash value and credits a rate of interest to the accumulation. Variable policies typically offer a series of investment options that often include investment funds managed by the insurer and outside investment managers. When a client purchases a variable life insurance policy, the cash value of the policy is held in a separate account and the policy owner bears all of the investment risk associated with his or her investment choices. If the cash value is invested in funds that increase in value at a rate greater than the crediting rate that the insurance company offers on whole life insurance, the policy-owner can benefit from either a decrease in insurance costs (if an option A level death benefit with a decreasing amount at risk is chosen), or increased death benefits (if an option B increasing death benefit is chosen), or, in some cases, both.

If the policyowner experiences losses from the investments he or she chooses, this can result in either:
1. increased premium costs for the owner, or
2. a lapse of the policy.

Variable Universal Life Insurance Policies (VULs) are often used by young individuals who have the risk tolerance and time frame necessary to weather equity market downturns. Since VULs have a flexible premium payment option like universal life insurance policies, the policyowner can make large premium payments in early years to fund the cash value accumulation pot, and, if the investments do well over a period of time, have sufficient resources in the cash-value pot to continue to pay the term insurance premium without further premium payments. From a planning perspective, early funding of VULs usually produces the best results, but owners should be aware of the Modified Endowment Contract (MEC) rules. If the policy is funded too fast, lifetime benefits that the owner can receive from the policy may become subject to income tax.

The ability to control the investments in a VUL policy causes the policy to be considered a registered investment security. Life insurance agents and financial planners who sell VULs must be licensed to sell both life insurance and securities.

FEATURE COMPARISON OF COMMON LIFE INSURANCE POLICIES — EXHIBIT 2.7

	Term Life	Whole (Ordinary) Life	Universal Life	Variable Life	Variable Universal Life
Premium $	Fixed or Variable	Fixed	Variable, subject to a required minimum	Fixed	Variable, subject to a required minimum
Death Benefit	Fixed	Fixed	May increase above initial face amount, depending on cash value accumulation	Has a guaranteed minimum, but can increase if investment experience on cash value is good	Has a guaranteed minimum, but can increase if investment experience on cash value is good
Policyowner's Control Over Investments	None	None	None	Complete	Complete
Rate of Return on Investment	None	Fixed rate	May have a minimum guaranteed rate, but can be higher depending on interest rates	No minimum guarantee, but positive investment experience can yield very high returns	No minimum guarantee, but positive investment experience can yield very high returns
Application	Large need, limited resources	Want guarantees	Flexibility without investment responsibility	Flexibility with investment responsibility, fixed premiums	Flexibility with investment responsibility, variable premiums

MODIFIED ENDOWMENT CONTRACTS (MECs)

A Modified Endowment Contract (MEC) is not really another type of life insurance policy but rather a cash value life insurance policy that has been funded too quickly (faster than a 7-equal-pay corridor).

In the 1980s life insurance became a popular tool for taxpayers who wished to defer income. Income tax rates in the early 1980s were as high as 50 percent and it made sense for taxpayers in those high brackets to purchase universal, whole life, or variable universal life insurance policies as an investment to defer the growth on the policy cash value until they retired, cash in the policy, and pay tax on the growth at a lower rate. Since life insurance policy cash values grow on a tax-deferred basis (if the policy is cashed-in during lifetime) or a tax-free basis (if a death benefit is paid when the insured dies), they became popular tools used to defer investment income into the future. In theory, life insurance is a product designed to hedge against the mortality risk faced by the insured but for high income taxpayers in the 1980s life insurance became a tool to lower tax rates on investment income. Needless to say, Congress was not amused with this use of life insurance.

In the Tax Reform Act of 1986 Congress enacted the modified endowment contract (MEC) rules. These rules state that if a single premium life insurance contract is purchased, or if a regular life insurance policy is purchased and is funded too quickly, lifetime benefits received under the policy (in particular, the ability to obtain a loan against the policy cash value without income tax consequences) would trigger income tax liability.

Congress imposed two tests to determine whether a life insurance contract meets the definition of a MEC:
1. the corridor test; and
2. the 7-pay test.

The corridor test calls for the policy to be tested using actuarial principles and requires the premiums to represent no more than a specified portion of the death benefit. The calculation of the corridor test is beyond the scope of this text. The 7-pay test states that if the cumulative premium payments made on the policy are in excess of the net level premium for the policy during the first seven years it is in existence (or following a material change to the policy), the life insurance contract will be considered a MEC.

When the insured dies and a MEC pays a death benefit, the death benefit is exempt from income tax. If the insured wishes to access policy values during lifetime, however, distributions in the form of loans or withdrawals are taxed on a last-in first-out (LIFO), or interest first, basis. The LIFO treatment of MEC contract means that, to the extent that the value of the policy exceeds the owner's basis in the policy and the owner takes some form of lifetime benefit, distributions are subject to income tax. In the event that the owner is under the age of 59½, the distribution may also be subject to a 10 percent penalty tax.

GROUP-TERM INSURANCE

As part of their employee benefit packages, many employers offer group term insurance to their employees. **Group-term insurance** covers all eligible employees under a master contract that is obtained by the employer. Employers may offer the group term insurance as a flat amount (for example, $50,000 or $100,000 of death benefit protection for all employees) or as a percentage of income (one, two, or three times the employee's annual income).

When offering group term life insurance to its employees, an employer is able to deduct the premium costs that it pays as an ordinary and necessary business expense. An income tax doctrine called the economic benefit doctrine states that when a person receives property in return for services, the value of the property received must be included in his or her income for income tax purposes. The first $50,000 of death benefit protection received by the employees, however, has been excluded from tax by Congress, which means that the employee is not taxed on the value of up to $50,000 of group term insurance paid for by the employer.

To the extent that the employer pays the entire premium on the group policy and the death benefit protection for an employee exceeds $50,000, the value of the death benefit protection must be included in the employee's income and is subject to income tax. The amount subject to tax equals the amount of death benefit protection in excess of $50,000 multiplied by the applicable premium rate found in the IRS Premium table. If the employee contributes to the cost of the group term insurance through payroll deduction, that portion of the insurance received is not subject to tax under the economic benefit doctrine.

Group term insurance is a very cost effective way of obtaining life insurance protection, even when the employee has to include in his or her income the imputed premium on insurance provided in excess of the $50,000 group term limit. In this case, the employee receives the life insurance protection at a fraction of the cost that he or she could have purchased the insurance for in the private market. In essence, the employee only pays tax on the imputed premium; the employee does not pay the premium itself. Depending on the employee's marginal income tax rate, this results in a significant reduction in the cost of insurance protection.

EXAMPLE 2.15

Godfrey works for Pennant Enterprises, Inc. As part of Pennant's employee benefit program, Godfrey receives $150,000 of group term insurance paid for by the company. Based on the IRS Premium Table Rates and Godfrey's attained age, the imputed premium on the $100,000 of insurance in excess of the tax-free group term limit of $50,000 is $328. At the end of the year, Pennant Enterprises will include an additional $328 in Godfrey's W-2, which will be reported on his annual tax return. Since Godfrey's marginal income tax rate is 25%, the tax he will incur on the inclusion of the imputed premium is $82. For an out of pocket annual cost of $82, Godfrey receives $150,000 of term life insurance protection.

If an employee terminates from service, he or she typically has the option of converting the group term policy into a permanent, cash-value policy at a rate specified in the group contract (and based on the employees age at the time). This conversion feature may be valuable for individuals who are not insurable since evidence of insurability is not required and the conversion will preserve the employee's ability to purchase death benefit protection. If a terminating employee is insurable, it may be wise to first consider the cost of commercially available life insurance since the insurance companies underwriting the group plan often assume that those wishing to convert their group term insurance to permanent insurance upon termination of employment are uninsurable and may therefore charge a higher premium.

OTHER TYPES OF GROUP LIFE INSURANCE

Employers can also provide group whole life insurance, group universal life insurance, and group variable universal life insurance to their employees. Often making these types of insurance contracts available on a group basis results in cost savings for the insurer that are passed on to the employees participating in the plan in the form of lower premiums. Sometimes employers pay the premiums on these policies as an employee benefit, while others make the plans available and permit the employees to pay the premiums with after-tax dollars at the lower group rates.

Planners should be aware, however, that the income tax exclusion for the first $50,000 of death benefit protection only applies to group-term insurance plans. Employer provided group whole life, group universal life, or group variable universal life insurance benefits will subject the employee to tax on the economic benefit the employee receives, which is measured by the imputed term cost of the insurance protection received.

COMMON LIFE INSURANCE CONTRACT POLICY PROVISIONS

GRACE PERIOD

Life insurance policy premiums are typically structured to be payable on a monthly, quarterly, or annual basis. To keep the life insurance policy in force, the premium must be paid on time. This is particularly true for term insurance policies, which do not have cash value that can be used to keep the policy in force (permanent policies are often structured to borrow from the cash value to pay the premium on the due date unless the insured has already paid the premium). Most life insurance policies provide a **grace period**, typically spanning one month (31 days), after the premium due date for the policyowner to pay an overdue premium. Generally, the insured would not have to provide further evidence of insurability if the premium is paid within the grace period, but once the policy lapses and the grace period expires, the insured may be required to undergo additional underwriting for the policy to be reinstated.

During the grace period the policy remains in force. If the insured dies during the grace period the insurance company will pay the death benefit to the named insured and deduct from that death benefit the premium that is due. Some policies may also charge interest on the overdue premium since the insurance company loses the ability to invest the premium proceeds on the due date.

INCONTESTABILITY

In the early days of life insurance some companies would issue policies to insureds and collect premiums over several years, yet contest the validity of the contract when the death benefit was due based on an alleged misrepresentation, omission of information, or concealment of information by the insured that would have been relevant making a proper underwriting decision when issuing the policy. The incontestability clause found in life insurance policies today combats this abuse and states that once the policy has been in force for a period of time, typically two years, the insurer may not cancel the policy if they later discover a material misrepresentation, omission, or concealment.

Key Concepts

Underline/highlight the answers to these questions as you read:

1. Highlight the typical clauses found in life insurance contracts.

2. Describe the difference between a survivorship clause and a simultaneous death clause.

3. Describe the settlement options: lump-sum, interest only, and the various annuity options.

MISSTATEMENT OF AGE OR GENDER

The cost of life insurance protection is based on the age and gender of the insured. As individuals get older, the likelihood that they will die within the year (as expressed in mortality tables) increases, thereby increasing the risk for the insurer. Furthermore, females tend to live longer and therefore have lower mortality risk when compared to males at the same age. To compensate for this increased risk the insurance company charges a higher premium for the life insurance protection. If the insured misstates his or her age or gender on a life insurance application the insurance company can, at any time (even after the death of the insured), adjust the face amount of the policy to the amount that the specified premium would have purchased at the correct age or using the correct gender of the insured. Since the date of the insured's birth will be listed on the insured's death certificate and in the Social Security death index, when processing death claims insurance companies routinely check to make sure that the insured's age, as disclosed in the policy, was correct prior to paying the claim.

EXAMPLE 2.16

Gloria is trim, fit, and gorgeous at age 48. People think she is close to 30 years old and she has been lying about her age for years. Gloria purchases a 30 year term policy with a death benefit of $3,000,000 paying the level premium for a 30 year old, which is $0.60 per $1,000 of average. Her total annual premium is $1,800. Unfortunately, three years later she is killed in an automobile accident. The executor of her estate sends the certified death certificate to the insurer who then discovers how old she really was at the inception of the policy. The level premium for a 48 year old female at the time of inception was $2.00 per thousand. The insurer will pay to the beneficiary $900,000 ($1,800 ÷ 2 x 1,000).

SUICIDE

The risk that insureds facing an almost certain risk of loss will seek to transfer that risk to an insurance company is known as adverse selection risk. Adverse selection risk is experienced with all kinds of insurance policies, including life insurance. As discussed above, the individuals most likely to seek to convert their group term life insurance contracts to permanent insurance when they separate from service are those who are sick or who expect to have a shorter than average life expectancy.

The **suicide clause** in a life insurance policy is designed to hedge against the risk that individuals with suicidal thoughts will purchase life insurance and, shortly thereafter, commit suicide. Since a person who commits suicide has an actual mortality risk of one (or 100%), the normal pricing of a life insurance policy that takes into consideration the actuarial life expectancy of the individual will not result in a premium sufficient to hedge the risk of death for the insurance company. The suicide clause states that if an insured commits suicide within a specified time (in most states, this is two years), the insurance policy will not pay the death benefit to the beneficiary but will refund the premiums paid on the policy to the named beneficiary. Since it is unlikely that a person would plan to purchase life insurance several years before planning to commit suicide, a two-year exclusion is usually considered sufficient to balance the adverse selection risk of the insurer against the potential loss of the life insurance death benefit for the beneficiaries in the event a suicide does occur.

REINSTATEMENT

If a life insurance policy lapses due to non-payment of premium and expiration of the grace period, the policy may permit reinstatement provided that the requirements specified in the policy are satisfied. Typically, the policy will specify that reinstatement without evidence of insurability is available for a short time after expiration of the grace period (usually 31 days). Provided that past premiums plus interest on those premiums are paid to the insurer, and satisfactory evidence of insurability is provided, it may be possible to reinstate a life insurance policy up to five years after the policy lapse.

POLICY LOAN PROVISIONS

One of the benefits of using a permanent life insurance policy is the cash value accumulation that is attached to the insurance. The purpose of the cash value is to accumulate funds to permit the policy-owner to spread the cost of the risk of protection over a long period of time, preferably until the death of the insured. The cash value can also be accessed by the policyholder in the form of a policy loan. When a policy loan is issued there are no income tax consequences for the policy-owner (provided that the life insurance policy was not classified as a modified endowment contract (MEC)) and the interest rate charged on the loan is typically a low rate that is specified in the contract. Any loan outstanding at the death of the insured, plus accrued interest on the loan, is deducted from the death benefit paid to the policy beneficiary.

In financial planning the cash value of life insurance policies can be considered part of a client's emergency fund since the loan provides easy access to cash at a reasonable rate of interest and can be repaid at any time. Sometimes a policy will offer an option that permits the policy owner to use life insurance policy cash values to pay the ongoing policy premium. This option may be particularly useful when cash values have accumulated substantially and the policyowner no longer wishes to pay the premium.

BENEFICIARY DESIGNATIONS

At the insured's death, the policy death benefit is paid to the beneficiaries named by the contract owner or, if no beneficiary has been named, to the estate of the insured individual.

Most beneficiary designations on life insurance policies are revocable, which means that the policy owner can change the beneficiary at any time. In some cases an irrevocable beneficiary will be named on a policy. For example, a divorced client may be required to maintain life insurance for the benefit of an ex-spouse and/or children, in which case the beneficiary designation is typically irrevocable. In order to change the beneficiary on a policy that has an irrevocable beneficiary designation, the original beneficiary must consent to the change.

The individual or organization that will receive the death benefit upon the death of the insured is referred to as the **primary beneficiary**. More than one primary beneficiary may be named on a life insurance policy, which allows the primary beneficiaries to share the death benefit in the manner specified by either the policy-owner or the policy itself.

Contingent beneficiaries will receive the death benefit if the primary beneficiary is not available to receive the policy proceeds. If individuals are named as the primary beneficiaries on a life insurance policy, it is important to consider the possibility that the primary beneficiary may die before the insured causing the death benefit to be transferred to someone else. If no contingent beneficiary is named, the death benefit is generally paid to the policyowner or to the policy owner's estate (if the policy owner was also the insured). Naming a contingent beneficiary is not as important when the policy death benefit will be paid to either a trust or a corporation since these entities do not have a natural life and are likely to be in existence when the insured dies.

SURVIVORSHIP CLAUSES

A **survivorship clause** specifies that the death benefit will only be paid to the beneficiary if the beneficiary survives the insured by a specific number of days (usually 30-60 days). If the beneficiary does not survive by the specified number of days, the death benefit is paid to the contingent beneficiary, or, if there is no contingent beneficiary to the policy owner or the policy-owner's estate. A survivorship clause protects the testamentary intent of the policy owner by ensuring that the appropriate party receives the policy proceeds and can also minimize estate and probate complexities that might be encountered if the policy proceeds are subject to administration in two estates in quick succession.

SIMULTANEOUS DEATH PROVISIONS

A **simultaneous death provision** is similar to a survivorship clause and is effective whenever the insured and the beneficiary die within a short time of one another and it is not possible to determine who died first. Under the Uniform Simultaneous Death Act, if the insured and the beneficiary die in a common accident and the order of deaths is uncertain, the policy death benefit is distributed as if the beneficiary had predeceased the insured. When the policy owner has named a contingent beneficiary, that beneficiary will receive the death proceeds. If no contingent beneficiary is named, the policy proceeds will be distributed to the policy owner or the policyowner's estate.

ASSIGNMENT

Assignment is the process of transferring all or part of the policy's ownership rights. A policyholder might wish to assign his interest in a life insurance contract to a bank as collateral for a loan, with or without the insurance company's consent. Two main types of assignments exist in today's insurance industry: absolute and collateral. An absolute assignment gives the entity that has received the assignment all policyownership rights subject to any limitations set forth in the assignment. A collateral assignment is used to serve as security for debt and gives the lender or "assignee" limited ownership rights under the policy. The assignment automatically terminates when the debt is paid and policyownership rights are usually exercisable only if the borrower defaults on the loan.

AVIATION EXCLUSION

Though no longer a common exclusion in policies issued today, the aviation exclusion denies coverage for those who die in noncommercial flights, such as private pilots, their passengers, and military pilots. Premiums are usually returned to the beneficiary but the death benefit is not paid.

Quick Quiz 2.3

Highlight the answer to these questions:

1. An owner of a life insurance policy is always free to change the beneficiary of the policy.
   a. True
   b. False

2. The suicide clause states that if the insured commits suicide at any time while a life insurance policy is in place, there will be no pay out.
   a. True
   b. False

3. If a client is concerned that his or her surviving spouse will not be able to effectively manage the benefit amount, an interest only option should be considered.
   a. True
   b. False

4. Only that portion of the annuity amount that is attributable to the growth of the death benefit is taxed to the beneficiary.
   a. True
   b. False

False, False, True, True.

WAR EXCLUSION

This exclusion allows the insurer to deny the death claim if the insured dies while in the military or as the result of a military action. Premiums are usually returned to the beneficiary with interest and the death benefit is not paid.

SETTLEMENT OPTIONS FOR LIFE INSURANCE

When an insured individual dies and the insurance company is notified of the death, the life insurance benefit becomes payable. The beneficiary can receive the proceeds in a lump-sum payment but most insurance policies provide several alternative options for the beneficiary to receive the death benefit.

LUMP-SUM PAYMENT

Receiving a lump-sum benefit is perhaps the simplest way to complete the life insurance transaction. Sometimes the insurance company will pay the lump sum directly in the form of a check to the beneficiary. More recently life insurance companies have been creating an account for the beneficiary at the life insurance company in which the policy proceeds are deposited. The beneficiary receives a check book and can draw any or all of the death benefit out of the account by simply writing a check. Amounts left in the account will earn interest until withdrawn. This approach may be valuable for beneficiaries who would like to receive a lump-sum distribution but who have not yet decided how to invest or otherwise deploy the life insurance death benefit.

INTEREST ONLY

The interest only option allows the beneficiary to keep the death benefit on deposit with the insurance company and receive periodic payments of interest on the policy proceeds. If the owner/insured is concerned about the ability of the beneficiary to manage the insurance proceeds, the interest only option should be considered. In some cases the beneficiary is given the opportunity to access some of the principal amount (the death benefit) in addition to receiving payments of income. The primary beneficiary is permitted to name a contingent beneficiary to receive any amounts remaining when the primary beneficiary dies.

ANNUITY PAYMENTS

Fixed Amount

When the fixed amount annuity method of distributing the death benefit is chosen the policy death benefit will be deposited with the insurance company and the beneficiary will receive a fixed payment each year until the proceeds are depleted. The balance on deposit with the insurance company will be credited with interest each year. As the beneficiary receives payments, the portion of each payment that represents interest earnings will be taxable to the beneficiary but the remaining portion of the payment, which represents part of the death benefit, will not be subject to income tax.

The beneficiary should choose a contingent beneficiary in case the primary beneficiary dies prior to receiving all of the payments from the insurance company. If no contingent beneficiary is named the remaining amount in the account is typically paid to the estate of the deceased beneficiary.

Life Income

The life income option converts the death benefit into an annuity contract for the life of the beneficiary. When the life income approach is chosen the amount of the annuity payment will depend on the size of the death benefit paid, the age, and the health of the beneficiary. Each year as payments are received the beneficiary will pay income tax on a portion of each payment representing the growth in the annuity contract and the remaining portion will be exempt from income tax. This result relies on the calculation of the exclusion ratio for the policy. The portion of the payments representing the return of the death benefit paid under the life insurance policy will be received by the beneficiary income tax free. Since the payments will stop when the beneficiary dies, there is no need to name a contingent beneficiary if a life income option is chosen.

Fixed Period

Instead of receiving an annuity payment over the lifetime of the beneficiary, the death benefit proceeds could be used to purchase an annuity certain, which is an annuity that will make payments for a specified number of years. When the fixed period option is chosen, the beneficiary's age and health will not be considered in the pricing of the annuity. The only factors that will matter are: (1) the size of the death benefit received and (2) the crediting rate of interest on the annuity contract. If the beneficiary dies prior to receiving all of the fixed payments, a contingent beneficiary can be named to receive the remaining payments or, if a contingent beneficiary is not named, the payments will be made to the primary beneficiary's estate.

A fixed period annuity with a term less than the life expectancy of the beneficiary, all else equal, will result in a higher payment than a life income annuity. In financial planning engagements, using a fixed period annuity payout may be preferential to the life income method when: (1) the beneficiary needs additional cashflow for a fixed period of time, such as until retirement age (when distributions from retirement accounts will begin), or (2) when the beneficiary suspects that he or she will have a shorter than average life expectancy and would like to preserve some of the death benefit value for a successor beneficiary if the primary beneficiary dies young.

Life Income with Period Certain

The life income with period certain payout method combines the benefits of the life income method with the benefits of the fixed period method. This approach will transform the death benefit into a life annuity contract based on the age and health of the beneficiary, yet will promise to make a specified number of payments under the contract. If the beneficiary dies early, a contingent beneficiary will receive the remaining payments promised under the contract.

All else equal, a life income with period certain payout will provide a lower periodic payment than a straight life payout because the insurance company is promising to make payments for a minimum period of time. It may be useful in financial planning contexts, however, when the beneficiary would like to have the security of annuity payments, but suspects that they might have shorter than average life expectancy.

> **EXAMPLE 2.17**
>
> Bryan was named as the beneficiary of his Aunt Josephine's life insurance policy. In his earlier years, Bryan was a bit free-wielding, and engaged in several activities that could have the impact of shortening his lifespan. Since Bryan has not had a good track record with managing money, he would like to choose a payout method that will give him income for life, but would like to make sure that his son, Garrett, gets something if he dies too soon. Bryan elects to take a life income with a 15 year period certain. If Bryan lives beyond 15 years, he will continue to receive payments for the rest of his life and the payments will stop at Bryan's death. If Bryan dies 10 years after the payments begin, however, the insurance company will continue to make payments for an additional 5 years to Bryan's son, Garrett, whom Bryan named as contingent beneficiary of the proceeds.

Joint and Last Survivor Income

With the Joint and Last Survivor Income settlement option, annuity payments will be made over the joint lives of two individuals and, when one of them dies, the survivor will receive a reduced payment for the rest of his or her life. Sometimes, a period certain is also incorporated into this option as well. If the beneficiary of a life insurance policy would like to ensure that another person, such as a spouse, will continue to get benefits from the policy even after the beneficiary's death, this settlement option would be a good one to consider.

TAXATION OF LIFE INSURANCE POLICIES

While this chapter discusses some of the tax consequences of life insurance in the context of the individual policies and techniques, it may be helpful to summarize the tax characteristics of life insurance policies in one section. In this section, we will also introduce a few advanced tax concepts concerning life insurance, such as tax-free exchanges of insurance policies, and viatical settlements.

PREMIUM PAYMENTS

Premium payments on life insurance policies are not tax deductible, with a few rare exceptions. For example, group term insurance premiums on insurance protection of up to $50,000 are deductible by the employer and not included in the income of the employee. Furthermore, certain types of employee benefit plans, such as VEBAs and 415 plans, can be created by an employer and funded with life insurance policies allowing the employer to deduct the premium. Life insurance purchased within a qualified pension plan effectively achieves a tax deduction since the money used to fund the pension plan was tax deductible (many restrictions apply to this, however, and they are covered in detail in a retirement planning course). Finally, life insurance purchased pursuant to a divorce decree may be deductible by the ex-spouse paying the premiums (as alimony), provided that the other ex-spouse is the owner of the policy. Except for these circumstances, however, life insurance premiums are not tax deductible.

Since the premiums cannot be deducted for income tax purposes, the owner of the policy will have a basis in the policy (representing after-tax investments in the vehicle) equal to the cumulative premiums paid for the policy. The owners basis may be reduced when the insurance company issues dividends or when the owner makes a withdrawal from the cash value of the policy, both of which are discussed below.

Key Concepts

Underline/highlight the answers to these questions as you read:

1. Highlight some of the income tax benefits to be derived from life insurance planning, both to the policy beneficiary(ies) and the owner.

2. Describe FIFO and LIFO treatment.

3. Describe the possible tax consequences for policy exchanges.

4. Describe a viatical.

DEATH BENEFIT TAXATION

IRC Section 101(a) states that the death benefit received by a beneficiary of a life insurance policy due to the death of the insured is exempt from federal income tax. The income tax-free character of the death benefit is an important planning consideration. While Congress could subject life insurance death benefits to income tax, it chooses not to as a means of encouraging individuals to purchase life insurance (and, as a consequence, providing for their beneficiaries so that the beneficiaries will not have to rely on public assistance after the insured's death).

If an individual owns a life insurance policy on his or her own life, or if the proceeds of the policy are made available to the executor of his or her estate, the death benefit will be included in the owner/insured's gross estate and may be subject to estate tax. Many individuals confuse the income tax and estate tax rules concerning life insurance – they believe that the death benefit is "tax free." If the insured does not own the policy covering his or her life and the proceeds of that policy are not made payable to the executor of his or her estate, this understanding is correct. Many individuals, however, own the life insurance policies that cover their own lives so when this situation applies the death benefit is free from income taxation but is potentially subject to estate taxation (if the decedent had a taxable estate).

TAXATION OF LIFETIME BENEFITS

One of the benefits of owning a permanent life insurance policy during lifetime (even on your own life) is that the owner can obtain several tax-free benefits from the policy prior to the payment of the death benefit.

As discussed earlier, dividends are issued on life insurance policies when the pool of individuals insured experience better than anticipated life expectancies. Dividends are treated as a return of premium (a rebate of previously taxed income) and are therefore not subject to income tax. A dividend distribution does, however, reduce the owner's basis in their life insurance policy. If dividends exceed the owner's basis, the owner would be subject to tax on those excess dividends, since he or she has already recouped the capital investment in the life insurance policy.

Owners may also withdraw cash value from permanent life insurance policies without being subject to income tax. Withdrawals are treated first as a distribution of basis (which would not be subject to income tax), using the first-in-first-out, or FIFO, method of accounting. The exception is a MEC, which follows LIFO rules. Once the owner of the policy withdraws all of his basis, any further withdrawals would be subject to income tax since they would represent policy earnings which are not paid by reason of the death of the insured.

When the owner of a policy has reduced his or her basis in the policy down to zero (through receipt of dividend distributions or withdrawals) and would like to access additional policy values without triggering a taxable event, the owner can borrow from the cash value of the policy. The loan will carry a favorable rate of interest specified in the life insurance contract and does not have to be paid back provided that the life insurance policy remains in force during the life of the insured. When the insured dies, the loan plus accumulated interest will be subtracted from the death benefit received by the beneficiary. Provided that the policy remains in force until the death of the insured, the owner of the policy can access cash values on an income tax-free basis.

Quick Quiz 2.4

Highlight the answer to these questions:

1. If the insured dies while owning the life insurance policy, the value of the policy is not includible in his or her estate for estate tax purposes.
   a. True
   b. False

2. The FIFO method of accounting is preferable to the LIFO method because income tax is deferred until the distributed amount exceeds basis.
   a. True
   b. False

3. If a client exchanges a policy for a similar policy there is no income tax due at the time of exchange; rather the basis is carried over to the new policy and it is not increased by additional premium payments.
   a. True
   b. False

4. If your terminally ill client sells his life insurance policy and uses the proceeds to pay for a vacation rather than medical expenses, those proceeds, to the extent they exceed the client's basis in the policy, will be subject to income tax.
   a. True
   b. False

False, True, False, False.

When a permanent life insurance policy is terminated during the life of the insured (the policy is surrendered), a taxable event may result. The difference between the amount received by the owner on the surrender of the policy and the basis of the policy in the hands of the owner will be subject to income tax. If the owner receives less than his or her basis, the payment is considered a return of capital and is not subject to tax. When a policy is surrendered, the owner may receive the proceeds in a lump sum, may leave the proceeds with the insurer and receive interest payments on the proceeds, or may choose an installment payment method specified in the life insurance contract. When the installment payment method is chosen, it is possible to spread the taxable gain on surrender of the policy over several tax years using the exclusion ratio approach to calculating the taxable portion of each payment. The installment method may be valuable to a high-bracket income tax payer who realized a large gain upon surrender of a life insurance policy.

POLICY EXCHANGES

Often, clients may wish to change life insurance policies, or transform them into other types of insurance products as their needs change. Fortunately, the Code specifies that when certain exchanges take place there is a deferral of gain from one product to the next. Under IRC Section 1035, deferral applies to certain exchanges made between life insurance policies, modified endowment contracts (MECs) and annuity contracts.

As our discussion above highlights, life insurance policies are uniquely tax-favored products due to the income tax exclusion of the death benefit and the ability to access lifetime benefits on a tax-free basis. Modified endowment contracts (MECs) also provide income tax-free death benefits but if the owner of a MEC attempts to receive lifetime benefits from the policy, those benefits may be subject to income tax (MECs use LIFO, not FIFO treatment when considering the tax consequences of withdrawals and loans). Annuity contracts provide tax deferral but ultimately all gains in the contract will be subject to income tax. Purely from a tax perspective, therefore, life insurance contracts are the best of the three, MECs come in second, and annuities are the least attractive, since they always result in taxable income.

Section 1035 of the Code states that if a policy is exchanged for another similar policy (for example, life insurance for life insurance, MEC for MEC, or annuity for annuity), or for an insurance product that increases the potential for assessment of income tax, the exchange of the policies is a tax-deferred exchange and no income tax will be due at the time of the exchange. If a tax-deferred exchange is desired, therefore, life insurance policies can be exchanged for other life insurance policies, MECs, or annuity contracts. MECs can be exchanged for other MECs or annuity contracts, and annuity contracts can be exchanged only for annuity contracts.

EXCHANGE TREATMENT FOR LIFE INSURANCE AND ANNUITIES

	EXCHANGE FROM	
EXCHANGE TO	Life Insurance	Annuity
Life Insurance	OK	Taxable Event
Annuity	OK	OK

The basis of the original contract will carry over into the new contract and will increase by additional premium payments made to the insurance company.

TRANSFER FOR VALUE

If an existing life policy is transferred for valuable consideration (transfer for value), the insurance proceeds are includible in the gross income of the transferee to the extent the proceeds exceed the basis. Thus, the usual income tax exclusion for life insurance proceeds is lost. There are five instances when the transfer of a policy will not result in inclusion of proceeds in the income of the transferee. They are:
- A transfer to the insured
- A transfer to a business partner of the insured
- A transfer to a partnership of which the insured is a partner
- A transfer to a corporation of which the insured is an officer or shareholder
- A transfer that results in the transferee's basis being determined by reference to the transferor's basis, such as a gift

VIATICAL SETTLEMENTS

A **viatical settlement** is the sale of a life insurance policy to a third party. As previously discussed, the surrender of a life insurance policy (which could be thought of as a sale of the policy back to the insurer) results in a taxable event for the owner if the value of the life insurance policy exceeds the owner's basis at the time of surrender. Generally, the same rule applies to viatical settlements – the original owner of the policy will be subject to income tax to the extent that the sale proceeds exceed his or her basis in the policy.

As is the case with most income tax rules, there are exceptions to this tax treatment. If the owner-insured of a life insurance policy is terminally ill at the time the policy is sold, the gain in the policy will not be subject to income tax. Terminal illness is defined as having a life expectancy of less than 24 months, which must be certified by a health care professional. In many cases, when an insured sells a life insurance policy shortly before death, the proceeds are used to pay for their medical care. To encourage use of private, as opposed to public funds to cover those medical expenses, Congress exempts the gain on the policy realized by the insured from income tax. Note that the actual use of the proceeds does not change the result – as long as the insured was terminally ill when the policy was sold, there will be no income tax on the gain.

If the owner-insured is chronically ill and the proceeds of the life insurance policy sale are used to pay for long-term care costs for the insured, any gain on the sale of the policy is exempt from income tax. Chronic illness implies that the insured has either a substantial cognitive impairment (suffers from advanced stages of Alzheimer's disease or senile dementia), or is unable to perform two of the six activities of daily living (eating, bathing, dressing, transferring, toileting, and continence) without assistance.

When the purchaser of a policy under a viatical settlement receives the death benefit, the death benefit will be subject to income tax to the extent that the policy death benefit received exceeds the purchaser's basis in the policy. Under the transfer-for-value rule, when a life insurance policy is sold for valuable consideration (as in the case of a viatical settlement), the death benefit is subject to income taxation. The transfer-for-value rule is covered in more detail in income tax and estate planning courses.

ACCELERATED BENEFITS PROVISION

An **accelerated benefits provision** entitles a qualified insured to receive a lifetime benefit deemed nontaxable. This is similar to a viatical settlement and follows the same rules except the parties involved are only the original insurer and the original insured. There are no third parties as in a viatical settlement.

ANNUITY CONTRACTS FOR LIFE OR FOR TERM

A life annuity is not life insurance but is a product often sold by life insurance companies. A life **annuity** contract provides protection against superannuation, outliving assets by providing a series of periodic payments to the annuitant. Payments are made for as long as the annuitant lives. Annuities are commonly used to fund retirement benefits. For example, a retiree might retire with $2 million in retirement funds. Instead of trying to budget the money over the retirement years, the retiree can simply purchase a life annuity that will guarantee a steady stream of income until death.

Similar to life insurance, annuity payments are based on the pooling of the risk and life expectancy of a group. Some annuitants live to be 85 or 90, others die at much younger ages. Thus, some persons will be paid more money than others and the risk of living "long" is thus shared among the group. The remaining principal from those who die at younger ages is applied to a fund, which is used by the group to pay those who survive longer than their life expectancies. Annuity payments are comprised of a combination of premium payments, interest earnings, and unliquidated principal of annuitants who die early.

TYPES OF ANNUITIES

Immediate vs. Deferred
The insured has the option of having annuity payments made monthly, quarterly, semiannually, or annually. In addition, the insured may also specify whether the payments are to be immediate or deferred. An immediate annuity is one whose first payment is due one payment interval from its purchase date. Immediate annuities are purchased with one, single lump-sum premium.

A deferred annuity provides income at some future date. The most popular form of a deferred annuity is a retirement annuity in which the account value accumulates for a number of years and is then paid in installments when the insured reaches retirement age. Deferred annuities may be purchased with either a single premium or periodic level or varying premiums.

Flexible Premium vs. Single Premium
A flexible premium annuity allows the insured the option to vary premium deposits. The amount of retirement income will be directly related to the accumulated sum in the annuity

when it becomes due. Under a flexible premium plan the insured spreads payments out over a designated period of time by paying periodic premiums.

An annuity purchased with a single lump sum is known as a single premium annuity. Proceeds from life insurance policies can be used to purchase single premium annuities at special rates under life income settlement options.

TIMING OF ANNUITY PAYMENTS

Pure Life Annuity

Often referred to as a straight life annuity, a pure life annuity provides a lifetime income to the annuitant, whether he lives one year or 30 years after payments begin. Once the annuitant dies, no further payments are made. For a given purchase price, the highest amount of lifetime annuity income per dollar spent is paid by the pure life annuity.

For many people, the single life annuity is unsuitable because it is possible to purchase a pure life annuity, receive one payment, and then die. Since there is no guaranteed minimum number of payments the insurer must make the dependents of the annuitant receive nothing from the contract once the annuitant has died. For this reason the pure life annuity is ideal for the person who needs maximum income spread out over his lifetime and has no living dependents to whom he wishes to leave assets.

Life Annuity with Guaranteed Minimum Payments

A life annuity with guaranteed minimum payments ensures that the annuitant or his heirs either receives a minimum number of payments or will have lifetime income, whichever is greater. Two common guarantee options are the ten-year period certain and the twenty-year period certain. If the annuitant dies before the end of the guarantee period, the named beneficiary receives the remaining guaranteed payments. If the annuitant outlives the guarantee period, payments continue until the annuitant's death.

Installment Refund Annuity

This annuity is similar to the one described previously, except the insurer promises to continue periodic payments after the annuitant has died until the sum of all annuity payments equals the purchase price of the annuity or, with the cash refund option, the balance is paid in cash at the annuitant's death.

Joint and Survivor Annuity

A **joint and survivor annuity** is based on the lives of two or more annuitants, usually husband and wife. Annuity payments are made until the last annuitant dies. A true joint and survivor annuity pays the full monthly payment to both parties and continues the same payment to the survivor. Some persons, however, choose a joint and survivor annuity that pays the survivor only a portion of the payment that was paid on both lives. A common amount might be 75 percent, in which case the annuity would be called a joint and 75 percent survivor annuity. Joint and last survivor is the most popular form of the multi-life annuity today. Premiums are higher than those charged for single life annuities, because the insurer guarantees payment for what is almost always a longer time period.

TAXATION OF ANNUITIES

Each annuity payment is considered a partially tax-free return of basis and partially taxable income using an inclusion/exclusion ratio similar to that for the installment method settlement option of life insurance death benefits. The numerator for the exclusion ratio is the cost basis in the annuity. The denominator is the total expected benefits. Unlike annuities resulting from life insurance settlements, any annuity payments from purchased annuities that are received beyond the original life expectancy are fully taxable as ordinary income to the annuitant.

DISABILITY INSURANCE

One of the greatest risks faced by clients is the prospect of not being able to work during their earning years – the prospect of becoming disabled. While life insurance acts as a hedge against the prospect of early death, **disability insurance** acts as a hedge against being unable to work. The risk of being unable to work (referred to by actuaries as morbidity risk) at any age is greater than the risk of death (mortality risk). According to statistical data derived from the Society of Actuaries, the National Safety Council, and the Disability Fact Book, the likelihood of disability over death at various ages is:

Age	Likelihood
30	4 to 1
35	3.5 to 1
40	2.7 to 1
45	2.1 to 1
50	1.8 to 1
55	1.5 to 1

Furthermore, as medical science has improved treatments and has substantially reduced the risk of death from heart disease and cancer, the risk of disability from these diseases has remained the same or increased. Individuals who rely on employment related income to meet their current and future financial planning needs should consider hedging their risk of disability with disability insurance policies.

AMOUNT OF COVERAGE

As a rule of thumb, individuals should have between 60 and 70 percent of their gross income protected with a disability insurance policy. In some cases the replacement percentage may be greater, particularly for younger individuals with few assets who have families with young children. Due to the moral hazards that can present themselves with this type of insurance, insurance companies will not issue disability insurance policies that will cover more than 100 percent of the insured's income (alone or in combination with other policies), and often will limit coverage to a fraction of the insured's income. The reasoning behind this is that if the insured has no incentive to work, this may increase disability insurance claims for the insurer, particularly when own occupation policies (covered below) are issued.

TERM OF COVERAGE

Coverage under disability insurance policies is typically split between short-term coverage and long-term coverage. Short-term disability insurance policies often provide benefits for a period of one to two years, while long-term disability insurance policies provide coverage until normal retirement age or death. When an individual is covered under both short-term and long-term disability insurance policies the benefit periods should be coordinated so that there is no gap in coverage. For example, if a short-term disability insurance policy covers benefits for two years, the insured's long-term disability policy should provide benefits beginning two years after the disability began (when the short-term disability benefits terminate) to normal retirement age or death. Once the individual reaches normal retirement age, disability coverage is no longer needed, since retirement income will commence.

Key Concepts

Underline/highlight the answers to these questions as you read:

1. Describe the moral hazard that is associated with disability insurance.

2. Describe how any occupation disability insurance works in regard to highly skilled professionals.

3. Describe what is meant by a split definition of disability.

4. Describe the possible tax consequences of disability benefits.

TYPES OF DISABILITY INSURANCE POLICIES

Disability insurance policies typically cover periods when the insured is unable to work due to suffering an accident or sickness. There are three primary types of disability policies:
- own occupation policies,
- any occupation policies, and
- split definition policies.

TYPES OF DISABILITY POLICIES

EXHIBIT 2.8

Own occupation policies state that if the insured is unable to perform each and every duty associated with his or her own occupation the insured is deemed to be disabled and the policy will provide benefits.

DISABILITY INSURANCE 99

EXAMPLE 2.18

Rosemary is a concert pianist and has spent her lifetime practicing and performing piano concertos around the world. She recently contracted a disease which affected the dexterity of her hands and has therefore prevented her from being able to perform at concerts. She purchased an own occupation disability insurance policy 25 years ago so the insurance policy will pay disability benefits to Rosemary since she can no longer perform the duties of her occupation as a pianist.

Own occupation policies used to be popular tools in the late 1980s and early 1990s, particularly with physicians, musicians, and other professionals whose income was dependent on their ability to perform specific tasks. Over time insurance companies recognized that there was a large adverse selection risk associated with these policies, which are now less available. When an own-occupation policy (as they are referred to) is issued, the premium is high due to the risks being undertaken by the insurance company.

An **any occupation** disability insurance policy provides benefits to a policy owner if he or she is unable to perform the duties of any occupation. This type of policy is not attractive to individuals in high-skill professions. The surgeon, for example, would probably not want a policy that will not pay benefits unless he/she could not perform telemarketing services. The courts have limited the interpretation of this definition of disability to mean that the insured can collect benefits if he/she is unable to perform any occupation for which he/she is suited based on training, experience, and educational degrees. Continuing our example, if the surgeon is unable to perform surgery due to an injury to his hands, but could teach medical school to new physicians, he would be expected to earn income in that fashion, and would not receive benefits under the policy. The surgeon would not, however, be required to perform telemarketing services as a means of minimizing benefits received under the policy.

Many disability insurance policies today use a **split definition** of disability in their disability insurance policies. Under a split definition policy, an insured will be covered against the risk of not performing his or her own occupation for a period of time and, after that period expires, an any-occupation definition of disability would be used. This gives the insured a period to adjust to his or her new reality and perhaps get the training necessary to perform other occupations that will allow him/her to replace the lost income from the old profession.

TYPICAL PROVISIONS IN DISABILITY INCOME POLICIES

Most disability policies begin to provide benefits after an elimination period has been satisfied. The elimination period ensures that benefits will not be paid unless the insured experiences a disability that has the potential of depriving the insured of income for a long period of time, and also helps the insurance company manage the moral hazard associated with fraudulent disability insurance claims. The elimination period may be as short as one month and can be extended depending on the needs of the insured. If, for example, the insured's employer will continue to pay salary to the insured for up to three months in the event of a disability, the elimination period on the disability insurance policy can be set to three months, which would ensure continuous income for the insured while lowering the cost of the insurance protection. As the elimination period increases up to a point (usually

180 days), all else equal, the premium on the policy will decrease. High quality disability policies are either noncancelable or guaranteed renewable (discussed in Chapter 3).

Disability policies today typically provide a **partial disability rider**, which states that if the insured is partially disabled, but is able to continue to work and perform some of his or her prior duties, the policy will pay a specified amount to the insured even though he or she is still working. The terms of the partial disability rider vary significantly from company to company, so the financial planner should attempt to use the policy that best meets the needs of the individual insured. Usually, these riders only provide coverage for a short period, such as three to nine months. Providing partial disability insurance benefits to an insured encourages the insured to return to work, which helps minimize the risk undertaken by the insurance company in issuing the policy.

BENEFIT PERIOD

Disability insurance distinguishes between short-term and long-term coverage. **Short-term disability** typically has a short elimination period (5 - 30 days), the period an insured must wait before receiving benefits, and provides coverage for up to two years. Many employers offer group short-term disability insurance that provides employees with a percentage of their salary while disabled. **Long-term disability** typically has a longer elimination period (30 -180 days) and provides coverage until normal retirement age, until death, or for a specified term. Some employers offer group long-term disability insurance with premiums generally paid for by the employee. Employer-sponsored plans are usually not portable and terminate when the employee leaves the firm unless the reason for leaving employment is directly related to the disability.

PARTIAL DISABILITY

Many policies include coverage for partial disability, defined as the inability to perform at least one important duty of the insured's normal occupation. The partial disability provision provides payments that are less than those paid for total disability but these benefits usually last for only a short time (such as six months). By covering partial disability in this manner, the insurer gives the insured some incentive to return to work sooner than he or she otherwise might.

OTHER DISABILITY POLICY PROVISIONS

Benefits awarded under a disability income policy are provided because the insured no longer has income, or has reduced income, from employment. Most disability insurance policies, therefore, will waive future premium payments under the policy once the elimination period has been met and the insured is receiving benefits under the policy. If the insured regains his or her health and returns to work, the premiums on the policy must be paid in order to keep the policy in force.

Some disability insurance policies also provide a cost of living (COLA) adjustment to the benefit payments. Since the cost of items that the insured consumes will increase as inflation increases, a COLA adjustment will help the insured maintain his or her purchasing power during a long period of disability. Typically, COLA adjustments are tied to the consumer price index (CPI). All else equal, a disability insurance policy with a COLA provision will have a higher premium than one without a COLA provision.

In addition to protecting current income, some insureds would like assurance that, as their income increases, they will be able to get additional disability income insurance. Two riders are commonly used to achieve this:
- the future increase option rider - permits the insured to increase the monthly benefit as the insured gets older, and
- an automatic increase rider - automatically increases the monthly benefits by a stated percentage every year.

If either of these two options is chosen, the premium on the policy, all else equal will be greater than a policy that does not provide these protections.

RENEWABILITY

Insured individuals who have policies that are renewed each year are potentially subject to a risk of policy cancellation. In fact, it would be in the best interest of the insurance company to cancel policies held by individuals who are likely to become disabled as a means of avoiding benefit payments. To prevent this from happening, and to give policy holders some protection against policy cancellation, different renewability rights are provided for in disability insurance contracts, which include: (1) non-cancellable policies, and (2) guaranteed renewable policies.

Non-cancelable

Non-cancelable policies prevent the insurance company from cancelling the policy for any reason provided that the policy premium is paid. Usually, the policy will specify that it is non-cancelable for a specific period of time or until the insured reaches a stated age. Some policies also specify that, during the non-cancelable period, no changes to the policy may be made, including changes to the premium. Non-cancelable policies provide the greatest degree of protection to the insured since the insured can force the insurance company to provide continued coverage simply by paying the premium on the policy.

Guaranteed Renewable

Guaranteed renewable disability insurance policies require the insurance company to renew the policy for a specified period of time or until the insured attains a certain age. Provided the insured pays the premium, the insurance company must renew the policy during the period stated in the contract. Unlike the case with non-cancelable policies, which do not permit increases in premium, the premium on a guaranteed renewable policy may be increased on a class basis (i.e., increased across the board for all similarly situated insureds), but may not be increased for one participant simply because he or she has been exposed to a disease or health condition that increases the likelihood of suffering a period of disability.

RESIDUAL BENEFIT PROVISION

Experiencing a condition that prevents an insured from working for a period of time may lead to a permanent loss of income. This may be particularly true when an insured is covered by an any-occupation disability policy or an own-occupation disability policy that morphs into an any-occupation policy after a specified period of time. While the insured may be able to work, it is possible that the conditions causing the disability will prevent him/her from being able to perform all of the requirements of the prior job, resulting in a loss of income. A **residual benefit provision** will provide continuing benefits for an insured who returns to work but suffers a loss of income due to the disability.

Insurance companies typically use two approaches to determine eligibility for residual benefits: (1) the loss of earnings method or (2) the loss of earnings and loss to time/duties method. Under the loss of earnings method, residual benefits are usually payable if the insured's earnings loss exceeds 20 percent. Under the loss of time or duties test, if, as a result of the insured's disability, compensation is adjusted for time away from the job, or the income is adjusted because the insured cannot perform the same duties, a residual benefit may also be available. To qualify for benefits, the insured is required to prove an earnings loss (usually by submitting earnings statements before and after the period of disability). Disability insurance policies often compare income before and after on an average basis, such as the average monthly earnings for the 12 month period immediately preceding disability.

Some residual benefit provisions also index benefits for inflation, usually based on the Consumer Price Index. While this increase may not match future increases in income that would have been attained had no disability been suffered, at least it attempts to preserve the purchasing power of the benefit.

Quick Quiz 2.5

Highlight the answer to these questions:

1. A thirty year old has a lower morbidity rate than a fifty year old.
   a. True
   b. False

2. Disabled insureds generally continue to pay premiums while they receive benefits to avoid cancellation of the policy.
   a. True
   b. False

3. The "own occupation" policy is the most widely sold disability insurance policy.
   a. True
   b. False

4. Generally, it is more effective to pay disability insurance premiums with after-tax dollars, to avoid paying income tax on disability benefits.
   a. True
   b. False

False, False, False, True.

GROUP DISABILITY INSURANCE

Disability insurance is also available on a group basis, and is a benefit that is popularly available to employees of larger companies. Group disability insurance can be provided on a short-term or long-term basis, and in many cases both short-term and long-term policies are provided. The elimination periods for these policies are typically coordinated so that there is continuous income coverage for the insured. Often, the short-term group coverage will begin after employer coverage for sick time ends, and the long-term group coverage will begin when the short-term coverage terminates. Long-term group disability coverage usually terminates when the insured reaches normal retirement age or dies.

The advantage of group disability coverage is that the premiums are typically much lower than the premiums on individual coverage. Employers may pay for the premiums on behalf of the employees, or may permit the employees to pay for the coverage directly by payroll deduction. While group policies provide coverage to employees at a reasonable cost, they are not as portable as personal policies. Consequently, employees who anticipate frequent changes in employment may wish to consider the purchase of individual coverage.

TAXATION OF DISABILITY INSURANCE BENEFITS

The taxation of benefits received under a disability insurance policy depends on who paid the policy premiums. If the insured paid the premiums with after-tax dollars (as is the case when individual disability insurance is purchased, or when group insurance is purchased with after-tax dollars), the benefits received under the policy will not be subject to income tax. Benefits provided under a policy paid for with pre-tax dollars (such as when the employer provides disability benefits at no cost to the employees as an employee benefit) are subject to income tax.

If given a choice, an employee with access to employer group disability insurance should pay for the coverage with after-tax dollars to ensure that benefit payments are received on a tax-free basis. If the employee receives benefits under the policy, that implies he or she is unable to work, and that would probably not be the best time to have to worry about an additional cash outflow – in the form of income tax. Many employers who offer group disability policies to their employees permit them to pay for the policies with after tax dollars to achieve this benefit.

CONCLUSION

Life Insurance and disability insurance are tools that can be used by a financial planner to hedge against the mortality and morbidity risk that all clients face. Having a basic understanding of how each policy works, when it is appropriate to use them, and how much coverage should be obtained is important for anyone wishing to provide comprehensive financial planning advice to clients.

Key Terms

Accelerated Benefits Provision - Entitles a qualified insured to receive a lifetime benefit deemed nontaxable.

Annual Renewable Term (ART) - Type of term insurance that permits the policyholder to purchase term insurance in subsequent years without evidence of insurability, but premiums on the policy increase each year to reflect the increasing mortality risk being undertaken by the insurer.

Annuity - Periodic payment to an individual that continues for a fixed period or for the duration of a designated life or lives

Any Occupation - Type of disability insurance policy that provides benefits to a policy owner if he or she is unable to perform the duties of any occupation.

Assignment - The process of transferring all or part of the policy's ownership rights.

Asset Accumulation Phase - This phase is usually from the early 20s to late 50s when additional cash flow for investing is low and debt to net worth is high.

Beneficiary - A person or institution legally entitled to receive benefits through a legal device, such as a will, trust or life insurance policy.

Capitalized Earnings Approach - Method to determine life insurance needs that suggests the death benefits of a client's life insurance should equal an income stream sufficient to meet the family's needs without depleting the capital base.

Conservation (Risk Management) Phase - This phase is from late 20s to early 70s, where cash flow assets and net worth have increased and debt has decreased somewhat. In addition, risk management of events like employment, disability due to illness or accident, and untimely death become a priority.

Contingent Beneficiaries - Person(s) or organization named to receive the death benefit if the primary beneficiary is not available to receive the policy proceeds.

Decreasing-Term Insurance - Type of term insurance that allows the owner to pay the same premium for the insurance protection each year. The death benefit on the policy will, however, decrease each year to offset the increasing mortality cost due to the passage of time.

Disability Insurance - A type of insurance that provides supplementary income in the event of an illness or accident resulting in a disability that prevents the insured from working at their regular employment.

Distribution (Gifting) Phase - This phase is from the late 40s to end of life and occurs when the individual has high additional cash flow, low debt, and high net worth.

Key Terms

First-to-Die - Type of joint life insurance policy that covers two individuals, but the death benefit is paid upon the death of the first individual.

Grace Period - A provision in most insurance policies which allows payment to be received for a certain period of time after the actual due date without a default or cancellation of the policy.

Group Term Insurance - A type of life insurance coverage offered to a group of people (often a component of an employee benefit package) that provides benefits to the beneficiaries if the covered individual dies during the defined covered period.

Human Life Value Approach - Method to determine life insurance needs that suggests the death benefit of a client's life insurance should equal to the economic value of the client's future earnings stream.

Insured - Specifically named individual or institution with whom an insurance contract is made, and whose interests are protected under the policy.

Joint and Survivor Annuity - An annuity based on the lives of two or more annuitants, usually husband and wife. Annuity payments are made until the last annuitant dies

Level Premium Term Insurance - Type of term insurance that charges a fixed premium each year over a specified period of years, so the premium does not increase over that period.

Limited-Pay Policies - Type of whole life policy with a payment schedule (typically 10 or 20 years). At the end of the payment period, the policy is considered to be paid-up, at which time no additional premium payments are due.

Long-Term Disability - Provides coverage for specified term, until specified age, or until death

Modified Endowment Contract (MEC) - A cash value life insurance policy that has been funded too quickly. Under a MEC, the death benefit payable to the beneficiary is not subject to income tax.

Modified Whole Life Policies - Type of whole life policy with lower premiums than a regular policy for an initial policy period (often 3 to 5 years), and increase to a higher level premium at the end of the initial period.

Mortality Risk - The risk that an individual will die within the year.

Needs Approach - Method to determine life insurance needs that suggests the death benefits of a client's life insurance should equal the cash needs that the family will require at death.

Key Terms

Ordinary (or Straight) Life - Type of whole life policy that requires the owner to pay a specified level premium every year until death (or age 100).

Owner - Person or institution who owns the policy and can exercise the economic rights in a policy, including assignment, sale, etc. Also the person who is obligated for the payment of premiums.

Own Occupation - Type of disability policy which states that if the insured is unable to perform the duties associated with his or her own occupation, the insured is deemed to be disabled and the policy will provide benefits.

Partial Disability Rider - Provision that provides payments less than those paid for total disability.

Primary Beneficiary - Person(s) or organization named to receive the death benefit upon the death of the insured.

Residual Benefits Provision - Provision that provides continuing benefits for an insured who returns to work but suffers a loss of income due to the disability.

Second-to-Die - Type of joint life insurance policy that is often used in estate planning to provide liquidity at the death of the second spouse to die. A second-to-die policy names two insureds, and pays the death benefit only when the second insured dies.

Short-Term Disability - Typically has a short elimination period (5 - 30 days), the period an insured must wait before receiving benefits, and provides coverage for up to two years.

Simultaneous Death Provision - Provision in a life insurance policy for situations where the insured and the beneficiary die within a short time of one another and it is not possible to determine who died first, generally the policy death benefit is distributed as if the beneficiary had predeceased the insured.

Single Premium Policy - Type of whole life policy that requires the owner to pay a lump sum in return for insurance protection that will extend throughout the insured's lifetime. These policies require a substantial initial cash outlay, and are typically used for estate and generation-skipping transfer tax purposes.

Split Definition - Type of disability policy where an insured is covered against the risk of not performing his or her own occupation for a period of time, and after that period expires, an any-occupation definition of disability is used.

Suicide Clause - Provision in a life insurance policy specifying that the insurance company will not pay the benefit if the insured attempts or commits suicide within a specified period from the beginning of the coverage. The clause is designed to hedge against the risk that individuals with suicidal thoughts will purchase life insurance, and shortly thereafter, commit suicide.

Key Terms

Surrender Charge - A fee levied on a life insurance policyholder upon cancellation of the policy to cover the up front costs of issuing the policy in the first place.

Survivorship Clause - Provision in a life insurance policy specifying that the death benefit will only be paid to the beneficiary if the beneficiary survives the insured by a specific number of days.

Term Insurance - Life insurance policy that states that if the premium has been paid and the insured dies during the term of the policy, the insurance company will pay the specified death benefit.

Universal Life Insurance - Type of term insurance with a cash value accumulation feature allowing individuals to make premium contributions in excess of the term insurance premium. The excess premiums are deposited into an account with various investment options.

Variable Life Insurance - Type of life insurance policy that permits the owner of the life insurance policy to direct the investment of the policy's cash value. Variable policies typically offer a series of investment options that often include investment funds managed by the insurer and outside investment managers.

Variable Universal Life Insurance Policies (VULs) - Type of life insurance policy that combines variable and universal life insurance and gives the policyholders the option to invest as well as alter insurance coverage.

Variable Whole Life Policies - Type of life insurance that provides for a fixed premium payment and permits the cash value of the policy to be professionally managed by the insurance company or an outside investment manager.

Viatical Settlement - An arrangement in which a policyholder sells their life insurance policy to a third party.

Whole Life Insurance - type of life insurance that provides guarantees from the insurer that are not found in term insurance and universal life insurance policies.

DISCUSSION QUESTIONS

1. List and explain the three Life Cycle stages.

2. List and explain the three methods used to determine clients' life insurance needs.

3. List the benefits of term life insurance.

4. List the options available with term life insurance.

5. List the benefits of whole life insurance.

6. List the options available with whole life insurance.

7. Describe the income tax consequences associated with whole life insurance plans.

8. Define a modified endowment contract (MEC).

9. Describe the benefits associated with group life insurance plans.

10. List and describe provisions commonly found in life insurance policies.

11. List the settlement options that are available to life insurance beneficiaries.

12. Why are beneficiaries not taxed on life insurance proceeds?

13. Describe why a client might want to take a loan out from a whole life insurance policy; and what the consequences of that loan would be.

14. Define a viatical settlement.

15. List and define the three types of disability insurance.

16. List and describe provisions commonly found in disability insurance policies.

17. What are the various needs for insurance on the person in general, and life insurance in particular?

18. What are three recognized methods used to determine the amount of life insurance one should purchase?

19. What are component needs that make up the needs approach to the amount of life insurance needed?

20. How do term and whole life insurance differ, and what are the advantages/disadvantages of each?

21. What are the various types of term life insurance?

22. What are the various types of whole life insurance?

23. What differentiates variable life insurance from variable universal life insurance?

24. At what threshold is an employee taxed on group term life insurance provided by an employer?

25. What are the various types of annuities that are settlement options from life insurance?

26. What are the tax implications of life insurance and annuities?

27. What are the various contractual provisions and options that pertain to life insurance contracts?

28. What are the important policy provisions and major contractual features of group health and disability coverages?

29. What is the purpose of disability income insurance, and what are some of the various definitions of disability?

MULTIPLE-CHOICE PROBLEMS

1. Which of the following life insurance policies provide the highest benefit, for the lowest premium, and is simply a pure death benefit policy?

    a. Term.
    b. Whole life.
    c. Universal life.
    d. All of the above.

2. Joe, age 33, is married and has a newly born son. Joe is concerned about providing for his family in the event of his premature death. He is concerned about the long-term affordability of life insurance, but is able to budget a fixed amount for a period of time. Which of the following policies would you recommend?

    a. Annually renewable term.
    b. Level premium term.
    c. Whole life insurance.
    d. Single premium annuity.

3. Ryan and Jody are age 68 and 72, respectively and are married. They have significant assets that will be subject to estate taxes upon the second spouses death. Which of the following life insurance policies would you recommend?

    a. Annually renewable term.
    b. Second to die whole life policy.
    c. First to die whole life policy.
    d. Ordinary whole life.

4. Which of the following life insurance policies contain a cash value savings component that reaches the face value of the policy at age 100?

    a. Term.
    b. Whole life.
    c. Universal life.
    d. Lifetime annuity.

5. Which of the following life insurance policies have a fixed premium, a cash value and death benefit that can fluctuate based on investment performance?

    a. Annually renewable term.
    b. Variable renewable term.
    c. Variable whole life.
    d. Variable lifetime annuity.

6. All of the following statements concerning whole life insurance are true except?

   a. Level premium whole life insurance accumulates a cash value that eventually reaches the face value of the policy at age 100.
   b. Whole life insurance offers permanent protection throughout the insured's lifetime.
   c. Whole life insurance can be participating which means the insured must participate in self directed investments for the cash value.
   d. Whole life insurance premiums paid throughout the insured's lifetime are ordinary life policies.

7. All of the following statements concerning universal life insurance are true except?

   a. The insured has the flexibility to adjust premiums, face value and cash value of the policy.
   b. Insured has flexibility without the investment responsibility of the cash value.
   c. Cash value of the policy can be used to pay the premiums.
   d. The death benefit of a universal life insurance policy is fixed.

8. All of the following statements regarding disability insurance are correct except?

   a. The longer the elimination period, the less expensive the policy.
   b. An own occupation policy will provide disability benefits if the insured is unable to perform the duties of their own occupation.
   c. An any occupation policy is less expensive than an own occupation policy.
   d. A residual benefit clause provides the insured with benefits that extend beyond the disability period.

9. An individual has decided to purchase life insurance and comes to you as his agent. In order to program a system of life insurance to meet his individual needs, your first step is:

   a. Review his will or have him write a will if he does not have one.
   b. Selection of an insurance company.
   c. Selection of policy type he wants to purchase.
   d. Analysis of his needs and determination of the amount of life insurance coverage needed.

10. When utilizing the needs approach in the determination of the amount of life insurance, which factors should be considered?
    1. The family expenses that will remain after the wage earner dies.
    2. The value of the wage earner's life in the event he or she dies.
    3. The income that can be generated by the surviving spouse.
    4. The number of dependents.
        a. 1 only.
        b. 3 only.
        c. 1, 2, and 3.
        d. 1, 3, and 4.

11. The blackout period is:
    a. The period of time immediately following the death of the wage earner.
    b. The period of time after the death of a wage earner when the family is adjusting to life without the individual.
    c. The period of time when the widow or widower and dependents receive Social Security benefits.
    d. The period of time when the dependents have reached age 18 and the spouse's Social Security retirement benefits have not started.

12. Fred is 30 years old and recently began a job with a salary of $60,000. He is single but has been dating Lisa for 3 years. He expects to marry her within the next 5 years. Fred lives with his parents. What is the amount of life insurance that Fred currently needs?
    a. $0.
    b. $100,000.
    c. $60,000 x 6 = $360,000.
    d. $60,000 x 10 = $600,000.

13. Which of the following is needed to calculate the client's human life value?
    1. Average annual earnings to the age of retirement.
    2. Estimated annual Social Security benefits after retirement.
    3. Costs of self-maintenance.
    4. Number of years from the client's present age to the contemplated age of retirement.
        a. 3 and 4.
        b. 1, 2, and 4.
        c. 1, 3, and 4.
        d. 1, 2, 3, and 4.

14. Jack has a disability income policy that pays a monthly benefit of $2,400. Jack has been disabled for 60 days, but he only received $1,200 from his disability insurance. Which of the following is the probable reason that he only received $1,200?

    a. The policy has a deductible of $1,200.
    b. The elimination period is 45 days.
    c. The policy has a 50% coinsurance clause.
    d. Jack is considered to be only 50% disabled.

Quick Quiz Explanations

Quick Quiz 2.1
1. False. The asset accumulation phase generally lasts from the time one enters the workforce until retirement.
2. True.
3. False. In the event that the decedent's health insurance policy did not cover all of his or her medical expenses, life insurance proceeds are appropriately used to pay these expenses.
4. False. As clients age, the human life value and the need for life insurance protection decreases.

Quick Quiz 2.2
1. True.
2. True.
3. False. Option B provides for increasing death benefits - the stated policy amount plus the cash value. Option A provides a level death benefit or the cash value, whichever is greater.
4. True.

Quick Quiz 2.3
1. False. The owner could be under a legal obligation (for example, divorce) to keep a specific beneficiary if the beneficiary designation is an irrevocable election.
2. False. The suicide clause is generally only in effect for a specific amount of time (usually 2 years) and during that time, there is no payout, regardless of the reason for death or the cash value.
3. True.
4. True.

Quick Quiz 2.4
1. False. If the insured is the owner, the policy is includible in the decedent/owner/insured's estate.
2. True.
3. False. There is no income tax due, and the basis carries over, but additional premiums increase basis.
4. False. Regardless of what the money is actually used for, no gain on the sale of the policy is realized, if the seller was terminally ill at the time of the sale.

Quick Quiz 2.5
1. False. Morbidity rates fall with age.
2. False. Generally, once an insured becomes disabled and the elimination period has passed, future premiums are waived.
3. False. Own occupation disability insurance is the least sold type of disability insurance.
4. True.

Health Insurance and Long-Term Care

CHAPTER 3

INTRODUCTION

Effective financial plans assist clients in making appropriate financial choices that improve the client's financial health but a client who has a financial plan without physical health will not have a good quality of life. Unlike the risks associated with death and disability, clients tend to understand health risks and know that having adequate protection against those risks, in the form of health insurance, is a desirable financial goal. When a client chooses to self insure against health risks and a major health problem emerges, all of the client's assets are at risk. Health care treatments can be expensive, and may deplete a client's accumulated savings (for retirement, educational costs for the children, and major purchases), leaving the client financially unsound. Transferring the risk of incurring major health care costs to an insurer is prudent, especially when there is a possibility that other financial goals will be jeopardized if proper risk management plans are not put in place.

In this chapter we review the basics of group and individual health insurance and long-term care insurance. Long-term care insurance provides medical and custodial care for individuals whose health has deteriorated to the point where they cannot perform some basic functions of daily living without assistance. As medical science advances have increased life expectancy, the risks associated with long-term care have become very real for many people, and long-term care insurance should also be considered as part of any personal risk management plan.

When a person who is fully insured under the Social Security system reaches age 65, that person can obtain government provided health insurance from the Medicare system. Medicare part A, which is paid for by payroll tax deductions during the participant's working career, covers hospital costs. Medicare part B, which is paid for by payroll deductions plus a monthly premium amount deducted from the participant's Social Security benefits, covers Medical costs (doctors bills, lab tests, and the like). Persons receiving Medicare benefits often obtain a Medigap insurance policy to pay for items not provided for by Medicare. The details of Medicare health insurance are covered elsewhere in this text. This chapter focuses primarily on private individual health and long-term care insurance that clients need to acquire during their working years.

GROUP HEALTH INSURANCE

The most popular type of health insurance coverage in the market today is **group health insurance**. Most working individuals obtain their health insurance coverage by participating in their employer's group health insurance plans. Self-employed individuals with employees may offer a group health insurance plan as well to attract and retain qualified employees.

The Patient Protection and Affordable Care Act of 2010 and the Health Care and Education Reconciliation Act of 2010 require large employers (an employer that, at any time during the year, employs at least 50 people) to provide a minimum level of health insurance coverage to employees or face significant tax penalties. Small Employers (employers who, at all times during the year, employ less than 50 workers) are encouraged to provide health insurance to employees through the creation of tax credits for small businesses. The 2010 Health Care legislation also requires all U.S. citizens and residents to obtain health insurance, or face tax penalties for failing to comply. The constitutionality of mandating health coverage has already been challenged in federal court and, as of the date of this writing, has been ruled unconstitutional and is being appealed. As a consequence of the 2010 legislation, it is likely that even more individuals than ever will be covered by Group Health Insurance Policies.

Key Concepts

Underline/highlight the answers to these questions as you read:

1. Highlight the two reasons that explain why group health insurance is the most popular type of health insurance.

2. Highlight the two reasons that explain why group health insurance can be provided so cost effectively.

3. Define the two primary types of group health insurance.

4. Describe how a co-pay, a deductible, and a maximum out-of-pocket amount work in conjunction with each other.

The most attractive features of group health insurance are the ability to obtain coverage at a reasonable **premium** and without a physical and proof of insurability. Underwriting a large group of individuals permits the insurer to spread the claims risk among the pool of participants. Having a large group of participants spreads the administrative costs of the plan across many people. Both of these factors contribute to smaller premiums for group insurance when compared to individual health insurance policies.

ELIGIBILITY

To be eligible to purchase group health insurance, an individual has to be affiliated with a group that is covered by a group health insurance policy. Typically, all individuals who are employed on a full-time basis (or are a member of a qualifying group) at a company that provides group health coverage are eligible to participate in the group plan. Sometimes non-employer groups provide coverage for their members as well. Common examples are local Chambers of Commerce (which may offer a group plan that can cover the employees of all member companies), labor unions, and professional associations (such as The American Bar Association or the American Institute of Certified Public Accountants).

FEATURES OF GROUP HEALTH INSURANCE

Unlike individual health insurance, which is underwritten by assessing the specific health risks of the individual requesting coverage, group policies are underwritten based on the characteristics of the group to be covered. Individual underwriting and proof of insurability is not required for group health insurance contracts. Instead, the characteristics of the group as a whole are considered, and include items such as the average age of the group, and the type of work performed at the company. Most group contracts require that either all full-time employees, or all members of a qualifying group, to be automatically covered (enrolled) under the plan. This helps prevent adverse selection risk for the insurer, which is the risk that healthy members of the group will opt out of coverage, leaving only those with greater expected health care needs covered in the plan.

Quick Quiz 3.1

Highlight the answer to these questions:

1. Reasonable premiums and no required proof of insurability (i.e., a physical) are two of the most attractive attributes of group health insurance.
   a. True
   b. False

2. Underwriting a large amount of people spreads the actuarial risk amongst the pool of group health insurance, but participants drive up the administrative costs.
   a. True
   b. False

True, False.

The employer typically enrolls all eligible employees in the plan, and pays all or some of the premiums for coverage. If the employee must pay part of the health insurance costs, those costs are typically paid through payroll deduction. Since the employer shoulders a large part of the administrative burden by enrolling employees and paying premiums, part of the administrative cost savings realized by the insurer can be passed on to the employer in the form of lower group-health insurance premiums.

Types of Group Health Insurance

There are two primary types of group health insurance:
- group basic medical insurance, and
- group major medical insurance.

When the features of these plans are combined into one policy, the policy is referred to as a Group Comprehensive Major Medical Insurance plan.

Group Basic Medical Insurance

Group basic medical insurance covers hospital and physician bills, and surgical bills, but typically has low policy limits. Due to the low policy limits, group basic medical coverage is often used in conjunction with group major medical insurance.

Group Major Medical Insurance

Group major medical insurance coverage supplements basic medical coverage by permitting a wider array of services and increasing policy maximums. Sometimes these policies are referred to as group supplemental insurance plans.

Group Comprehensive Major Medical Insurance

Group comprehensive major medical insurance plans combine the benefits of basic medical coverage and major medical coverage. Typically, plan deductibles are low, and the employee may be required to make a co-payment when receiving services. After the plan deductible has been met for the year, the insurance company usually pays 80 percent of the cost of health care and the participant pays the remaining 20 percent until a maximum annual out-of-pocket limit is reached. Once the annual out-of-pocket limit is reached, the insurance company pays 100 percent of the costs of care for that year.

Quick Quiz 3.2

Highlight the answer to these questions:

1. A Group comprehensive Major Medical Insurance Plan is a combination plan that covers both basic and major health risks.
   a. True
   b. False

2. Once the insured reaches his out-of-pocket limit, the insurer pays the cost of care in excess of the insured's co-pay.
   a. True
   b. False

True, False.

EXAMPLE 3.1

Dylan is a participant in his employer's Group Comprehensive Major Medical Insurance Plan. The plan has a $200 deductible, and a $1,500 out-of-pocket maximum. If Dylan is injured in an accident and his medical costs total $2,000, Dylan will have to pay the first $200 to cover the deductible, and will pay $360 (20% of the remaining $1,800 in medical costs), for a total of $560. The plan will pay the remaining portion of the cost, or a total of $1,440. The next time that Dylan needs medical attention within the same year, he will pay 20% of those costs (but he would not have to pay another deductible, since the deductible has to be satisfied only once per year) until his total out-of-pocket costs for the year (including the deductible) is $1,500. In other words, Dylan will have to pay a maximum of $1,140 more for the year before the insurer pays 100% of future costs for the year.

Traditionally, comprehensive major medical plans were not favored by employees, since they resulted in the employee paying up to the out-of-pocket maximum each year. Many employees and unions favored first-dollar pay type plans, where the employee would make a small co-payment (of, perhaps $5 or $10) each time they visited a physician, and the insurance company would pay for the balance of the bill. First-dollar-pay type plans have higher premiums than comprehensive plans due to the increase in benefit payments made by the insurance company, and the increased administrative costs incurred. More recently, however, with the creation of Health Savings Accounts (HSAs) and the new federal requirements concerning health insurance coverage for employees, high deductible plans have enjoyed a renaissance as a means to provide adequate healthcare coverage while cutting premium costs for employers.

INDIVIDUAL HEALTH INSURANCE

NEED FOR COVERAGE

When a client does not have health insurance coverage under a government sponsored program, such as Medicare, and does not have access to employer provided or other group health insurance, the client should consider purchasing an individual health insurance policy.

Premiums on individual health insurance are typically higher than premiums on group health insurance, which may encourage some individuals to self-insure instead of purchasing coverage. Everyone should have, at a minimum, coverage for catastrophic medical expense needs (such as unforeseen major surgery or hospitalization) even if they choose to self insure for routine medical expenses, such as annual physical exams, tests, and office visits.

Key Concepts

Underline/highlight the answers to these questions as you read:

1. Highlight how the Patient Protection and Affordable Care Act of 2010 is designed to spread the cost of mandatory health insurance.

2. Describe the inverse relationship between deductibles and premiums.

3. Define stop loss limit.

4. Describe what medical expense insurance covers, and name the subcategories of it.

EXAMPLE 3.2

Dermot is a healthy, unemployed individual who does not qualify for participation in any group health insurance plans. The cost of a health insurance plan that pays everything except a small co-payment per office visit is prohibitive, so Dermot decides to self insure for small recurring costs, and purchase insurance to cover only major, unexpected medical expenses. By choosing a policy that has a high deductible, Dermot can minimize the premium cost of obtaining the insurance protection, while also protecting his other assets should he get sick and need major medical treatment.

Subsequent to the passage of The Patient Protection and Affordable Care Act of 2010 and the Health Care and Education Reconciliation Act of 2010, all U.S. citizens and residents are required to obtain health insurance, or face tax penalties for failing to comply. The constitutionality of mandating health coverage has already been challenged in federal court. Under current law, obtaining adequate health insurance is no longer a choice, it is a civic obligation.

COST OF INDIVIDUAL POLICIES

Unlike group coverage, which is often subsidized by the employer, a person purchasing an individual health insurance policy will typically be responsible for paying the full premium, and will not receive the benefits of risk spreading within a group or administrative efficiencies that reduce premium costs. The individual health insurance plan is underwritten taking the peculiar risks facing the applicant into consideration, so those who have existing conditions that require regular medical treatment or oversight will likely pay greater premiums.

The Patient Protection and Affordable Care Act of 2010 attempts to lower the cost of individual health insurance for individuals whose income is no greater than 400 percent of the federal poverty level by requiring the states to administer a program to provide low-cost insurance protection to qualified persons. The Federal government will provide a tax credit, or will pay part of the cost of obtaining the insurance directly to the insurance carrier. The detailed rules governing this program have not yet been finalized, but as a result of the new health care legislation, individual health insurance policies should be more affordable for lower income individuals.

ELIGIBILITY

As with other forms of insurance, individual health insurance can only be obtained if the person seeking coverage is relatively healthy at the time the policy is issued. Those with existing conditions requiring extensive medical treatment will either have to pay large premiums to offset the risk that the insurer is undertaking, or the existing condition may be excluded from coverage. If the condition is discovered in a routine health examination, it may be excluded from the policy. The 2010 Health Care Legislation has changed some of the rules concerning pre-existing condition coverage, but as of the time of this writing the details and applications of those provisions are not yet known.

When applying for individual health insurance, the insurance company will often require the applicant to undergo a medical examination, and will obtain copies of prior medical records to support the underwriting decision.

TYPES OF INDIVIDUAL POLICIES

Major Medical Insurance
Similar to group major medical insurance plans, **individual major medical plans** provide coverage for hospital and physician's and surgeon's fees, medications, and durable medical equipment (such as wheelchairs and hospital beds). Routine eye and dental exams are usually not covered under a major medical insurance policy, and the policy often has exclusions for self-inflicted injuries and medical procedures that are purely cosmetic in nature. The coverage provided by major medical policies often differs from carrier to carrier, so it is important to pay attention to the policy terms, coverages, and exclusions when making

policy comparisons and selecting coverage. Many carriers, for example, impose maximum charges for various medical procedures or hospital stays, and may also impose additional limits on treatments such as mental health visits.

The lifetime policy limits on major medical insurance policies are usually high, and are often set at a $1 million lifetime maximum. One million dollars is generally the minimum lifetime maximum coverage amount that most financial planners recommend. The Health Care Act has removed the lifetime cap for all policies issued after September 2010.

The annual **deductible** for a major medical policy can vary from a few hundred dollars to several thousand dollars. If the major medical insurance policy covers a family, the deductible typically applies per person, per year. There is an inverse relationship between the amount of the deductible and the size of the premium - as the deductible grows, the premium gets lower since many of the first healthcare expenses encountered during the year will be paid for by the insured, reducing claims-flow and administrative burdens for the insurer.

For comprehensive individual medical and major medical coverage policies, after the deductible amount has been met, the insurance company pays a percentage of the medical costs (limited to the amount classified as a usual and customary expense), and the insured pays the remainder as a **coinsurance** amount. Typical structures for such a policy are 80%/20% or 60%/40%, up to an annual stop-loss limit. Once the insured's out-of-pocket expenses, including the deductible and coinsurance amounts, equals the annual stop-loss limit, the insurance company pays 100 percent of any additional health care costs for that year.

EXAMPLE 3.3

Randy and Kelly are married and have three children. They are covered by a comprehensive medical and major medical insurance policy with a $250 deductible per person, 80% / 20% coinsurance provision, and an annual stop-loss limit of $2,500. In a softball game this year, Randy slid into second base and dislocated his knee to the point that he needed knee replacement surgery. The surgery cost $25,000. Each of his children had their annual physical exam which cost $250 each. Aside from these expenses, there were no other health care costs incurred by the family this year.

Randy's knee replacement surgery will result in him paying a $250 deductible, as will the physical exams for each of the children, for a total of $1,000. In addition, Randy must pay 20% of the cost of the major medical knee surgery in excess of the deductible amount, up to his stop-loss limit of $2,500. Twenty percent of $24,750 would equal $4,950, but Randy will only have to pay $1,500 in addition to the $1,000 deductible, which is the amount that is necessary to bring his out-of-pocket expenses up to the annual stop-loss limit of $2,500. Note that if the policy was not comprehensive, but rather a major medical, stand-alone policy, any deductible would be in addition to the stop-loss limit.

Medical Expense Insurance

Medical expense insurance is similar to group basic medical expense coverage. Unlike major medical insurance policies, medical expense insurance policies only cover specified types of medical expenses. Medical expense insurance may pay for actual expenses incurred when receiving health care, or may pay a lump sum upon the occurrence of some event affecting one's health. In either case, the policy limits are likely to be very low compared with major medical policies. While obtaining medical expense insurance is better than having no health insurance at all, planners should recognize that the policy limits may not be sufficient to cover the expenses incurred.

The most common types of medical expense insurance include hospital expense insurance, physicians expense insurance, and surgical expense insurance.

Hospital expense coverage, as the name implies, pays for costs of medical care while the insured (or family members, if a family policy) is in the hospital. Amounts billed directly by the hospital are covered, subject to policy limitations, but separately billed items, such as doctors and surgeon's fees, and x-ray fees for services performed outside of a hospital are not covered by a hospital expense policy. Many policies limit coverage to a specified number of days, such as 60, 90, or 180 days.

Physicians expense insurance provides coverage for fees charged by physicians for office visits and tests that are not performed in the hospital (such as blood work, x-rays, and non-surgical procedures).

Surgical expense insurance pays for surgeon's fees when a surgical procedure is not conducted in a hospital (if the surgical procedure was conducted in the hospital, these expenses would be covered by the hospital expense coverage policy).

HEALTH INSURANCE POLICY PROVISIONS

Pre-Existing Conditions

A pre-existing conditions exclusion clause helps control adverse selection. A pre-existing condition generally is defined as a condition for which the insured person was treated during the six-month or one-year period prior to the policy's inception date. Pre-existing conditions are not covered under individual health insurance policies, although this exclusion usually lasts for only one or two years, after which treatment for the pre-existing condition will be covered, as it would be for any other medical condition.

Grace Period

A grace period of 31 days is granted to the insured in the event that he or she is late making a premium payment. During the grace period, a policy may not be canceled by the insurer. However, if payment of the overdue premium is not received by the last date of the grace period, the coverage automatically lapses.

Reinstatement

Included in every health insurance policy is a procedure for policy reinstatement should coverage lapse due to nonpayment of premium. Certain policies specify a time limit within which the insured may reinstate the policy without proof of insurability. Other policies require the insured to again submit to the underwriting process before coverage is reinstated. Reinstated policies usually exclude coverage for illnesses incurred during the first ten days after reinstatement (again to control adverse selection problems).

Time Limit Clause

The time limit clause is attached to the policy so that an insurer may void a policy on the grounds of misrepresentation made by the insured on the application for coverage. The insurer must usually discover and contest the misstatement during the first two years the contract is in force. After that time, the policy is incontestable and misstatements may not be used against the insured to void a policy or deny a claim. This is similar to the incontestability clause in a life insurance contract.

Renewal Clauses

Renewal clauses in the individual health insurance policy specify the length of time that an insurance policy can remain in force. This can have a serious effect on the duration of coverage. In the case of group insurance policies, as long as the insured is employed by the group, then he or she may retain coverage.

Quick Quiz 3.3

Highlight the answer to these questions:

1. Once an insured meets the stop-loss limit, not taking into account the deductibles paid, the insurer pays the full amount, up to a specified ceiling.
   a. True
   b. False

2. The high cost of individual health insurance is partly due to the inability of the insurer to spread the risk amongst a group's participants.
   a. True
   b. False

3. The Patient Protection and Affordable Care Act requires states to administer a program to provide low-cost health insurance to qualified persons.
   a. True
   b. False

4. The most common types of medical expense insurance are: hospital expense insurance, pharmacy expense insurance, and surgical expense insurance.
   a. True
   b. False

False, True, True, False.

Guaranteed Renewable

Under a guaranteed renewable clause, the company promises to renew the policy to a stated age, usually 65. The insurance company cannot cancel the insured at any time during the benefit period, regardless of bad health or the number of claims filed by the insured. The renewal of the policy is at the sole discretion of the insured. The insurance company, however, reserves the right to increase premiums as deemed necessary, as long as such premium increases are for the entire group covered.

Noncancelable

A health insurance policy with a noncancelable renewal clause provides the greatest amount of security for the insured. The insurer guarantees the renewal of the policy until age 65 and the premiums may not be increased. Noncancelable premiums are about 25 percent higher than they are for a similar guaranteed renewable policy because the insured is afforded much more protection.

Renewable at Insurer's Option

With this renewal clause, the insurer may not cancel the policy during its term (usually one year), but it may refuse to renew the policy for a subsequent term. Clearly, this provision is not safe for the insured. One should carefully consider the purchase of a policy with this provision.

Conditionally Renewable

A conditionally renewable contract cannot be canceled by the insurer during the policy term (again, usually one year), but it may refuse to renew the contract for another term if certain conditions exist. For example, if full-time employment ceases, the insurer reserves the right to cancel the policy at the end of the last month of employment. Also, renewal may be denied on the basis of unpaid premiums or the insured reaching age 65 and becoming eligible for Medicare coverage. This renewal clause gives the insured more protection than the one discussed previously, but still is not as safe as the guaranteed renewable and noncancelable options.

EXHIBIT 3.1 — **SAMPLE INDIVIDUAL HEALTH INSURANCE MONTHLY PREMIUMS**

ZIP CODE: 70068 (97 PLANS)	27 Year-Old Female	27 Year-Old Male	47 Year-Old Female	47 Year-Old Male
Premiums	$46.93 - $321.33	$33.28 - $224.58	$78.39 - $536.80	$66.50 - $472.27
Deductibles	$0 - $10,000	$0 - $10,000	$0 - $10,000	$0 - $10,000
Types of Plans	PPO, POS, Network*	PPO, POS, Network*	PPO, POS, Network*	PPO, POS, Network*
Office Visits	Not Covered to $50/Visit	Not Covered to $50/Visit	Not Covered to $50/Visit	Not Covered to $50/Visit
Co-Insurance	0 - 30%	0 - 30%	0 - 30%	0 - 30%

Zip Code: 30303 (115 Plans)	27 Year-Old Female	27 Year-Old Male	47 Year-Old Female	47 Year-Old Male
Premiums	$50.25 - $401.46	$39.81 - 259.86	$94.00 - $665.88	$78.00 - $591.46
Deductibles	$500 - $20,000	$500 - $20,000	$500 - $20,000	$500 - $20,000
Types of Plans	HMO, PPO, POS, Network*	HMO, PPO, POS, Network*	HMO, PPO, POS, Network*	HMO, PPO, POS, Network*
Office Visits	Not Covered to $50/Visit	Not Covered to $50/Visit	Not Covered to $50/Visit	Not Covered to $50/Visit
Co-Insurance	0 - 30%	0 - 30%	0 - 30%	0 - 30%

*Network plan is a variation of a PPO plan.
www.ehealthinsurance.com

TYPES OF GROUPS AND INDIVIDUAL PLANS

Both group and individual health insurance plans can be written on an indemnity basis (reimbursement) or on a managed care basis.

INDEMNITY HEALTH INSURANCE

Indemnity health insurance is also referred to as a traditional health insurance plan. Indemnity health insurance plans allow participants the benefit of having a whole range of health care practitioners at their disposal and not be locked into a service network system for medical care. Indemnity health insurance is the most flexible type of insurance policy, but participants also pay some of the highest premiums in order to have the flexibility of choosing their own health care providers. Typically, indemnity plans have deductibles, no copays, and coinsurance for major medical.

Key Concepts

Underline/highlight the answers to these questions as you read:

1. Describe the differences and similarities between an HMO and a PPO.

2. Explain the reasoning behind the criticism of managed care insurance plans.

MANAGED CARE INSURANCE

Managed care insurance emerged from a desire to reduce the costs of health care while increasing competition among service providers. When compared to major medical plans, managed care approaches to health care restrict participant choice of health care providers, and often require participants to obtain pre-approval from insurance company representatives (who are not always medically trained) as a condition of obtaining covered treatment that is not considered emergency care. Companies offering managed care have also been criticized for prohibiting physicians from discussing alternative options to care with the patients, creating an ethical dilemma for the health care provider who is determined to act in the best interest of the patient. Despite their shortcomings, managed care approaches to health insurance have assisted in somewhat containing the cost of medical services over time.

There are three main types of managed care approaches to health insurance coverage:
- Health Maintenance Organization (HMO),
- Preferred Provider Organization (PPO), and
- Point-of-Service Plans (POS).

Health Maintenance Organizations (HMOs)

Health Maintenance Organizations (HMOs) were authorized by the HMO Act of 1973. HMOs consist of a group of physicians who provide comprehensive care for their patients, and are organized in an effort to control the rising cost of healthcare. Physicians are employed by the HMO directly or may be physicians in private practice who have chosen to participate in the HMO network. The independent physicians are paid a fixed amount for each HMO member that uses them as a **primary care physician**. Some HMOs require medical services be performed by the pre-approved physicians who are either employees or independent contractors of the HMO, and will not pay for health care services obtained outside of the HMO's physician network. Other HMOs permit their members to obtain coverage outside of the insurance company's provider network, but claim payments made for services performed by an out-of-network provider will typically be smaller than claims allowed for similar services provided within the network (which effectively increases the cost to the participant).

One major disadvantage of HMOs is that patient choice is limited by establishing a network of approved health care providers. Americans, as a group, do not like having their options limited, which may explain why HMOs never became popular vehicles for providing health care services.

EXHIBIT 3.2 ADVANTAGES AND DISADVANTAGES OF HMOS

ADVANTAGES
• Fixed fee for health care
• Low co-payments
• Total health care costs is generally lower and more predictable than with PPO or POS
DISADVANTAGES
• Gatekeeper for specialists services so it is often difficult and complicated to get specialized care
• Longer waits for non-emergency doctor appointments
• Any health care costs from out-of-network providers, except in emergencies, is not covered much or at all

Quick Quiz 3.4

Highlight the answer to these questions:

1. PPOs typically have a wider network of health care providers, from which to choose, than HMOs.
   a. True
   b. False

2. The emergence of managed care plans was born from a desire to decrease competition amongst health care providers.
   a. True
   b. False

True, False.

Preferred Provider Organizations (PPOs)

A **Preferred Provider Organization** is an arrangement between insurance companies and health care providers that permits members of the PPO to obtain discounted health care services from the preferred providers within the network. Unlike an HMO, which limits choice of physicians and other health care providers, a PPO typically has a larger provider pool for participants to choose from. Participants are not required to receive services from preferred providers, but higher deductibles and coinsurance payments may apply when services are obtained from providers outside of the network. Health care providers are not employed by the PPO, but do receive a fee for serving as primary health care provider for a member of the PPO.

ADVANTAGES AND DISADVANTAGES OF PPOs

EXHIBIT 3.3

ADVANTAGES
• Health care costs are low when using in-network providers
• Consultations with any specialists, including out-of-network providers
• Primary care physician is not required
• Yearly out-of-pocket costs are limited
DISADVANTAGES
• Out-of-network treatment is more expensive
• Co-payments are generally larger than with HMOs
• May need to satisfy a deductible, especially with out-of-network providers

Point of Service Plans (POS)

A **point of service plan (POS)** is considered a managed care/indemnity plan hybrid, as it mixes aspects of in-network and fee-for-service, for greater patient choice. Members choose which option that they will use each time they seek health care.

Like an HMO and a PPO, a POS plan has a contracted provider network. POS plans encourage members to choose a primary care physician from within the health care network. This physician becomes the patient's "point of service." The in-network, primary care physician may make referrals outside of the network, if the patient prefers an out-of-network provider, but higher deductibles and coinsurance payments may apply if the insured is receiving services on the indemnity side.

POS plans are becoming more popular because they offer more flexibility, lower costs, and freedom of choice than standard HMOs, PPOs, or indemnity plans.

EXHIBIT 3.4   ADVANTAGES AND DISADVANTAGES OF POS PLANS

ADVANTAGES
- Freedom of choice for managed care
- Not limited to only HMO network providers
- Costs are minimal for in-network care
- Annual out-of-pocket costs are limited
- No referral is needed for choosing an out of network doctor

DISADVANTAGES
- Copays for out-of-network providers are high
- There are deductibles for out-of-network providers
- Sometimes difficult and complicated to get specialized care within network providers

POLICY PROVISIONS

Health insurance policy provisions for groups are very similar to the provisions typically found in individual policies and in disability insurance policies. A summary of some of the more important policy provisions that are relevant for financial planners is provided below.

PREEXISTING CONDITIONS

Insurance works by spreading unknown risks (such as the risk of contracting health conditions that require medical treatment) across a pool of individuals. If it were possible for consumers to purchase insurance when they had a known condition or disease requiring medical treatment for a fraction of the cost of the treatment itself, a rational consumer would wait until he or she had a need for insurance (a pending medical expense) to obtain it. Under these circumstances, it would be impossible for the insurance company to spread those risks across the pool of insureds and generate a profit for performing that service.

Key Concepts

Underline/highlight the answers to these questions as you read:

1. Describe some health insurance policy provisions that are particularly relevant to financial planners.

2. Briefly describe the taxation of an individual's health care benefits.

3. Explain the different coverage periods for different individuals, under the COBRA plan.

4. Describe how HSAs work.

When an applicant for health insurance has an existing condition that requires medical treatment, that condition is typically excluded from coverage provided under the health insurance policy for a specified period of time. The purpose of the pre-existing condition clause is to prevent adverse selection against the insurance company, and to permit the risk-spreading function to work. If healthy individuals who will not require medical services for the current year are not part of the premium paying pool, there is no way to spread the risk across the pool, and the purchase of a policy by a sick person would be little more than a disguised attempt to transfer a known cost to the insurance company.

The exclusion of preexisting conditions when issuing health insurance policies has been a subject of interest in the debate over national health care, and the Patient Protection and Affordable Care Act of 2010 and the Health Care and Education Reconciliation Act of 2010 have attempted to alter how preexisting condition limitations are employed in the issuance of health insurance policies.

Many group policies do not have a pre-existing conditions exclusion if the member of the group joins the plan within a specified period (e.g. for employer plans, generally a period of days from the date of hire).

INCONTESTABILITY CLAUSE

When a health insurance policy is issued on a noncancelable or guaranteed renewable basis, the policy often includes an **incontestability clause**. The incontestability clause protects the insured by preventing the insurer from challenging the validity of the health insurance contract after it has been in force for a specified period of time unless the insured initially obtained coverage fraudulently.

GRACE PERIOD

As is the case with all insurance policies, an insurance company will only undertake the risk the insured is trying to transfer when the insured compensates the company for undertaking the risk. If policy premiums are not paid by the due date, the health insurance policy will lapse. When the policy includes a **grace period**, however, the policy will remain in force and will not lapse as long as the premium is paid within a specified number of days after the due date. A one-month grace period (which usually translates to a period of 31 days), is very common in health insurance policies.

RENEWABILITY

Health insurance that is underwritten on an annual basis may prevent insureds from obtaining access to needed health care if they get sick. If, for example, the health insurance company does not reissue the policy when the renewal date is reached simply because the insured had contracted some form of disease or health condition in the prior policy period, access to treatment may be jeopardized. This is the opposite of adverse selection risk. In this instance, once a person becomes sick, the insurance company could decide to drop them from coverage so that it does not have to pay health care providers for the care given to the participant.

To prevent this from happening, and to give policy holders some protection against policy cancellation, different renewability rights are provided for in health insurance contracts, including:
- noncancelable,
- guaranteed renewable,
- conditionally renewable, and
- optionally renewable.

Noncancelable

Noncancelable policies prevent the insurance company from cancelling the policy for any reason provided that the policy premium is paid. Usually, the policy will specify that it is noncancelable for a specific period of time, or until the insured reaches a stated age. Some policies also specify that, during the noncancelable period, no changes to the policy may be made, including changes to the premium. Noncancelable policies provide the greatest degree of protection to the insured, since the insured can force the insurance company to provide continued coverage simply by paying the premium on the policy.

Guaranteed Renewable

Guaranteed renewable health insurance policies require the insurance company to renew the policy for a specified period of time, or until the insured attains a certain age (such as age 65, when eligibility for Medicare is established). Provided the insured pays the premium, the insurance company must renew the policy during the stated period. Unlike the case with noncancelable policies, which do not permit increases in premium, the premium on a guaranteed renewable policy may be increased on a class basis (i.e., increased across the board for all similarly situated insureds), but may not be increased for one participant simply because he or she has contracted a disease or health condition requiring treatment.

Conditionally Renewable

When a policy is conditionally renewable, it may not be cancelled by the insurance company during the policy term (which is typically one year), but the insurance company reserves the right to cancel the policy when it is up for renewal. The conditions that will cause the policy to be cancelled on the renewal date are often specified in the contract itself. Planners should be attentive to these provisions when placing conditionally renewable insurance with clients.

Optionally Renewable

An Optionally Renewable policy permits the insurance company to cancel the policy at any time, except during the term of the existing contract. Unlike a conditionally renewable policy which specifies the conditions that will result in loss of coverage, under an optionally renewable policy the insurance company can cancel coverage for any reason. Optionally renewable health insurance contracts give the client little peace of mind, and should be carefully considered prior to purchase.

TAXATION AND HEALTH INSURANCE

When an individual receives benefits under a health insurance policy, and those benefit payments are used to pay for the health care of the insured, no taxable event occurs. In this instance, the benefits are received tax-free. Some health insurance policies, such as dread disease policies (for example, a policy that pays a specified amount if the insured in diagnosed with cancer), pay a lump sum to the insured regardless of the actual expenses incurred in the treating the condition or disease. When lump-sum payments such as these are received, there are no federal income tax consequences to the extent that the proceeds are used to pay for medical care. Amounts received in excess of the actual cost of care, however, are subject to income tax.

When group health insurance benefits are provided for and paid for by an employer, there is no taxable event for the employee. Furthermore, when the policy pays the actual cost of medical care (as specified above), the insured will not have to report the benefits received as income. Normally, when an employee receives property (such as a health insurance policy) from an employer in return for his or her labor, the fair market value of that policy is subject to income tax the year it is received under a tax doctrine known as the economic benefit doctrine. Congress has enacted a specific exception to this rule that allows employees to receive health benefits on an income tax-free basis in an attempt to encourage employers to provide health insurance coverage to their employees. The employer can deduct the cost of providing group health insurance to its employees as an ordinary and necessary business expense.

CONSOLIDATED OMNIBUS BUDGET RECONCILIATION ACT OF 1985 (COBRA)

In 1985, Congress passed the Consolidated Omnibus Budget Reconciliation Act, which permits individuals who were covered under a group health insurance plan to continue to purchase health insurance coverage at group rates for a certain period of time after they separate from the group. Premiums for group health insurance coverage are typically much lower than the premiums for similar individual health insurance policies. By extending group coverage to individuals who were formerly members of a covered group, Congress made health insurance a bit more affordable for affected individuals.

Employers who offer group health insurance to their employees and have at least 20 employees are required to provide COBRA continuation coverage to their covered employees.

The most common situation in which COBRA applies is when a worker is either laid off or separates from service with an employer that sponsors a group health insurance plan. The former employee can purchase group insurance at the same rate that applies to members of the group plan. In addition, the employer can charge an additional two percent of the premium amount to defray administrative costs.

Quick Quiz 3.5

Highlight the answer to these questions:

1. Adverse selection occurs when health insurance plans refuse to renew health insurance for people if they become ill.
   a. True
   b. False

2. Employers may deduct the costs of providing health insurance only if the employer includes, as income, the monetary benefit derived from that insurance.
   a. True
   b. False

False, False.

To be eligible for COBRA continuation coverage, the employee must not have been discharged for gross misconduct. Circumstances that create eligibility for COBRA continuation coverage include:

1. the voluntary or involuntary termination of an employee;
2. a reduction in employment status from full time to part time (part-time employees are not usually covered under an employers benefit programs);
3. the death of a covered employee (the employee's dependents may be eligible to purchase group coverage under COBRA);
4. the divorce or legal separation of the covered employee from his or her spouse;
5. the employee becomes eligible for Medicare (which usually occurs at age 65); or
6. a dependent child of the employee no longer qualifies for coverage under the employer plan.

In order to balance the interest of employees (who may wish to continue to receive health insurance coverage at reasonable rates) and employers (who are typically not interested in providing services for individuals who are no longer providing services to the company), COBRA continuation coverage is not perpetual. Individuals eligible for COBRA continuation coverage can obtain coverage for the following periods and reasons:

18 Months	• Termination of employment • Moving from full-time to part-time status
29 Months	• The employee meets the Social Security definition of disability
36 Months	• Death of a covered employee • Divorce or legal separation of a covered employee • Loss of dependent status • Eligibility for Medicare

Note that COBRA continuation is typically available for 18 months for the covered worker, and 36 months for survivors or dependents of the covered worker.

EXAMPLE 3.4   Roger, the Senior Vice President of The Amazing Company, died last week. His widow, Rosemary, does not work and is 56 years old. Rosemary can obtain group health insurance coverage under Roger's plan for 36 months after his death.

EXAMPLE 3.5   Charlie, an employee of Electrical Engineering Contractors, Inc., was recently divorced from his wife, Jane. Jane is unemployed, but may obtain group health insurance coverage under Charlie's plan for 36 months after the divorce.

EXAMPLE 3.6   Danielle has recently finished Medical School at the age of 27, and is no longer eligible to receive health insurance coverage as a dependent under her parent's group health insurance plan. During her residency, Danielle will not have access to employer provided group health insurance, so she may receive COBRA continuation benefits under her parent's group plan for 36 months.

EXAMPLE 3.7

Rennie recently retired at the age of 65, and is currently covered by Medicare. His wife, Pat, is 63 and does not yet qualify for Medicare coverage. Pat can obtain health insurance under Rennie's group plan for up to 36 months under COBRA.

HEALTH SAVINGS ACCOUNTS

Health Savings Accounts (HSA) may be set up by individuals or employers and allow eligible individuals to save for health care costs on a tax-advantaged basis. Contributions made to the HSA by the plan participant are tax-deductible as an adjustment to gross income (above the line), and distributions from the HSA to pay for qualified medical expenses are excluded from income. If an employer makes contributions to an HSA on behalf of an employee, and the contribution limits are not exceeded, the employer contribution is not included in the taxable income of the employee.

A similar tool, the **Flexible Spending Account (FSA)**, is commonly used by employers as an employee benefit that permits employees to defer income to the FSA to pay, typically for health care premiums with pre-tax dollars. FSAs require the employee to either use the contributed amounts for medical expenses by 2½ months after the end of the year, or forfeit the unused amounts to the company. HSAs permit employees to carry over unused amounts to future years, and to invest those amounts so that over time, the value inside of the HSA can grow.

EXHIBIT 3.5 ADVANTAGES AND DISADVANTAGES OF HSAs AND FSAs

	ADVANTAGES	DISADVANTAGES
HSA	• Pre-tax contributions • Funds carry over from year to year • Funds can be invested • Permits reimbursement of over-the-counter medication purchases, if with a prescription • No prescription necessary for insulin	• Must have a high deductible health plan to qualify • Some HSAs have high annual fees • Ability to purchase over-the-counter medications without a prescription (expires January 2011)
FSA	• Pre-tax contributions • Participants have total control over how to spend the money within the related health care or dependent care options • Can be used for "optional" medical procedures (LASIK eye surgery, braces, etc.) • Can be used for child care or dependent care • Permits reimbursement of over-the-counter medication purchases, if with a prescription • No prescription necessary for insulin	• Money must be used by 2½ months after end of plan year • Cannot receive distribution amounts that are covered under another health plan

From a financial planning standpoint, HSAs are effectively emergency funds for medical care costs. Younger individuals who are less likely to incur large medical expenses may choose to use a high deductible health insurance plan and establish an HSA to begin to accumulate a pool of money that can be used for future medical expenses. As the individual ages, and more medical services are needed, he or she can continue to use a high deductible health insurance plan (which will have a substantially lower premium compared to plans that pay the first dollar of medical-care costs) due to the presence of the health care emergency fund - the HSA. Over the insured's lifetime, accumulation of funds in an HSA during early years, and use of high deductible health insurance plans throughout the work life expectancy of the individual will help minimize insurance, or risk transfer, costs.

ELIGIBILITY

To be eligible to make HSA contributions, an individual must be covered by a high deductible health insurance plan. Individuals who are covered by Medicare, another health insurance policy, or individuals who are dependents of another person for income tax purposes are not eligible to make contributions to HSAs. One major exception to the dependent eligibility rule is that spouses who independently meet the requirements to establish an FSA may open up their own FSA even though they are listed with the spouse on a jointly filed income tax return.

HIGH DEDUCTIBLE HEALTH INSURANCE PLANS

High deductible health insurance plans (HDHP) include plans with a deductible of at least $1,200 for individual coverage and $2,400 for family coverage in 2011, with a maximum out-of-pocket stop-loss amount of $5,950 for single coverage and $11,900 for family coverage in 2010.

HDHP DEDUCTIBLES AND OUT-OF-POCKET EXPENSES (2011)

EXHIBIT 3.6

	Individual Coverage	Family Coverage
Minimum annual deductible	$1,200	$2,400
Maximum annual deductible and other out-of-pocket expenses*	$5,950	$11,900

* This limit does not apply to deductibles and expenses for out-of-network services if the plan uses a network of providers. Instead, only deductibles and out-of-pocket expenses for services within the network should be used to figure whether the limit applies.

There are some family plans that have deductibles for both the family as a whole and for individual family members. Under these plans, if you meet the individual deductible for one family member, you do not have to meet the higher annual deductible amount for the family. If either the deductible for the family as a whole or the deductible for an individual family member is below the minimum annual deductible for family coverage, the plan does not qualify as an HDHP.

Bob's annual deductible for the family plan is $3,500. This plan also has an individual deductible of $1,500 per family member. The plan does not qualify as an HDHP because the deductible for an individual family member is below the minimum annual deductible ($2,400) for family coverage.

EXAMPLE 3.8

CONTRIBUTION LIMITATIONS

The maximum amount that can be contributed to an HSA for the calendar year is $3,050 for individual coverage, and $6,150 for family coverage in 2011. Amounts contributed by both the employee and the employer count in this total. In addition, individuals can make a one-time transfer of funds from their IRA to their HSA without tax consequences.

CONTRIBUTION LIMITS (2011)

EXHIBIT 3.7

Individual Contribution Limit	Family Contribution Limit	Additional Catch-Up Contribution (55 or older / Single and Family)
$3,050	$6,150	$1,000

DISTRIBUTIONS

Distributions from an HSA that are used to cover medical expenses are exempt from income tax. All other distributions before age 65 are subject to both income tax and (beginning in 2010 under the new Health Care Legislation) a 20 percent penalty tax. Once the account owner reaches age 65 (and is therefore eligible for Medicare health insurance coverage), distributions from the HSA that are not used to pay for medical expenses will be subject to income tax, but no penalty tax will apply.

HSA owners are permitted to roll the funds in one HSA to another once per year without triggering adverse income tax consequences (i.e., the imposition of an income tax on the amount distributed plus, if applicable, the 20 percent penalty). If the rollover is not completed as a trustee to trustee transfer, the participant has 60 days from the date of distribution to rollover the distribution to a new HSA to avoid the imposition of income tax on distributed amounts that were not used to pay for medical costs.

Quick Quiz 3.6

Highlight the answer to these questions:

1. Upon voluntary termination of employment, one may stay on with his former employer's group insurance plan for 36 months.
   a. True
   b. False

2. If one dies prior to spending all of his HSA's funds, the balance can be paid to someone other than the owner's spouse; but that balance is subject to income tax in the hands of the nonspouse beneficiary.
   a. True
   b. False

False, True.

When the owner of an HSA dies prior to distributing all of the assets in the account, the remaining balance can be transferred to another person. If the beneficiary is the spouse, the spouse is treated as owner of the HSA and the normal HSA distribution rules apply. If the account is left to anyone other than the spouse, the death of the participant terminates the HSA, and the remaining balance will be subject to income tax (but not penalty) in the hands of the beneficiary.

LONG-TERM CARE INSURANCE

As medical advances continue to increase life expectancy, advanced age presents additional medical problems for individuals. Prolonged illness, or mental impairments, such as senile dementia and Alzheimer's disease often require an affected individual to receive assistance for medical and custodial care. Based on recent experience, experts suggest that over 40 percent of people over the age of 65 will require nursing home care at some point during their lives. Sometimes, nursing home care will be required for rehabilitation after surgery and will be of a relatively short duration. Cognitive impairments, however, may prevent a person from engaging in the normal **activities of daily living (ADL)** without assistance, and in these circumstances nursing home stays may last for several years. The cost of receiving nursing home care is high. Depending on the area of the country where services will be provided, the costs can range from about $60,000 a year on the low side to over $120,000 a year. While medical insurance plans may cover a short stay in a nursing home for rehabilitation purposes after surgery or a hospital stay, medical insurance does not cover the costs of extended nursing home stays. **Long-term care insurance** can be used to cover the cost of nursing home care that exceeds the coverage provided by medical insurance and Medicare.

WHO NEEDS LONG-TERM CARE

EXHIBIT 3.8

40% of persons receiving long-term care are between 18 and 64.

The likelihood of a disability grows as we age:
Ages 44-54: 22.6%
Ages 55-64: 35.7%
Ages 65-69: 44.9%

At least 70 percent of people over age 65 will require some long-term care services at some point in their lives.

* *GuidetoLongTermCare.com*

LONG-TERM CARE ROOM RATES

EXHIBIT 3.9

	National Average Room Rates		Annual Range Across States	
	Daily	Annual	Low	High
Nursing Home - Private	$219	$79,935	$49,275 (LA)	$213,160 (AK)
Nursing Home - Semi-Private	$198	$72,270	$47,693 (LA)	$225,570 (AK)
Nursing Home - Alzheimer's & Dementia Care	6.4% increase over nursing home rates			
Assisted Living	$103	$37,578	$24,492 (ND)	$56,548 (DE)
Assisted Living - Alzheimer's & Dementia Care	42% increase over assisted living rates			

* *2009 MetLife Market Survey of Long-Term Care Costs*
LA = Louisiana/AK = Alaska / ND = North Dakota / DE = Delaware

EXHIBIT 3.10 **LONG-TERM CARE ASSISTANCE RATES**

	Average	Range
Home Health Aides	$21/hr.	$15 - $30/hr.
Homemaker/Companion	$19/hr.	$13 - $25/hr.
Adult Day Services	$67/day	$27 - $150/day

2009 MetLife Market Survey of Long-Term Care Costs

EXHIBIT 3.11 **AVERAGE MONTHLY BASE COSTS FOR ASSISTING LIVING BY SERVICES INCLUDED**

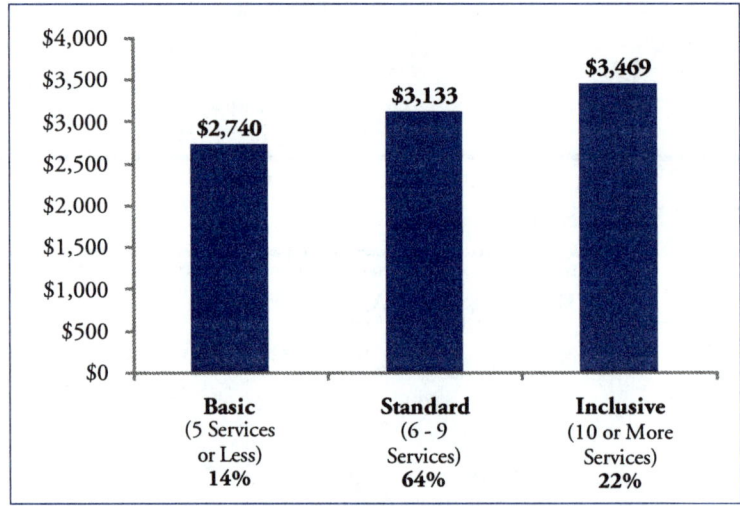

* 2009 MetLife Market Survey of Long-Term Care Costs

NEED FOR COVERAGE

Clients and planners often overlook the need for long-term care insurance. There are two primary issues that a client should consider when deciding whether or not to purchase long-term care insurance:
- the health of the client and his or her family, including an assessment of the family's average life expectancy; and
- the financial circumstances facing the client.

If a client is expected to have a long life expectancy (perhaps due to family history or current health status), long-term care insurance should be considered. In fact, the longer the client's life expectancy, the greater the need, all else equal, for long-term care insurance. Recall that, as noted earlier, 40 percent of adults over the age of 65 will need nursing home care at some point during their lifetime. The general health of the family should also be considered. If older family members suffer from health ailments that are likely to require nursing home care, such as Alzheimer's disease or senile dementia, the client's risk of contracting that disease might be heightened, which will also indicate that the client has a greater need for long-term care insurance protection.

Key Concepts

Underline/highlight the answers to these questions as you read:

1. Describe what risks long-term care insurance covers.

2. Describe what options are available to those persons who don't have long-term care insurance and who find themselves in need of long-term care.

3. Explain the two different types of long-term care coverage.

4. Describe the six activities of daily living, and why they matter.

The client's financial status is also an important consideration. If long-term care services are needed, and the client does not have insurance to cover the costs, the client's assets will have to be liquidated to pay for the cost of care.

Clients with relatively low net worth and low income may not be able to afford long-term care insurance premiums. Long-term care insurance can be expensive, particularly at older ages, and if the premium represents a significant portion of the client's net worth, it may not be a prudent risk management tool. Lower net worth clients have less to lose by self-insuring, and once their assets are spent down, they may be able to qualify for long-term care coverage through the Medicaid system, which is a government health care payment system for indigent persons.

Clients with a moderate level of net worth may wish to protect those assets for the benefit of family members (spouse and descendants), and therefore may not want to spend down assets to pay for long-term care needs. Long-term care insurance may be an appropriate solution for these clients, since the risk of paying for long-term care needs is shifted to an insurance company in return for premium payments. Moderate net worth clients with bequest motives should definitely consider long-term care insurance as a risk shifting tool.

There appears to be an urban legend circulating in client and planner circles that wealthy individuals do not need to consider long-term care insurance, since they can afford to self insure against long-term care needs and at the same time they can take steps to make sure that some of their assets are transferred to their heirs. Since long-term care insurance premiums, particularly at older ages, is perceived to be high, risk retention is viewed as an appropriate choice. After all, while 40 percent of people over age 65 will need long-term care services, 60 percent will not. In some cases, however, it may be more prudent for high net worth individuals to carry long-term care insurance, particularly when bequest motives are strong. In order to self-insure, the client would have to retain enough assets to pay for their care over an extended period of time, and those assets would have to be retained until the death of the client since long-term care expenses are often incurred shortly before death. By retaining assets to self-insure against the long-term care risk, the client cannot transfer those assets to family members as part of their gift and estate planning strategy, which can result in higher gift and estate tax consequences for the family.

Paying the long-term care premiums so that the insurance company will cover those costs if necessary will free-up assets that can be used for transfer tax planning purposes, and may result in saving a significant amount in gift and estate taxes. Instead of considering the long-term care premiums solely in dollar terms, which may be perceived as high, it may be more beneficial for higher net worth individuals to consider the premiums as a percentage of their asset portfolio which is being protected with the long-term care insurance. If the dollar amount of the premium is high, but that dollar amount only represents a few basis points when compared to the size of the client's asset base, incurring that basis point charge to protect the entire asset base seems a reasonable move, and doing so also opens up opportunities for gift and estate planning.

One final consideration is necessary when determining whether or not to purchase long-term care insurance - whether the client wishes to retain the ability to choose care providers. When a client decides not to purchase long-term care insurance and self-insures, when the client's assets are spent down he or she can go on public assistance (Medicaid or "Title 19"), but the client will receive care at the facility where the first bed becomes available. There is great diversity in the quality of care, particularly when considering long-term care services. If the client relies on public assistance to pay for these costs, he or she loses the ability to choose the facility where care will be provided. Individuals who purchase long-term care insurance, however, will have a choice in picking the care provider, and can ensure that they will receive a higher quality of care. For some clients, having the ability to choose the care provider is a more important consideration than preserving assets for family members or avoiding taxes, and should be taken into account when developing a comprehensive financial plan.

Exhibit 3.12 Long-Term Care Premium Factors

- Age
- Benefits
- Deductible Periods
- Inflation Protection

Exhibit 3.13 Common Features of Long-Term Care Policies

- Renewability - Guaranteed renewability
- Nonforfeitures Benefits - Return of premium or shortened benefit period
- Waiver of premium while receiving benefits

Types of Coverage Provided by Long-Term Care Insurance

While long-term care insurance policies are often perceived as policies that cover nursing home costs, the benefits provided under the policy are much more extensive, and includes custodial care, home health care, fees for assisted living facilities, adult day care, and hospice care.

When a person's health or cognitive abilities require a high level of care, a long-term care policy will pay for skilled or intermediate-care nursing facilities. A **skilled care facility** provides the highest level of service, and combines daily medical and custodial care. An **intermediate-care nursing facility** typically provides custodial care along with intermittent, as opposed to daily, medical care. Services in either a skilled-care or intermediate-care facility are ordered by a physician, and medical treatments are provided under the supervision of a physician.

Sometimes individuals need assistance for **custodial** purposes as opposed to medical purposes. A healthy individual with a cognitive impairment, for example, may not need constant medical attention but may need assistance so that he does not pose a risk to himself or others. Individuals who find themselves in this category often are unable to perform some or all of the six activities of daily living (eating, bathing, transferring, dressing, toileting, and continence).

Full-time custodial and medical care is expensive, and, if given the choice, most individuals would probably prefer to live at home rather than move into a nursing home. Long-term care policies pay for the cost of care provided at home (referred to as a home health care benefit), in some cases may pay for all or part of the costs of an assisted living facility (an independent living arrangement where assistance with daily living tasks is provided to the client in the form of prepared meals, cleaning services, and the like), and paying for adult day-care services. Individuals needing supervision who live with other family members may not need around the clock assistance. Adult day care facilities provide supervision during the day while family members are at work. Given the opportunity, insurance companies prefer to pay for these lower-cost alternatives to nursing home or custodial care.

For individuals with incurable illnesses in the terminal stages of life, long-term care insurance policies typically pay for the cost of hospice care. Hospice care does not provide therapeutic treatment (treatment designed to cure the individual of their condition), but rather provides pain management treatment and psychological and spiritual support services for patients to permit them to die with dignity and comfort. Hospice services can be provided in a dedicated hospice facility, in a hospital, or at home.

IMPORTANT COVERAGES IN LONG-TERM CARE POLICIES

EXHIBIT 3.14

- Coverage for Alzheimer's.
- At least one year of nursing home and/or home health care coverage, not limited primarily to skilled care.
- Inflation protection.
- No requirement to first be hospitalized to receive benefits.

LONG-TERM CARE BENEFIT PERIODS

Long-term care insurance policies will provide coverage for long-term care costs in one of two ways:
- benefits are provided for a fixed period of time, or
- a fixed dollar amount is available for the payment of long-term care benefits.

Policies that provide coverage for a defined benefit period may specify the maximum number of months or years for which coverage will be provided, or may provide coverage for the life of the insured once the need for long-term care services is established and the elimination period has been met.

Clients who are relatively conservative, or who have family histories indicating that they may be prone to non-life threatening diseases requiring long-term care services (such as Alzheimer's and senile dementia), may wish to choose policies that provide lifetime coverage.

Clients who are willing to retain more risk themselves, and whose family histories indicate that they are not prone to long-term debilitating diseases (such as Alzheimer's or senile dementia) may wish to choose a shorter coverage period, such as three or five years. The average stay in a nursing home is approximately 18 months, but that is no guarantee that the client will fall into the average category.

Long-term care policies that specify a maximum benefit payment amount may also be appropriate, depending on the client circumstances. Once the maximum benefit amount has been distributed, the long-term care policy will not pay for additional care, so the dollar limit should be chose carefully by the planner and client after considering the client's health and family history.

TAX-QUALIFIED LONG-TERM CARE CONTRACTS

Most long-term care contracts issued today are tax-qualified contracts. Tax-qualified implies that the long-term care insurance policy is treated as health insurance for federal income tax purposes, and is therefore deductible on income tax returns either as self-employed health insurance (an above the line, or adjustment to income deduction), or as a medical expense itemized deduction (below the line deduction). If long-term care insurance premiums are paid for by an employer, the employer may deduct the premium cost as an employee benefit and the employees will not be required to report the value received in their income for the year. Long-term care contracts cannot, however, be provided as a benefit under cafeteria plans.

To meet the definition of a tax-qualified contract, the long-term care insurance policy:
1. must provide benefits that are limited to long-term care services;
2. does not provide a cash surrender value or access to funds that can be paid, assigned, borrowed, or pledged as collateral for a loan;
3. provides that refunds may be used only to reduce future premium payments or increase future policy benefits;
4. must meet consumer protection standards defined in the Health Insurance Portability and Accountability Act of 1997 (HIPPA); and
5. must coordinate benefits with Medicare.

Long-term care contracts that do not meet the above requirements are not considered to be tax qualified, and will not permit the policy-owner to take a tax deduction for premium payments made on the policy.

CONDITIONS THAT TRIGGER LONG-TERM CARE COVERAGE

To receive benefits under a long-term care policy, an insured individual must be classified as either terminally or chronically ill.

Terminal illness is defined as having a life expectancy of less than 24 months, and must be certified by a qualified health professional.

Chronic illness is defined as having a physical or cognitive impairment that:
- prevents the insured individual from performing at least two of the six activities of daily living for at least a 90 day period, or
- requiring substantial supervision to prevent the insured from posing a danger to himself or others.

To be considered chronically ill, the insured individual must be certified as such by a qualified health professional within the previous 12 months.

The six activities of daily living include:
1. eating,
2. bathing,
3. dressing,
4. transferring,
5. toileting, and
6. continence.

Benefit payments cover expenses paid or pay a flat daily or monthly amount regardless of expenses depending on the contract.

Quick Quiz 3.7

Highlight the answer to these questions:

1. Long-term care insurance does not cover hospice care.
   a. True
   b. False

2. Because everyone qualifies for Medicaid, long-term care insurance is only for those who want more choices in long-term care than Medicaid offers.
   a. True
   b. False

3. Long-term care insurance is payable only for either a time certain or an amount certain.
   a. True
   b. False

4. One way to qualify as chronically ill is the inability to perform three of the six activities of daily living.
   a. True
   b. False

False, False, True, False.

CONCLUSION

Health insurance and long-term care insurance permit clients to purchase a hedge against the risk of incurring large medical and/or nursing home and long-term care expenses. All U.S. citizens are required, under current law, to maintain adequate health insurance. Long-term care insurance should be considered by any client who wishes to retain the ability to choose service providers or who has bequest motives that could be thwarted (or, possibly, be subject to higher gift and/or estate taxes) if long-term care coverage is not purchased. Planners and clients should carefully consider the most appropriate forms of insurance to purchase so that the appropriate amount of client risk exposure is transferred to insurance companies while protecting the client's asset base to achieve the client's other financial goals.

Key Terms

Activities of Daily Living (ADL) - Physical functions that an independent person performs each day, including bathing, dressing, eating, transferring, toileting, and maintaining continence.

Assisted Living - Senior housing that provides individual apartments, which may or may not have a kitchenette. Facilities offer 24 hour on site staff, congregate dining, and activity programs. Limited nursing services may be provided for an additional fee.

Coinsurance - The amount a patient must pay for major medical care after meeting the deductible.

Custodial Care - Board, room and other personal assistance services (including assistance with activities of daily living, taking medicine and similar personal needs) that may not include a skilled nursing care component.

Deductible - The amount a patient must pay each year before the health insurance plan begins paying.

Flexible Spending Account (FSA) - Employer-sponsored plan that permits employees to defer pre-tax income into an account to pay for health care expenses. FSAs require the employee to either use the contributed amounts for medical expenses by the end of the year, or forfeit the unused amounts to the company.

Grace Period - A provision in most insurance policies which allows payment to be received for a certain period of time after the actual due date without a default or cancellation of the policy.

Group Health Insurance - Health plans offered to a group of individuals by an employer, association, union, or other entity.

Health Maintenance Organizations (HMOs) - A form of managed care in which participants receive all of their care from participating providers. Physicians are employed by the HMO directly, or may be physicians in private practice who have chosen to participate in the HMO network. The independent physicians are paid a fixed amount for each HMO member that uses them as a primary care physician.

Health Savings Accounts (HSA) - Employer-sponsored plan that permits employees to save for health care costs on a tax-advantaged basis. Contributions made to the HSA by the plan participant are tax-deductible as an adjustment to gross income (above the line), and distributions from the HSA to pay for medical expenses are excluded from income.

High Deductible Health Insurance Plans - Plans with a deductible of at least $1,200 for individual coverage and $2,400 for family coverage in 2011, with a maximum out-of-pocket stop loss amount of $5,950 for single coverage and $11,900 for family coverage in 2011.

Key Terms

Incontestability Clause - Clause in a health insurance policy that prevents the insurer from challenging the validity of the health insurance contract after it has been in force for a specified period of time unless the insured fraudulently obtained coverage in the beginning of the policy.

Indemnity Health Insurance - Traditional, fee-for-service health insurance that does not limit where a covered individual can get care.

Individual Major Medical Plans - Coverage purchased independently from an insurance company (not as part of a group).

Intermediate-Care Nursing Facility - A licensed facility with the primary purpose of providing health or rehabilitative services. Typically provides custodial care along with intermittent, as opposed to daily, medical care.

Long-Term Care Insurance - Coverage that pays for all or part of the cost of home health care services or care in a nursing home or assisted living facility.

Managed Care Insurance - Health-care delivery systems that integrate the financing and delivery of health care. Managed care plans feature a network of physicians, hospitals, and other providers who participate in the plan. Managed care includes HMOs, PPOs, and POS plans.

Point of Service Plan (POS) - A form of managed care that is considered a managed care/indemnity plan hybrid, as it mixes aspects of HMOs, PPOs, and indemnity plans for greater patient choice. A primary care physician coordinates patient care, but there is more flexibility in choosing doctors and hospitals than in an HMO.

Preferred Provider Organization - A form of managed care in which participants have more flexibility in choosing physicians and other providers than in an HMO. The arrangement between insurance companies and health care providers permits participants to obtain discounted health care services from the preferred providers within the network.

Premium - The amount participants pay to belong to a health plan.

Primary Care Physician - A physician that is designated as a participant's first point of contact with the health care system, particularly in managed care plans.

Skilled-Nursing Care Facility - 24-hour nursing care for chronically-ill or short-term rehabilitative residents of all ages and provides the highest level of service, and combines daily medical and custodial care.

DISCUSSION QUESTIONS

1. Describe the benefits associated with group health insurance plans.

2. What is the difference between basic and major health insurance?

3. What is the difference between an indemnity plan and a managed care plan?

4. Describe the different types of renewal provisions.

5. Explain what a preexisting condition clause does.

6. Which employers are required to provide COBRA continuation coverage to their employees?

7. Who, besides the employee, qualifies for COBRA coverage?

8. Explain the tax benefits of HSAs.

9. Describe the greatest disadvantage associated with FSAs.

10. Describe the purpose of long-term care.

11. Describe how a stop loss limit works.

12. What are the two primary issues a planner should consider when advising regarding the purchase of long-term care insurance?

13. What conditions will trigger long-term care coverage?

14. What are the major types of individual health and disability coverages?

15. What is the tax treatment of health and disability coverages?

16. How do indemnity plans and managed care plans differ?

17. How can group health coverage be continued or transferred when employment terminates?

MULTIPLE-CHOICE PROBLEMS

1. Noncancelable health insurance contracts are different from guaranteed renewable contracts because:

    a. Noncancelable policies are not guaranteed renewable.
    b. Noncancelable policies cannot be canceled in mid-term.
    c. Noncancelable policies cannot have a premium change.
    d. Noncancelable policies have more liberal disability benefits.

2. Medical insurance is commonly known as health insurance and can be purchased from private insurance companies. Which of the following best describes the classes of medical insurance?

    a. Coverage for hospital expense, surgical expense, physician expense, and major medical expense.
    b. Coverage for hospital expense, nonmajor medical expense, surgical expense, and physician expense.
    c. Coverage for hospital expense, comprehensive major medical expense, nonmajor medical expense, and physician expense.
    d. Coverage for comprehensive major medical expense, nonmajor medical expense, surgical expense, and physician expense.

3. Mr. Johns has a major medical insurance policy with a $1,000 deductible and an 80% coinsurance clause. He becomes ill and is admitted to the hospital for several days. When he is discharged, his hospital bill is $5,000, and his doctor bills are $2,500. What is the amount that his insurance co-pay will pay?

    a. $5,200.
    b. $6,000.
    c. $6,500.
    d. $7,500.

4. In which of the following events would COBRA rules apply for the benefit of the covered employee, employee's spouse, or dependent child?
   1. The death of the covered employee.
   2. The covered employee is fired for incompetence.
   3. The employee changes status from full-time to part-time and, as a result, loses coverage.
   4. The covered employee gets a divorce.
      a. 1 only.
      b. 1 and 4.
      c. 2, 3, and 4.
      d. 1, 2, 3, and 4.

5. Due to a recession, Pat has voluntarily changed her status from full-time to part-time with her employer. Prior to the change, she and her husband were covered under the company health plan. Which statement regarding COBRA is correct?
   a. Because her change is voluntary, COBRA rules do not apply.
   b. COBRA rules allow continuation of health coverage in this situation for up to 36 months.
   c. COBRA rules allow continuation of health coverage in this situation for up to 18 months.
   d. COBRA rules allow continuation of health coverage in this situation for 29 months.

6. COBRA coverage is available for which of the following persons?
   1. A retiring employee.
   2. An employee who is terminated.
   3. Spouses and dependents of a deceased employee.
   4. An employee no longer able to work due to disability.
      a. 3 only.
      b. 3 and 4.
      c. 1, 2, and 3.
      d. 1, 2, 3, and 4.

7. Black Smith is an employee of ABC Corporation. He has just divorced Phyllis who was on all of his group health plan coverages. Phyllis wants to know to what COBRA coverage she is entitled. The following is a list of Black's group health plan benefits, all of which are integral parts of the plan. Which of Black's benefits is/are subject to COBRA rules?

   1. Medical expense plan.
   2. Dental plan.
   3. Vision care plan.
   4. Prescription care plan.

   a. 1 only.
   b. 1 and 4.
   c. 2, 3, and 4.
   d. 1, 2, 3, and 4.

8. The Watson family has a family medical policy that provides the following coverage:

   - $250/person deductible (3 person maximum)
   - $1,000 out-of-pocket limit
   - 80/20 coinsurance provision

   On a family trip, the Watson's were involved in a car accident. Four family members were hurt. Each person incurred medical expenses of $7,500. How much will the insurance company pay?

   a. $29,250.
   b. $29,000.
   c. $28,250.
   d. $23,400.

9. All of the following are activities of daily living (ADLs) as provided under the Health Insurance Portability and Accountability Act (qualified plans), except:

   a. Eating.
   b. Bathing.
   c. Maintaining continence.
   d. Cognitive thinking.

10. Which of the following most accurately describes the criteria required for an insured to qualify for long-term care benefits for a qualified plan under the Health Insurance Portability and Accountability Act?

    a. The insured is unable to perform two of the six ADLs for 90 days.
    b. The insured has substantial cognitive impairment requiring substantial service.
    c. The insured must meet both a and b.
    d. The insured may qualify by meeting either a or b.

11. Mr. Butler, who has recently turned 85, has been blind for two years. He has trouble walking and is unable to cook for himself since he lost his sight. His family has told him that he needs to consider entering an assisted living home. Assuming he has a qualified long-term care plan, is he considered chronically ill under the Health Insurance Portability and Accountability Act?

    a. Yes, he has been unable to perform two activities of daily living for over 90 days.
    b. Yes, but he does have to prove to the insurance company he is unable to perform these tasks.
    c. No, sight is not considered an activity of daily living, although cooking is.
    d. No, neither sight nor cooking is considered an activity of daily living.

12. Which of the following is a characteristic of guaranteed renewability?
    1. The insurer guarantees to renew the policy to a stated age.
    2. The policy is noncancelable and the premium may not be increased.
    3. Renewal is solely at insurer's discretion.
    4. The insurer has the right to increase the premium rates for the underlying class in which the insured is placed. Note: not for a single individual.
        a. 1 only.
        b. 1 and 4.
        c. 1, 2, and 4.
        d. 1, 2, 3, and 4.

Quick Quiz Explanations

Quick Quiz 3.1
1. True.
2. False. When underwriting a large number of people, the risk, as well as the administrative costs, are spread amongst all participants.

Quick Quiz 3.2
1. True.
2. False. Once the insured reaches his out-of-pocket limit, the insurer pays 100 percent of the cost of care. After the plan deductible is met and until the insured reaches his out-of-pocket limit, the insurer pays the cost of care in excess of the co-pay.

Quick Quiz 3.3
1. False. The stop limit takes into account deductibles paid, as well as co-pay amounts.
2. True.
3. True.
4. False. The most common types of medical expense insurance are: hospital, physician, and surgical expense insurances.

Quick Quiz 3.4
1. True.
2. False. Managed care plans emerged from a desire to decrease health care costs and increase completion amongst health care providers.

Quick Quiz 3.5
1. False. This is actually the opposite of anti-selection, which refers to ill people - or those who would derive the most benefit from insurance - being the only ones who seek insurance, thereby denying the company the ability to spread risk amongst both sick and healthy participants.
2. False. The monetary benefit derived from an employer funded health insurance plan is specifically excluded as income.

Quick Quiz 3.6
3. False. Upon voluntary termination, one may stay on the employer's policy for no longer than 18 months.
4. True.

Quick Quiz Explanations

Quick Quiz 3.7
1. False. Long-term care insurance coverage includes: nursing homes, home health, and hospice.
2. False. One must qualify financially for Medicaid.
3. True.
4. False. One way to qualify as chronically ill is the inability to perform two of the six activities of daily living.

CHAPTER 4

Property and Liability Insurance

INTRODUCTION

The professional planner should be as knowledgeable about property and liability risks associated with a client's property as with life, health, disability, and long-term care insurance. While property insurance protects the assets the client already owns, liability insurance protects the client against financial loss from legal action. Therefore, both property and liability insurance coverages are essential parts of a client's overall risk management and financial plan.

Property insurance includes homeowner's insurance, renter's insurance, automobile insurance, and insurance on boats and other assets. The home is one of the largest single purchases that individuals make during their lifetime. Although the frequency of perils causing financial losses to the home is small, the severity of any loss is potentially large. The automobile insurance policy is used to mitigate against the risk of loss to the automobile and those involved in an automobile accident. It may be among the most expensive aspects of owning a car for the client. The personal liability umbrella policy (PLUP) provides coverage in excess of the underlying liability coverage provided by the homeowners, automobile policies, and other property insurance policies.

The commercial package policy, the business owner's policy, professional insurance, and business automobile insurance policies provide protection for business owners and self-employed professionals for property and liability risks.

This chapter introduces each of these types of insurance to help the planner adequately evaluate his client's property and liability needs, and recommend appropriate coverage.

PERSONAL PROPERTY AND LIABILITY INSURANCE

This chapter introduces the three insurance policies most commonly used to protect against personal property and liability risks. The three insurance policies are:
- the homeowners insurance policy,
- the automobile insurance policy, and
- the personal umbrella liability insurance policy.

Homeowners and automobile insurance are package policies that provide both property and liability coverage in one contract. The personal liability umbrella policy provides a layer of personal liability protection above the coverages provided in the underlying homeowners and automobile policies, in the unfortunate event that those policies do not provide sufficient coverage for injury to another party or property.

Each of the following discussions is based on the standard policy forms issued by the Insurance Services Office (ISO). Since insurance is regulated at the state level, each state may require certain modifications to the standard ISO form. Thus, the ensuing discussions are general in nature. Absolute statements cannot be made about any particular policy without thoroughly reading that particular policy.

Key Concepts

Underline/highlight the answers to these questions as you read:

1. Identify the three types of insurance that are most commonly purchased to protect against liability and risks to personal property.

2. Identify and describe the four areas of coverage in Section I of a homeowners' insurance contract.

3. Describe coinsurance.

4. Identify and describe the two areas of coverage in Section II of a homeowners' insurance contract.

HOMEOWNERS (HO) INSURANCE: BASIC COVERAGES

Homeowners insurance is usually provided in a package policy covering both property and liability. There are a variety of alternative contractual forms that a homeowner may select. Each different **homeowners insurance** form includes two sections: Section I provides property insurance coverage, and Section II provides liability coverage. Exhibit 4.1 presents an overview of the different types of perils covered as well as the different forms of homeowners insurance available. The specific HO forms and their general and unique contractual provisions are discussed later in this chapter.

EXHIBIT 4.1   LIST OF COVERED PERILS

BASIC-NAMED PERILS	
1. Fire	2. Vehicles
3. Lightning	4. Smoke
5. Windstorm	6. Vandalism or malicious mischief
7. Hail	8. Explosion
9. Riot or civil commotion	10. Theft
11. Aircraft	12. Volcanic eruption

BROAD-NAMED PERILS
Includes Coverage for Basic-Named Perils (1-12) plus 13-18
13. Falling objects
14. Weight of ice, snow, sleet
15. Accidental discharge or overflow of water or steam
16. Sudden and accidental tearing apart, cracking, burning, or bulging of a steam, hot water, air conditioning, or automatic fire protective sprinkler system, or from within a household appliance
17. Freezing of a plumbing, heating, air conditioning, or automatic fire sprinkler system, or of a household appliance
18. Sudden and accidental damage from artificially generated electrical current

OPEN PERILS
(Include Coverage for Basic and Broad Perils)
Open perils means the insurance covers any risk that is not excepted in the policy.

COVERAGE FOR DIFFERENT FORMS OF HOMEOWNERS INSURANCE - SECTION 1						
	HO-2	**HO-3**	**HO-4**	**HO-5**	**HO-6**	**HO-8**
Coverage A Dwelling	Broad	Open	N/A	Open	Broad	Basic
Coverage B Other Structures	Broad	Open	N/A	Open	N/A	Basic
Coverage C Personal Property	Broad	Broad	Broad	Open	Broad	Basic
Coverage D Loss of Use	Broad	Broad	Broad	Open	Broad	Basic

SUMMARY OF GENERAL EXCLUSIONS (PERILS EXCLUDED)

Each HO form specifies which causes of loss (perils) it covers and which it excludes. Later in this chapter, the different HO forms and the perils covered by each are presented. Listed below are the general exclusions to all homeowners' policies:
- Movement of the ground (earthquake, mudslide, and sink hole)
- Ordinance or law
- Damage from rising water
- War
- Nuclear hazards
- Power failure
- Intentional acts
- Neglect

Movement of the Ground
Property damage arising from earth movement is excluded. This includes damage from an earthquake, volcanic eruption, landslide, and sink hole. Sink hole collapse and earthquake coverage are available by endorsement.

Ordinance or Law
A loss due to an ordinance or law that regulates the construction, repair, or demolition of a building or structure is excluded.

Damage from Rising Water
Property damage from the following are specifically excluded from coverage under the homeowners policy:
- Floods, surface water, waves, tidal water, and overflow or spray of a body of water.
- Water below the surface of the ground that exerts pressure on or seeps through a building, sidewalk, driveway, foundation, swimming pool, or other structure.
- Water backing through sewers or drains.

Coverage for naturally occurring floods is available through the National Flood Insurance Program offered by the federal government. Coverage for sewer backup is available in some areas as an endorsement to the HO policy.

War or Nuclear Hazards
Property damage from war or nuclear hazard, including radiation, or radioactive contamination is excluded. If a radiation leak from a nuclear power plant near an insured's home contaminates his or her property, there is no coverage for the loss.

Power Failure
Losses due to power failure caused by an uninsured peril, such as a freezer thawing out and its contents spoiling because of local power plant malfunctions, are not covered. If, however, a covered peril such as fire or lightning on the premises causes the power failure, then the resulting damage is covered. Refrigerated property coverage is available by endorsement.

Intentional Acts
If a loss is discovered to be an intentional act on the part of any insured, it is not covered. For example, one cannot intentionally burn his house down and recover insurance benefits.

Neglect
If an insured fails to use all reasonable and necessary means to save and preserve his property during or after the loss, or when the property is endangered by an insured peril, the loss is not covered.

SUMMARY OF SECTION I COVERAGES
Section I consists of five sections, four specific property coverages (identified as A through D) and additional coverages:
- Section A - Dwelling
- Section B - Other structures

- Section C - Personal property
- Section D - Loss of use
- Additional coverage - Debris removal, damage to trees, credit card loss, etc.

Coverage A: Dwelling

This coverage pays for repair and/or replacement of damage to the house, attached structures, and building materials on the premises. The homeowner typically buys an amount of coverage equal to the replacement cost of the **dwelling**, and in some cases, will be required to maintain higher coverage if the property is mortgaged. A mortgage lender generally demands an amount of coverage on the dwelling at least equal to the total amount owed on the mortgage.

Covered losses to the dwelling and other structures are paid on the basis of replacement cost with no deduction for depreciation. **Replacement cost** is the amount necessary to purchase, repair, or replace the dwelling with materials of the same or similar quality at current prices. Many contracts require the insured to carry insurance of at least 80 percent of the replacement cost (coinsurance) at the time of the loss or the insured will not be fully covered for a loss that is partial. If the insured carries less than the coinsurance provision requires, the insured will receive the following for a partial loss:

$$\frac{\text{Amount of Insurance Carried}}{\text{Coinsurance Requirement}} \times \text{Amount of the Loss}$$

EXAMPLE 4.1

Bill owns a home with a replacement cost of $400,000. He purchases $200,000 of property insurance with a coinsurance requirement of 80 percent. If Bill experiences a $50,000 loss, the insurance company will pay:

$$\frac{\text{Insurance Purchased}}{\text{Coinsurance Requirement}} \times \text{Amount of Loss}$$

$$\frac{\$200,000}{80\% \times \$400,000} \times \$50,000 = \$31,250$$

Bill will receive $31,250 less his deductible. Note, he will not receive the loss of $50,000 even though his total coverage is $200,000.

Certain properties attached to the dwelling or considered an integral part of the dwelling are covered only on an actual cash value basis. These properties include awnings, household appliances, outdoor antennas, outdoor appliances, and non-building structures. Building glass is replaced with safety-glazing materials, if required by local building codes.

Coverage B: Other Structures (Detached)

In addition to the main house, some homeowners have small, detached structures on their property. These include detached garages, small greenhouses, or storage buildings. Coverage

B pays for damage to these structures. The limit of insurance in Coverage B is typically 10 percent of the Coverage A (dwelling) limit. This coverage also pays on a replacement cost basis (just as for the dwelling).

Keep in mind that **other structures** may not be eligible for coverage if they are used for business purposes. If another structure is rented to someone who is not a tenant of the dwelling, no coverage applies (unless the structure is rented for use solely as private garage space).

Coverage C: Personal Property (Tangible Personalty - Moveables)

The value of a homeowner's **personal property** should not be underestimated. Imagine what it would cost to replace the typical family room's furniture, entertainment equipment, music collection, videos, tables, paintings, lamps, and books. All of the HO forms provide coverage for the personal property of the insured (and resident family members), irrespective of where the property is located at the time of loss. The limit of insurance for Coverage C is typically equal to 50 percent of the Coverage A (Dwelling) limit.

Note that the standard HO form provides only actual cash value (ACV) coverage for personal property. An optional endorsement is available to add replacement cost coverage to personal property, and this option is strongly recommended for most homeowners. **Actual cash value** is the depreciated value of personal property. Since the contents of a home depreciate rapidly, a homeowner could suffer a serious financial loss if replacement cost coverage were not provided.

EXAMPLE 4.2

Lisa bought a new 52" television for $2,800. Three years later the television was stolen and had depreciated by 60% in the three years. Today, the same television costs $1,500. Lisa will receive $600 ($1,500 - $900 depreciation) in actual cash value. She will receive the full $1,500 if she has replacement cost coverage.

Certain kinds of personal property have dollar limits on the amount that the insurer will pay for any loss. A typical HO policy contains the following personal property limits:

$200	-	money, bullion, coin collections, and bank notes
$1,500	-	securities, bills, evidence of debt, airline tickets, and manuscripts
$1,500	-	theft of jewelry, watches, gems, precious metals, and real furs
$1,500	-	watercraft, including trailers (not boat affiliated) and equipment
$2,500	-	theft of firearms
$2,500	-	theft of silverware, goldware, pewterware, and similar property
$500	-	loss of business use property not on premises
$2,500	-	loss of business use property on premises
$1,500	-	loss of electronic apparatus

If the insured owns personal items that have values beyond the limits stated above, it may be possible to purchase additional amounts of insurance beyond the special limits listed above or purchase a separate policy for such coverage. The additional increments of insurance purchased are listed in what is referred to as a schedule. A **schedule** is a list of dollar limits or amounts of insurance provided for specified personal items attached to the homeowners policy. Note, however, that scheduled assets are no longer covered under the general HO. Scheduled items also have no deductibles and are valued at agreed upon values.

Certain items of personal property are excluded from coverage because they are either uninsurable or outside the "normal" range of properties owned by the typical homeowner. Homeowners having these unusual types of personal properties and, thus, unusual risk exposures, must request special coverage in addition to that provided by their HO form.

The following personal property items are specifically excluded from coverage in most package homeowners policies:
- Animals, birds, and fish
- Articles separately described and specifically insured
- Motorized land vehicles used off premises
- Property of roomers or boarders not related to the insured
- Aircraft and parts
- Furnishings on property rented out to others
- Property held as samples, held for sale, or sold but not delivered
- Business data, credit cards, and funds transfer cards
- Business property held away from the residence premises

Coverage D: Loss of Use

Loss of use is defined as a combination of additional living expenses for that part of the premises occupied by the insured and for any loss of rental income. Coverage is generally limited to a maximum of 30 percent of the Coverage A (dwelling) limit. However, for HO6 (condo), the limit is 50 percent of Coverage C; and for HO8 (modified), it is ten percent of Coverage A.

A direct property loss can result in a family having to live in a hotel or apartment for days, weeks, or even months. The incremental difference between the cost of living in these temporary arrangements and normal costs that would have been incurred had there been no loss is known as additional living expense. The increase in housing costs, food, transportation, laundry, and so on are all examples of additional living expenses. Benefits are provided only for the additional (incremental) costs required to maintain the homeowner's normal standard of living.

Under loss of use, a lessor may recover the loss of fair rental value on property held for rental purposes by the insured lessor. Benefits are paid on the basis of rental value less charges and expenses that do not continue during the period in which the property is uninhabitable.

EXAMPLE 4.3

George (lessor) owns a house in which he rents a room to a student (lessee) for $400 per month. If the house is deemed uninhabitable for two months following a fire, George can recover $800 for loss of rent if he is insured.

If a civil authority prevents an insured from using his or her premises due to damage by a covered peril to a neighborhood or neighbor property, loss of use coverage will be provided for up to two weeks. This is a unique feature of the HO form, considering that the insured need not suffer damage to his own property to collect from the policy. The value of this coverage should not be underestimated. Consider the various forest fires in California or hurricanes in Louisiana. If a civil authority orders a homeowner to vacate the premises, the cost of putting a family of four in a hotel room, plus paying for restaurant meals, laundry service, pet boarding, and so on, can amount to several thousand dollars in a very short period of time.

Additional Coverages

In addition to providing Coverages A through D, Section I provides supplementary coverages as follows:

- All-risk coverage is provided for *property while it is being moved from one place to another,* and for an additional thirty days thereafter.
- The cost of *removing debris of covered property* damaged by an insured peril is paid for.
- A *fire department service charge* is covered up to $500 for loss by an insured peril; however, a fire department call for rescuing a cat from a tree or people in a home being threatened by a flood is not covered.
- The additional coverages under the homeowners policy also pay for *reasonable repairs to protect the property from further damage* after a covered loss occurs.
- An additional amount of insurance is provided to *cover damage to trees, shrubs, plants, and lawns* from all covered perils except for wind (limited to five percent of the dwelling coverage, but not more than $1,000 for any one tree or plant).
- Up to $1,000 per loss for *assessments against an insured* by a group of property owners arising from loss or damage to property jointly owned by all of the members collectively (for example, condominium owners or cooperative apartment projects).
- Coverage may exist for damage to property arising from *the collapse of a building* caused by an insured peril in addition to several circumstances per the insurance contract.
- Damage caused by *breakage of glass or safety glazing material* that is part of the building, storm doors, or storm windows is covered.
- Up to $2,500 may be paid for *damage to landlord's furnishings* in an apartment on the insured's dwelling premises.
- Up to $500 of coverage for loss due to *unauthorized use of credit cards,* fund transfer cards, forgery of checks, acceptance of counterfeit money, and any incurred court costs or attorney fees may be available.

SUMMARY OF SECTION II COVERAGES

Section II coverages are all the same for homeowner's policies, except the policy limits may be different. The coverages are coverage E for various forms of personal liability and coverage F for medical payments to others.

Coverage E: Personal Liability

Coverage E protects the named insured and all resident family members against liability for bodily injuries and property damage they or their resident premises cause others to suffer. The minimum limit of coverage is generally $100,000 per occurrence, although some homeowners carry a $200,000 or $300,000 limit. In addition to the liability coverage, the insurer pays all legal defense and settlement costs associated with a claim for damages made by an injured party as long as the insurer is unwilling to pay the limit on the policy.

This coverage provides liability coverage for *personal* (that is, nonbusiness) activities. The insuring agreement is quite broad, and simply agrees to protect against claims or suits for bodily injury or property damage. The coverage is then narrowed to exclude most nonpersonal liability situations and other uninsurable exposures. Exhibit 4.2 lists the exclusions that apply to both Coverage E and Coverage F.

LIABILITY EXCLUSIONS APPLICABLE TO COVERAGES E AND F — EXHIBIT 4.2

Exclusion	Coverage E: Personal Liability	Coverage F: Medical Payments
Intentional Injury	✓	✓
Business & Professional Activities	✓	✓
Rental of Property	✓	✓
Professional Liability	✓	✓
Uninsured Premises	✓	✓
Motor Vehicles	✓	✓
Watercraft	✓	✓
Aircraft	✓	✓
War	✓	✓
Communicable Disease	✓	✓
Sexual Molestation or Abuse	✓	✓
Nuclear Exclusion	✓	✓
Workers Compensation	✓	✓
Controlled Substance	✓	✓
Contractual Liability	✓	–
Property owned by or in custody of Insured	✓	–
Residence Employee Away from Premises	–	✓
Persons Residing on Premises	–	✓

Coverage F: Medical Payments to Others

This coverage pays necessary medical expenses of others that result from bodily injury. The bodily injuries must arise out of the insured's activities, premises, or animal(s). Medical expenses must be incurred within three years of the accident, and it is important to note that this coverage will *not* pay for medical expenses incurred by the insured or any regular resident of the household, except a residence employee (such as a maid or butler).

This coverage may seem to duplicate the coverage provided in Coverage E; however, there is an important difference between the two. Coverage F is a "no-fault" coverage that will automatically pay for bodily injuries, while Coverage E pays for both bodily injuries and property damage *for which the insured is legally liable.*

Quick Quiz 4.1

Highlight the answer to these questions:

1. The three types of insurance most commonly purchased to protect against liability and risks to personal property are: homeowners insurance, automobile insurance, and personal umbrella liability insurance.
   a. True
   b. False

2. Section I of a homeowners insurance contract covers: the dwelling, other structures, personal property, and loss of use.
   a. True
   b. False

3. Both coverage E (Personal Liability) and coverage F (Medical Payments to Others) pay claims based on regardless of who is at fault.
   a. True
   b. False

True, True, False.

EXAMPLE 4.4

Jordan is celebrating her 6th birthday with a party at her house. One of her guests, Dylan, age 6, falls and hits his head causing a gash on his forehead. Donna, Jordan's mother, rushes Dylan to the emergency room where he receives 6 stitches and returns to the party as a hero. Coverage F of Donna's homeowners policy will pay for the emergency room expenses for Dylan. If Dylan's mother later sues, any judgment for the fault will be paid under coverage E.

In summary, Coverage F pays regardless of fault, while Coverage E pays only when the insured is legally liable. A typical amount of coverage purchased under this policy is $10,000 per person per occurrence.

EXAMPLE 4.5

If guests at John's party get sick from eating bad oysters, each one of them may receive up to $10,000 to cover necessary medical expenses that result.

The standard homeowners policy contains three different types of exclusions: those that apply to both Coverages E and F, those that apply only to Coverage E, and those that apply only to Coverage F.

Exclusions to Both Coverages E and F
Neither Coverage E nor Coverage F will pay for injuries or damages:
- That are *expected or intended* by the insured.
- Resulting from the *insured's business or professional activities.*
- Resulting from the *rental of premises* (however, coverage will be provided when:
  - Part of an insured location is rented either on an occasional basis, or when part of an insured location is rented out solely as a residence to no more than two roomers or boarders; and
  - Part of an insured location is rented out as an office, school, studio, or private garage).
- Arising out of premises the insured owns, rents, or leases to others that have not been declared an insured location.
- Arising out of the *ownership or use of watercraft, motorized vehicles, and aircraft* (however, certain vehicles and watercraft are covered for liability):
  - Trailers that are not connected to a motorized land conveyance.
  - A vehicle designed primarily for use off of public roads that the insured does not own or that the insured does own but that is on an insured location.
  - Motorized golf carts while being used on a golf course.
  - Vehicles not subject to motor vehicle registration that include lawn mowers, motorized wheelchairs, and vehicles in dead storage on the insured location.
  - Nonmotorized watercraft (canoes and rowboats, for example).
  - Low-powered boats the insured owns or rents, or small (under 26 feet long) sailboats.
  - Model or hobby aircraft that are not designed to carry people or cargo.
  - Note that the exclusions of watercraft liability are very detailed. Any time the insured plans to purchase, rent, or use a watercraft, the HO policy should be consulted to determine whether or not coverage exists.
- Caused by *war or nuclear weapons* of any kind.
- Caused by the *transmission of a communicable disease.*
- Arising out of *sexual molestation, corporal punishment, or physical or mental abuse.*
- Arising out of the *use, sale, manufacture, delivery, transfer, or possession of a controlled substance* (other than legally obtained prescription drugs).

An exception to all of these exclusions includes liability coverage for injuries to a residence employee (housekeeper, butler, nanny, and so on). This type of liability coverage is provided to protect homeowners against injuries to domestic help when the homeowner is not required to purchase workers compensation coverage for such workers.

Exclusions to Coverage E Only

Certain exclusions pertain only to Coverage E of the policy. They are:
- Damage to *property of any insured* (should be covered under Section I).
- Damage to *premises the insured is renting* or has control of, unless caused by fire, smoke or explosion.
- *Contractual liability* (however, two types of contractual liability are covered). First, where the insured has entered into a contract that directly relates to the ownership, maintenance, or use of an insured location, coverage is provided. Second, where the liability of others is assumed by the insured in a contract prior to an occurrence, coverage is provided.
- Liability for *loss assessments charged against the insured* as a member of an association or organization of property owners (one example is a condominium association, which may charge individual unit owners for damage to community property).
- Liability for injuries to employees that falls under a *workers compensation or other disability law.*
- Liability for bodily injury or property damage for which the insured is also covered by a *nuclear energy liability policy.*

Exclusions to Coverage F Only

Coverage F will not provide coverage for bodily injuries:
- Sustained by the *insured* or any *family member.*
- Sustained by a *regular resident* of an insured location.
- Sustained by a *residence employee* of the insured that occur outside of the scope of employment.
- Sustained by anyone eligible to receive benefits for their injuries under a *workers compensation or similar disability law.*
- Resulting from *nuclear reaction radiation*, etc., regardless of how caused.

Quick Quiz 4.2

Highlight the answer to these questions:

1. In a partial loss scenario, an insured could be paid less than the full loss amount due to coinsurance requirements.
   a. True
   b. False

2. Coverage F of a homeowners policy pays medical expenses relating to a bodily injury suffered by someone who lives in the home.
   a. True
   b. False

True, False.

HOMEOWNERS (HO) INSURANCE: BASIC FORMS

The basic homeowners (HO) insurance[1] forms available are:
- HO-2: Broad Form
- HO-3: Special Form
- HO-4: Contents Broad Form (designed for tenants)

---

1. HO-1 has been discontinued in most states.

- HO-5: Comprehensive Form
- HO-6: Unit Owners Form (for condominium owners)
- HO-8: Modified Form

HO-2: Broad Form

The HO-2 provides coverage for basic perils (1-12) plus coverage for seven additional perils: falling objects, weight of ice, snow, sleet, accidental discharge or overflow of water, bursting of steam appliances or hot water systems, freezing, and accidental damage caused by artificially generated electrical current. The dwelling is covered for replacement cost but the personal property is only covered for actual cash value (ACV).

HO-3: Special Form

The HO-3 provides all of Coverages A through F, but offers greater protection for the dwelling by providing coverage on an "open-perils" (formerly called "all-risks") basis. Specifically, the HO-3 covers physical damage to the dwelling and other structures on an open-perils basis and personal property on a named-perils broad form basis. The dwelling is covered for replacement cost but the personal property is only covered for actual cash value (ACV).

Key Concepts

Underline/highlight the answers to these questions as you read:

1. Describe the difference between Replacement Value and Actual Cash Value.

2. Describe the difference between Open Perils coverage and Broad coverage or Named Perils Coverage.

3. Describe an "endorsement."

"Open-perils" means that unless a peril is specifically excluded in the policy, it will be covered. All of the perils in the HO-2 are covered, and all of the exclusions mentioned previously (war, nuclear, etc.) are included in the policy. The value of the HO-3 is that it will cover certain unusual losses not specifically named as perils in the HO-2. For example, suppose the insured under a HO-2 has his house trampled by a herd of cattle. As none of the named perils addresses this particular situation, the loss would not be covered. With the HO-3, however, there is no such exclusion, so the damage would be covered.

HO-4: Contents Broad Form (Designed for Tenants/Renters)

The Contents form (HO-4) is designed for tenants who do not own their rented dwelling premises. In such cases, what the tenant really needs is personal liability coverage, plus coverage for personal contents and loss of use. Therefore, the HO-4 policy does not provide Coverages A or B. The Contents Broad Form provides coverage for the losses caused by the same perils as HO-2. Once again, the personal property (contents) is only covered for actual cash value (ACV).

The minimum amount of coverage sold under the HO-4 is $6,000 of personal property coverage (Coverage C). Coverage D (Loss of Use) limit is equal to 30 percent of the Coverage C limit.

HO-5: COMPREHENSIVE FORM

The HO-5 is similar to HO-3 except the coverage for personal property. HO-3 covers personal property on a broad perils basis. HO-5, however, covers personal property on an open perils basis. Until recently, this type of coverage was added to HO-3 policies through an HO-15 endorsement. In 2000, ISO created the HO-5 form and eliminated the HO-15 endorsement. Unfortunately, the coverage for personal property under this contract is once again only actual cash value basis unless the insured endorses the valuation to replacement cost.

HO-6: UNIT OWNERS FORM (FOR CONDOMINIUM OWNERS)

The condominium association insures most condominium buildings; however, certain components of real property, such as additions, improvements and betterments (carpeting, etc.), may be the responsibility of the unit owner to insure. The HO-6 provides the unique coverage needed for these special exposures. This form covers the same perils as the HO-2 and HO-4, but does not provide building coverage (other than for additions and alterations). The minimum amount of insurance that must be purchased for Coverage C (personal property) under HO-6 is $6,000. Loss of use coverage is limited to 40 percent of Coverage C. Content is covered on an actual cash value basis unless endorsed to replacement value.

HO-8: MODIFIED FORM

The HO-8 policy provides repair cost coverage instead of replacement cost coverage for damage to property by a covered peril. The HO-8 form makes homeowners' insurance affordable for persons who live in older homes that can be quite expensive to repair if the insurance is required to use original construction materials and workmanship. Therefore, the functional replacement cost of the home might be much less than the actual replacement cost. The HO-8 provides coverage for basic perils, except that it provides "functional replacement cost" coverage. The insured's damaged dwelling and other structures will be repaired or replaced in the event of a covered loss, but the insurer pays only for currently accepted building materials and workmanship.

HOMEOWNERS (HO) INSURANCE: AVAILABLE ENDORSEMENTS

REPLACEMENT COST FOR PERSONAL PROPERTY

All of the HO forms previously discussed provide only Actual Cash Value (ACV) coverage for personal property. This endorsement adds replacement cost coverage on the personal property of the insured. Since the ACV of household contents is typically only about 25 cents of the replacement cost value, the replacement cost coverage option is strongly recommended. (This may not be available in all states.)

ALL-RISKS COVERAGE FOR PERSONAL PROPERTY (OPEN PERILS)

All-risk coverage, also known as "**open-perils**" coverage, provides for a much broader and more comprehensive protection program than named-perils coverage. Under an all-risk policy, an insurance company must provide evidence that the loss is not covered under the policy before it can deny payment. The burden of proof lies with the insurer. Depending on the policy form purchased, some amount of all-risk coverage may be included on certain types of property. However, if it is not included, its purchase is recommended on both dwelling and personal property.

INFLATION PROTECTION

To avoid a coinsurance penalty, or an "under-insurance" situation, a homeowner should consider adding an inflation-guard endorsement to the homeowners policy. This endorsement increases the face value of insurance on both the dwelling and other coverages by a specified percentage every three months, such as 1, 1½, or 2 percent.

It is rare that insurance coverage amounts will increase at precisely the same rate as inflation in property values. Although an inflation-guard endorsement is a worthwhile purchase, it is not a complete form of protection against inflation and should not be a substitute for regular and careful review of the adequacy of insurance coverage. As expected, the insured's premiums will increase as coverage increases.

EARTHQUAKE AND SINK HOLE COLLAPSE INSURANCE

Earthquake or sink hole collapse endorsements can be added to any homeowners policy to provide coverage for earthquakes, landslides and earth movement. A minimum deductible of $250 applies to any one loss, and there is a two to five percent deductible of the total amount of applicable insurance that applies to the loss.

Quick Quiz 4.3

Highlight the answer to these questions:

1. Replacement cost is generally a higher than actual cash value.
   a. True
   b. False

2. In an open perils coverage policy the burden lies with the insured to prove that the damages were caused by an insured against event.
   a. True
   b. False

3. It is possible to obtain an endorsement for liability insurance against unintentional damage to another's reputation.
   a. True
   b. False

4. While you could insure a small sailboat (under 26 feet long) under a homeowners policy, it is wiser to purchase a separate boat owner's policy.
   a. True
   b. False

True, False, True, True.

REFRIGERATED PROPERTY COVERAGE

Refrigerated property coverage covers damage to property stored in refrigerators or freezers caused by the interruption of electrical service. There is usually a $500 limit and a $100 deductible.

SEWER BACKUP COVERAGE

Sewer backup coverage endorsement provides coverage under Section I for property damage caused by sewer backup problems.

Personal Injury

Section II of the standard HO policy protects the insured only against liability for bodily injury and property damage. An insured may be liable for personal injury or damage to someone's reputation, as well. The HO policies can be endorsed to provide limited personal injury protection to the insured. This endorsement adds coverage for the following *unintentional* offenses (remember that if the loss is intentionally caused, the policy will not provide coverage):

- False arrest, detention or imprisonment, or malicious prosecution.
- Libel, slander, defamation of character, or violation of the right of privacy.
- Invasion of right of private occupation, wrongful eviction, or wrongful entry.

Business Pursuits

A business pursuits endorsement provides the insured with liability for business activities, as long as the insured does not have an ownership or controlling interest in the business. This endorsement is designed to protect the insured as an employee of someone else who may or may not provide liability protection for the insured.

Watercraft

Certain types of watercraft can be added back to the homeowner's policy for coverage; however, a separate boat owner's policy is generally the wisest choice for any insured who owns watercraft. The boat owner's policy is quite similar in format and coverages to the Personal Auto Policy, which will be discussed later in this chapter.

Other Endorsements

Many other endorsements for additional premiums are available to meet the specific needs for coverage for various homeowners. The following are but a few of the wide variety of endorsements available.

- An "other members of your household" endorsement extends the definition of the insured to include non-relatives over 21. This endorsement is in response to our changing society and the increase in nontraditional households.
- An "assisted living endorsement" extends the definition of the insured to provide coverage for personal property of relatives, not necessarily a household member, in a care facility. The endorsement includes loss of use and liability coverages.
- An "open-perils endorsement" for computers used in the home.
- An "endorsement available for golf carts" can be added to the homeowner's policy and is generally owned to cover property damage. This endorsement is usually subject to a $500 deductible and can also include collision liability coverage.

HOMEOWNERS INSURANCE CONTRACTUAL CONDITIONS

SECTION I CONDITIONS

Duties of the Insured after a Loss

If there is a loss to an insured's property, the insured is required to fulfill a number of obligations before the loss can be settled. Immediately following the loss the insured must:
1. Give notice immediately to the insurance company or agent.
2. Protect the property from any further damage.
3. Prepare an inventory of loss to the building and personal property.
4. File written proof of the loss with the insurance company, given the company's time constraints. The insurer must provide a state-promulgated form for the proof of loss.

Loss Settlement

This condition specifies how certain property items will be valued (whether on an ACV basis or a Replacement Cost basis, etc.). The coinsurance provision of the policy is also contained in this clause.

Key Concepts

Underline/highlight the answers to these questions as you read:

1. Highlight the obligations of the insured.

2. Highlight the obligations of the insurer.

3. Describe how a claim will be paid when the loss is insured by more than one insurer.

4. Highlight the differences between the different standard HO forms 2 – 6.

Loss to a Pair or a Set

When there has been a loss to a pair or a set (such as a partial loss of a set of china, or the theft of only one earring), the insurer may either repair or replace the damaged/lost items, or pay the difference between the value of the property as a set (before the loss) and the value after the loss.

Appraisal

This clause gives the insured the right to dispute the amount of settlement offered by the insurer. If either the insured or the insurer disagrees on the amount of loss, either person may demand an appraisal by a competent appraiser. Then, both the insurer and the insured hire their own appraisers. If the two appraisers cannot reach an agreement on the loss amount, an umpire may be chosen to mediate their differences. Each party pays for its own appraiser, and both the insured and the insurer equally share the expense of hiring the umpire.

Other Insurance

When a loss covered under this policy is also covered by some other policy, the insured cannot collect from each policy in full. To do so would violate the principle of indemnity. The Other Insurance clause states that when another policy also covers a loss, the insurer will only pay a proportion of the loss based on the limits of coverage provided by each policy.

EXAMPLE 4.6

Suppose Phyllis has two HO policies. One provides a limit of $100,000 and one provides a limit of $200,000. Her house is worth $100,000; and after a fire destroys it, she will collect a proportion of the loss from each insurer. Because the first insurer provides 1/3 of all coverage provided ($100,000/$300,000), it will pay 1/3 of the loss, or $33,333. The second insurer will pay 2/3 of the loss, or $66,667.

Suit Against the Insurer

This clause gives the insured the right to sue the insurer *only after* all the policy provisions have been complied with. It also requires that the suit be brought within one year of the date of the loss.

Settlement at Insurer's Option

The insurer retains the right to repair or replace any part of damaged property with similar property, as long as it notifies the insured of this right within 30 days after receiving the insured's sworn proof of loss.

Loss Payment

The insurer has 60 days *after* an agreement is reached regarding the amount of loss to provide payment to the insured. Most insurers will of course pay sooner, but the standard HO policy does give the insurer 60 days to actually make payment.

Abandonment of Property

The insurer does not have to accept property abandoned by an insured. A homeowner who suffers fire damage, for example, might try to force the insurer to take control of the house and be responsible for cleanup and repairs, and even mortgage payments.

Mortgage Clause

Because many homes are mortgaged, the insurer includes this clause to protect the mortgagee's (lender's) interest in the insured home. This clause gives the mortgagee important rights. The mortgagee has the right to receive payment for valid claims on the property, even if the insurer has denied the insured's claim (which would happen in the case of misrepresentation by the insured or an intentionally caused loss). Next, the mortgagee has the right to receive notice of policy cancellation or nonrenewal at least 10 days before the coverage on the property ends.

This clause also imposes certain obligations on the mortgagee. The mortgagee is responsible for notifying the insurer if there is a change in ownership or occupancy of the mortgaged property. The mortgagee must also pay any homeowner premiums that are due but that the insured has neglected to pay, and file proof of loss statements if the insured fails to do so.

No Benefit to Bailee

If the insured has left property with a bailee, such as a moving company or dry cleaner, the insurer will not pay for loss or damaged property on behalf of the bailee. This clause does not say that claims by the insured will not be paid; it merely states that the coverage will not protect or benefit the bailee. If, for example, a fire on the premises of a dry cleaner destroyed the insured's personal property, the insurer would pay the insured's claim; however, it would then subrogate against the dry cleaner.

Recovered Property
When the insured or the insurer recovers property for which the insurer has already paid a claim (as might be the case following a theft), each must notify the other party of the recovery. The insured then has the option either to return the recovered property to the insurer or to keep the recovered property. If the insured keeps the property, the loss payment must be adjusted accordingly.

Volcanic Eruption Period
All volcanic eruptions occurring within a 72-hour period are considered one occurrence. Because volcanoes tend to erupt gradually over a period of days, this clause protects the insured from having to pay a new deductible for each eruption.

SECTION II CONDITIONS

Limit of Liability
The insurer will not pay more than the policy's coverage limit for each occurrence, regardless of the number of suits or claims filed against the insured for any one event.

Duties after a Loss
The insured is expected to give notice of any accident or occurrence to the insurer or its agent. The insured must also promptly forward to the insurer all summons and demand letters. The insured must cooperate and assist the insurer in the investigation and settlement of any claims. Finally, the insured must not voluntarily make payments for anything other than first aid at the time a bodily injury is sustained.

Duties of an Injured Person - Coverage F
An injured person or a representative must give the insurer written proof of a claim as soon as practical after a loss, and give the insurer permission to obtain medical records of the injured person. The injured person must also submit to a physical exam by the insurer's doctor, if instructed to do so by the insurer.

Payment of Claim - Coverage F
This clause states that paying any claim under Coverage F is in no way an admission of liability by the insurer or the insured.

Bankruptcy of an Insured
The bankruptcy or insolvency of any insured does not terminate coverage or relieve the insurer of its obligations under the policy.

SECTIONS I AND II CONDITIONS

Concealment or Fraud
Dishonesty either before or after a loss may void the policy. Examples of dishonesty that will void the policy include intentionally concealing or misrepresenting material facts, and intentionally causing losses to occur.

Cancellation and Nonrenewal
Every state imposes its own restrictions on the insurer's right of cancellation and nonrenewal, so it is important to examine the specific policy to understand what is allowed. Generally, however, the insured may cancel the policy at any time by notifying the insurer, while the insurer may cancel the policy only for certain reasons: nonpayment of premium, material misrepresentation of fact, or a substantial change in the risk. In most cases, the insurer must only provide a 10-day notice of cancellation when it is canceling a newly issued policy, or when it is canceling for nonpayment of premium. Other cancellations and nonrenewals usually require a 30-day notice. Cancellations generally result in a pro-rata refund of unused premium.

Assignment
The insured may not assign rights under the policy without the insurer's written consent.

Subrogation
The insurer may require the insured to assign rights of recovery for payments made by the insurer. This allows the insurer to take over the insured's subrogation rights against negligent third parties. The insurer does not, however, subrogate for claims made under Coverage F of the policy.

Exhibit 4.3 summarizes the preferred provisions of homeowners insurance.

Quick Quiz 4.4

Highlight the answer to these questions:

1. If a homeowner has two HO policies on the home, and suffers a loss, the formula for determining the payout by each insurer is to put the total amount of all insurance as the denominator, and each insurer's policy's limits in the numerator.
    a. True
    b. False

2. The insurer may owe a duty to the mortgagee of the home.
    a. True
    b. False

3. Generally, the insurer has one year to pay the insured for a loss suffered.
    a. True
    b. False

4. Generally, the insurer may cancel the policy at any time by notifying the insured.
    a. True
    b. False

True, True, False, False.

HOMEOWNERS CHECKLIST FOR PREFERRED PROVISIONS

EXHIBIT 4.3

Part A - Dwelling	• Replacement cost • Open perils
Part B - Other Structures	• Replacement cost • Open perils
Part C - Personal Property	• Replacement cost • Open perils
Additional Endorsements and Riders	• Extra coverage for valuable personal property • Aircraft • Watercraft • Furnishings on property rented out to others • Business property • Earthquake insurance • Sewer backup coverage

EXHIBIT 4.4 — SUMMARY OF HOMEOWNERS INSURANCE POLICIES

	HO-2 (Broad Form)	HO-3 (Special Form)	HO-5 (Comprehensive Form)	HO-8 (For Older Homes)	HO-4 (Renter's Contents Broad Form)	HO-6 (For Condominium Owners)
Perils covered	Perils 1 – 18	All perils except those specifically excluded on buildings; perils 1 – 18 on personal property	All perils except those specifically excluded	Perils 1 – 12	Perils 1 – 18	Perils 1 – 18
Section 1: Property coverages/limits						
House and any other attached buildings	Amount based on replacement cost, minimum $15,000	Amount based on replacement cost, minimum $20,000	Amount based on replacement cost, minimum $20,000	Amount based on actual cash value of the home	10% of personal property insurance on additions and alterations to the apartment	$1,000 on owner's additions and alterations to the unit
Detached buildings	10% of insurance on the home	10% of insurance on the home	10% of insurance on the home	10% of insurance on the home	Not covered	Not covered
Trees, shrubs, plants, etc.	5% of insurance on the home, $1,000 maximum per item	5% of insurance on the home, $1,000 maximum per item	5% of insurance on the home, $1,000 maximum per item	5% of insurance on the home, $1,000 maximum per item	10% of personal property insurance, $1,000 maximum per item	10% of personal property insurance, $1,000 maximum per item
Personal property (contents)	50% of insurance on the home	50% of insurance on the home	50% of insurance on the home	50% of insurance on the home	Chosen by the tenant to reflect the value of the items, minimum $6,000	Chosen by the home-owner to reflect the value of the items, minimum $6,000
Loss of use and/or add'l living expenses	30% of insurance on the home	30% of insurance on the home	30% of insurance on the home	10% of insurance on the home	30% of personal property insurance	50% of personal property insurance
Credit card, forgery, counterfeit money	$500	$500	$500	$500	$500	$500
Section 2: Liability						
Comprehensive personal liability	$100,000	$100,000	$100,000	$100,000	$100,000	$100,000
Damage to property of others	$250 – $500	$250 – $500	$250 – $500	$250 – $500	$250 – $500	$250 – $500
Medical payments	$1,000	$1,000	$1,000	$1,000	$1,000	$1,000
Special limits of liability	Special limits apply on a per-occurrence basis (e.g. per fire or theft): money, coins, bank notes, precious metals (gold, silver, etc.), $200; securities, deeds, stocks, bonds, tickets, stamps, $1,500; watercraft and trailers, including furnishings, equipment, and outboard motors, jewelry, watches, furs, $1,500; silverware, goldware, etc., $2,500; guns, $2,500.					

AUTOMOBILE INSURANCE

Automobile insurance is required in virtually every state, either expressly or implicitly. Mandatory automobile insurance laws exist in many states, and they expressly require the purchase of liability insurance before owning or operating a motor vehicle. Some states further require the purchase of "no-fault" coverages that pay for bodily injuries on a first-party basis, meaning that each insured pays for his and his passengers' injuries without regard to fault. Other states implicitly require automobile insurance by requiring motorists to be "financially responsible" for a minimum amount of bodily injury and property damage. Purchasing automobile insurance generally proves financial responsibility, although some automobile owners opt to post a bond or other proof of financial responsibility.

Key Concepts

Underline/highlight the answers to these questions as you read:

1. Describe the three major risks that should concern an automobile owner/operator.

2. Highlight what "your covered auto" could be defined as in a standard PAP.

3. Highlight the six parts / categories of a standard PAP.

4. Describe several exclusions are regularly found in standard PAPs.

In addition to these state statutory requirements, many people purchase automobile insurance because their automobile is financed, and the lender requires the borrower to carry coverage for direct physical damage to the automobile. Finally, many people purchase automobile insurance because they recognize that the financial burden associated with an automobile accident could be devastating to their financial well being. One at-fault accident could injure or kill one person or many people, and the insured could be responsible for those damages. In addition, with most new cars costing over $20,000, the damage to the insured's owned vehicle could cost thousands of dollars to repair.

THE LEGAL ENVIRONMENT FOR THE AUTOMOBILE

The automobile is one of the most widely-owned and used major asset of consumers in the United States. The automobile presents great risk of economic loss to the owner including both property and liability damage.

The liability of the owner or operator for an automobile is generally governed by the tort laws of negligence. However, some states have modified the negligence law to also include **vicarious liability** responsibility for owners of automobiles for the negligent acts of family members or members of the household who are operating the automobile or for damage caused by a minor while driving the insured automobile. These laws take the form of family purpose doctrine or permissive use statutes. Essentially these laws make both the driver and the owner jointly liable for damages.

All states have financial responsibility and compulsory automobile liability insurance laws with Maine having the highest requirements (expressed as 50/100/25) and Louisiana and Oklahoma having the lowest (10/20/10). In the case of Maine, the bodily injury liability per person minimum limit is $50,000, the bodily injury liability per accident minimum limit is $100,000 and the property damage per accident minimum liability limit is $25,000.

In spite of compulsory liability laws, there are many uninsured motorists. A few states have created special low-cost automobile insurance policies to deal with densely populated urban areas where the poor may not be able to afford the relatively high automobile liability insurance premiums. The fact that there are many uninsured motorists is an essential reason to consider adding uninsured motorists coverage for both bodily injury and property damage caused by an uninsured or under-insured motorist.

COST OF AUTOMOBILE INSURANCE

Automobile insurers determine premiums using three basic sets of factors:
- Age and sex of operators;
- Use of the automobile; and
- Driving record of the operators.

In addition, the premiums vary with the location in which the automobile is operated or garaged. For example, less populated areas are generally less expensive. Premiums are increased for increases in coverage and for more valuable automobiles. Some insurers have begun using credit ratings (FICO Scores) to adjust premiums up or down for perceived risk.

Initial premiums are adjusted down for youthful operator discounts (driver training and for good student), safe driving ratings (no tickets or accidents), and the number and types of automobiles.

SUMMARY OF AUTOMOBILE COVERAGE

To summarize, the owner and operator of an automobile should be concerned about the following risks:
- Liability for injuries and damages to persons outside of the insured vehicle.
- Liability for injuries and damages to persons inside the insured vehicle.
- The cost to repair or replace a damaged or stolen insured vehicle or other property.

In the next section of this chapter, the personal auto policy (PAP) is discussed. This package policy can provide protection against the three major losses listed above.

PERSONAL AUTO POLICY (PAP) COVERAGES

The ISO's **personal automobile policy** is the policy that is sold in almost every state; however, various state laws may result in different policy provisions and coverages. It is always important to read each policy and policy provisions carefully. The following discussion focuses merely on the basic ISO PAP.

ELIGIBLE AUTOS

The PAP may be used to insure four-wheel passenger automobiles, pickup trucks, and vans that are owned by individuals or leased for at least six months. Pickups and vans must have a gross vehicle weight of less than 10,000 pounds and not be used primarily for business purposes (other than farming, ranching, and some sole proprietors). The policy may be used to insure one vehicle or all the vehicles owned in a household (usually subject to a maximum of four vehicles on one policy). It is generally cheaper to insure all the vehicles in one household on the same policy than to insure each vehicle with a separate policy.

The PAP may be used to insure vehicles that are used for pleasure and recreation, driving to and from work, farming and ranching, and even for business use by a sole proprietor.

IMPORTANT POLICY DEFINITIONS

The PAP contains a section of definitions that are important for reference purposes when reading the policy. Each defined word is put in quotation marks whenever it is used in the policy. While many of the definitions are straightforward, one deserves explanation before the various coverages are discussed.

"Your covered auto" is defined as any of the following:
- Any vehicle shown in the policy declarations.
- Any new vehicle *in addition to* those shown in the declarations, but only for 30 days or until the new vehicle is reported to the insurer. The insurer will charge a premium from the date the vehicle was acquired. The new vehicle will have the broadest coverage provided on any declared vehicle for the 30-day period.
- Any new vehicle *that replaces* a vehicle shown in the declarations. The new vehicle will have the same coverage as the vehicle it replaced. The insured must report the new vehicle within 30 days *only if* coverage for damage to your auto is desired.
- Any trailer the insured owns.
- Any auto or trailer that the insured does not own, but that is used as a temporary substitute while a covered vehicle is unavailable due to loss, breakdown, repair, service, or destruction.

The reason this definition is so important is that sometimes coverages are provided for *any* auto, while others are provided only for "your covered auto." Thus, this distinction is important to remember when determining which losses the PAP covers.

Throughout the policy, "you" and "your" refer to the named insured. These terms will not be put in quotation marks, however, in the subsequent discussions throughout this chapter.
- Part A - Liability coverage
- Part B - Medical payments
- Part C - Uninsured motorists
- Part D - Damage to your auto
- Part E - Duties after an accident or loss
- Part F - General provisions

PART A: LIABILITY COVERAGE

Part A agrees to provide liability protection for bodily injuries and property damages caused by an auto accident for which any insured becomes legally liable. The insurer retains the right to defend or settle any claim or suit, and any settlement and defense costs are paid in addition to the policy limits.

Covered Persons and Autos

Who is an insured under Part A? The policy clearly defines an insured as one of four parties:
- You or any family member for the ownership, maintenance, or use of any auto or trailer (this includes the use of borrowed autos, and even rental cars).
- Any person using "your covered auto" with permission.
- Any organization that is responsible for the conduct of someone driving "your covered auto," (such as an employer or charitable organization).
- Any organization that is responsible for your conduct or the conduct of a family member, while you are driving a nonowned automobile (such as an employer that might be responsible for your actions when you are using a coworker's car for business purposes).

Exclusions

The PAP liability coverage is quite broad in nature. It excludes coverage only for the following persons and situations.
- *Vehicle used by auto dealer* - No coverage is provided for any auto dealer or other person in the auto business who is driving your car (the person in the auto business should have their own liability coverage).
- *Bodily injury to an employee* - No coverage is provided for injuries to an employee, because those should be covered by workers compensation benefits. One exception is that the insured will be covered for liability for injuries to a domestic employee.
- *Insured's owned property* - Liability insurance is designed to pay for damages to third parties that are caused by the insured. By definition, liability insurance cannot pay for damages to the insured's owned property. Therefore, in an auto accident, damages to the insured's car and its contents are not paid by the liability coverage. Damage to the car would have to be covered by Part D, and damage to contents of the vehicle would have to be paid by the homeowners coverage.
- *Property in the insured's care, custody, and control* - Along the same lines as the previous exclusion, this one prohibits the insured from recovering under his or her own liability insurance for items that are not true liability losses. When property such as a rental car is damaged in an automobile accident, the PAP treats it as if it were the insured's owned auto. The insured may not use the liability coverage to pay for damages to the rental car.
- *Intentional acts* - Any person who intentionally causes an auto accident is not covered for liability by the policy.
- *Public livery* - Coverage is not provided for any person or vehicle while transporting people or property for a fee. A share-the-expense car pool is not considered a for-fee activity and is, thus, covered.
- *Commercial vehicles used in business* - This exclusion eliminates coverage for business use of automobiles, but then gives back coverage for business use of any private pas-

senger auto, or any owned pickup or van, or any temporary or substitute pickup or van. The intent is to limit business coverage on autos to either private passenger autos or owned pickups and vans.
- *Using auto without permission* - No coverage is provided for any person who uses an automobile without having a reasonable belief that he or she has permission to do so.
- *Regular use of nonowned or nondeclared automobile* - When the insured has the regular use of an automobile that is not shown on the declarations page, either because the employer provides a company car or because the insured owns a nondeclared vehicle, coverage is not provided. If the insured has a company vehicle, the employer should provide coverage or the insured should declare the vehicle as a nonowned vehicle and purchase coverage for it. Recall that the named insured is covered while using "any" auto. If this exclusion were not in the policy, the insured could own ten vehicles, buy coverage on only one, but have coverage on all ten. This exclusion makes it clear that the insurer will only cover those owned vehicles that have been declared and for which a premium has been paid.
- *Autos with less than four wheels* - Motorcycles and recreational vehicles having fewer than four wheels must be specifically insured under a different policy. No coverage is provided for these types of vehicles, regardless of whether they are owned or borrowed.

Coverage Limits

The limits of coverage for Part A are shown on the declarations page, and in most cases there are actually three separate liability coverage limits: two for bodily injury and one for property damage. All limits are on a per occurrence basis. The first bodily injury limit is the per person limit. A per person limit of $100,000 indicates that any one injured person may not receive more than $100,000 for bodily injuries. The second bodily injury limit is the per occurrence limit for all bodily injuries. If this limit were $200,000, the insurer would pay up to $200,000 for all the bodily injuries sustained in one accident, regardless of the number of persons injured. The property damage limit is also a per occurrence limit, and specifies the most the insurer will pay for all property damages caused by one accident.

These "**split limits**" are often written as follows: 100/300/50. The first number is the per person bodily injury limit, the second number is the per occurrence bodily injury limit, and the third number is the property damage liability per occurrence limit. These numbers represent thousands of dollars. In other words, $100,000/$300,000/$50,000 of coverage.

EXAMPLE 4.7

Assume that the insured carried 100/300/50 limits and had a major accident that is deemed to be his fault. Imagine the following claims filed by injured parties in the other vehicle: X sustains $110,000 in bodily injuries, Y sustains $120,000 in bodily injuries, and Z sustains $170,000 in bodily injuries. X, the other driver, also incurs $35,000 in automobile repair and rental car costs. W, a nearby homeowner, sustained $21,000 in property damage. Assume that all claims are settled in the order they are mentioned above.

First, address the bodily injury claims. X is allowed to collect $100,000, because that is the per person liability limit. Note that X likely will sue for the $10,000 deficiency. Y will collect $100,000. Z will collect only $100,000 because at that point, the $300,000 per occurrence limit has been reached. Claims are paid in the order that they are settled, not on a prorata basis, so it is important that claimants begin the settlement process as soon as possible. Z will likely sue the insured for the $70,000.

Next, consider the property damage claims. The policy provides a total of $50,000 of coverage, yet there is a total of $56,000 in property damage claims. Thus, the insurer will pay all of X's damages, and W will receive only $15,000 and may sue for the additional $6,000.

Increased Limits While Driving in Another State
As mentioned previously, all states require some minimum level of financial responsibility or automobile liability insurance. When the insured, a resident in one state, drives within another state and has an accident, the insured must generally have sufficient limits to meet the minimum requirements of the state in which the accident occurred.

EXAMPLE 4.8

A driver from Louisiana, who has only the minimum required liability limits of 10/25/10 drives through Texas, where the minimum liability limits are 20/40/15, and would be expected to have those coverage limits if an accident occurred in Texas. The PAP automatically provides the increased limits required by the state law in which the driver has the accident. Therefore, the Louisiana driver's insurance policy would pay up to 20/40/15 if an accident occurred while the insured was driving in Texas.

It is important to note that this policy provision never reduces the limits of liability the insured has purchased. If a Texas driver has 20/40/15 coverage limits and drives to Louisiana, his policy will pay up to those purchased liability limits for any accident.

Liability Loss Sharing with Other Coverage
When more than one auto policy covers a liability loss, the general rule is that the insurance on the automobile is primary, while the insurance on the driver is secondary and excess. The same is true for damage to the insured's auto.

EXAMPLE 4.9

If Brian borrows Beth's car and has an accident while driving it, Beth's PAP coverage will pay first. When Beth's limits of coverage have been exhausted, then Brian's policy will pay on an excess basis. If more than one policy is primary (for example, if an automobile is declared and covered by two separate policies), then the primary policies share losses on a proportionate basis (as discussed under homeowners insurance).

PART B: MEDICAL PAYMENTS

Medical payments are optional no-fault, first-party coverage designed to pay for bodily injuries sustained in an auto accident. Expenses must be incurred within three years of the auto accident. Limits of insurance are provided on a per person, per occurrence basis. A typical limit of coverage is $5,000/person/occurrence. This means that if four covered persons are injured in an auto accident, each may collect up to $5,000 for reasonable and necessary medical and funeral expenses.

Who is Covered?

An insured in this coverage is defined as any of the following:
- You or any family member while occupying a motor vehicle.
- You or any family member as a pedestrian when struck by a motor vehicle.
- Any other person while occupying "your covered auto."

Exclusions

Medical payment coverages exclude the following:
- *Public livery* - Again, no coverage is provided while the vehicle is used to carry persons or property for a fee.
- *Auto used as a residence* - Although trailers are included as covered autos, this exclusion prevents someone from having medical payments coverage on a house trailer. This type of nonstandard risk must be specifically insured.
- *Injury while working* - Any benefits that are payable under workers compensation or other disability benefit laws preclude coverage under this policy.
- *Using auto without permission* - No coverage is provided for any person who uses an automobile without having a reasonable belief that he or she has permission to do so.
- *Regular use of nonowned or nondeclared auto* - Once again, when the insured has the regular use of an automobile that is not shown on the declarations page, either because the employer provides a company car or because the insured owns a nondeclared vehicle, coverage is not provided.
- *Autos with less than four wheels* - Motorcycles and recreational vehicles having fewer than four wheels must be specifically insured under a different policy. No coverage is provided for these types of vehicles, regardless of whether they are owned or borrowed.
- *Auto used in insured's business* - The same exclusion that was discussed in Part A applies here. Coverage is again provided for private passenger autos used in business and for owned pickups and vans used in business.
- *War and nuclear hazard injuries* - Consistent with other policies, this coverage does not apply to any injuries sustained because of acts of war or because of nuclear contamination or radioactive hazards.

- *Racing* - No coverage is provided when the vehicle is located inside a racing facility or when the vehicle is practicing for, preparing for, or competing in any type of racing or speed contest.

PART C: UNINSURED MOTORISTS

Purpose
Because so many drivers do not obey financial responsibility and compulsory automobile insurance laws, the PAP offers insureds the option of purchasing uninsured motorist coverage that acts as the liability insurance for an uninsured or underinsured motorist.

What is Covered?
Part C will pay for bodily injuries and, in many states, property damages that are sustained by an insured because of an uninsured or underinsured motorist. In simpler terms, this coverage will pay what the uninsured, at-fault motorist's liability insurance *should* have paid, had it existed.

Who is Covered?
An insured for this coverage is defined as follows:
- You or any family member.
- Any other person occupying "your covered auto."
- Any person who might also be entitled to damages (such as a spouse or child) for the injuries sustained by a person described above.

Definitions of an Uninsured / Underinsured Auto
An **uninsured or underinsured motorist** is defined as one who has no liability coverage, one who has limits of liability coverage less than those required by the insured's home state law, one who is an unidentified hit-and-run driver, or one who has liability insurance, but whose insurer cannot or will not pay the claim. Once again, it is important to emphasize that for the insured to collect from this coverage, the uninsured or underinsured driver *must be at fault* in the accident.

Exclusions and Limitations
Many of the exclusions contained in Part B are repeated in this coverage:
- Public livery
- Regular use of nonowned auto
- Injury while working
- Regular use of nondeclared auto
- Using auto without permission
- Auto used in insured's business

In addition, the insurer will not pay for any bodily injuries when the insured or their legal representatives settle a bodily injury claim without the insurer's consent. Furthermore, this coverage will not pay for punitive or exemplary damages.

PART D: COVERAGE FOR DAMAGE TO YOUR AUTO

Coverage D provides direct damage coverage on "your covered auto," plus any "nonowned auto." "Your covered auto" was defined previously, so it is only necessary to define "nonowned auto." A "nonowned" auto is any private passenger, auto, pickup, van or trailer not owned by or furnished for the use of a family member that is in your (or a family member's) custody. This would include a borrowed car, a rental car, and a temporary substitute auto.

Two Coverages Available

Part D provides the insured with two different direct damage coverages: collision and comprehensive. The insured may purchase one or both of these coverages (automobile lenders will generally require the insured to carry both coverages).

Collision coverage protects the insured against upset and collision damages, such as those sustained in an accident involving other vehicles, or those sustained when an auto runs off the road and into a lake. These types of accidents are generally viewed to be the insured's fault because if there were another party to blame for the accident, the insured could ask that party's liability insurance to pay for the damages.

Comprehensive (sometimes referred to as "other than collision") coverage protects the insured against the following perils: missiles or falling objects, fire, theft, explosion, earthquake, windstorm, hail, water or flood, malicious mischief or vandalism, riot or civil commotion, contact with bird or animal, and breakage of glass. These perils are typically viewed as accidental and out of the insured's control. Thus, the premium for this coverage is lower than that for collision coverage.

Dispute Resolution (Appraisal Clause)

If the insured and the insurer do not agree on the amount of a loss, the insured may demand an appraisal process similar to that provided for in the homeowners policy.

Loss Payment

The insurer retains the sole option either to pay for repairs or to declare the vehicle a "total loss" and pay the actual cash value of the vehicle, less any deductible. The collision coverage deductible is typically twice as high as the "other than collision" deductible. In most cases, insureds should carry a minimum $250 "other than collision" deductible and $500 collision deductible. Higher (and lower) deductibles are available. However, higher deductibles generally reduce premiums.

Loss Sharing with Other Policies - Collision

As with a liability loss, when more than one auto policy covers a loss (by collision), insurance on the automobile is primary, while insurance on the driver is excess. Therefore, if Joe borrows Fred's car and has an accident while driving it, Fred's collision damage coverage will pay first. Joe's policy will pay on an excess basis, but will not pay more than the loss, and will still require Joe to pay his own deductible.

If more than one policy is primary (for example, if an automobile is declared and covered by two separate policies), then the primary policies share losses on a proportionate basis (as discussed under homeowners insurance).

Exclusions

Many of the exclusions described in other coverages apply here:
- Public livery
- Custom furnishings on a pickup or van
- Using auto without permission
- Radar detectors
- Racing
- Most electronic equipment (except permanently installed sound reproducing equipment)
- War
- Nuclear damages

As with most direct property coverages, the PAP excludes coverage for normal wear and tear, and ordinary maintenance losses such as road damage to tires. Loss caused by destruction or confiscation by governmental authorities is also excluded, as could occur if the insured vehicle were involved in a crime. Losses to nonowned autos are not covered when the auto is used or maintained by anyone in the automobile business.

Finally, no coverage is provided for a rental vehicle if the insured has purchased a loss damage waiver from the rental car company. Loss damage waivers relieve the insured of liability for damage to the rented vehicle, so the insurer will not provide coverage.

PART E: DUTIES AFTER AN ACCIDENT OR LOSS

Most of the duties required of the insured are common sense: notify the insurer, file proof of loss, and cooperate with the insurer in the investigation and settlement of any claim. In addition, the insured must file a police report to have theft coverage for a stolen vehicle, or to have uninsured motorist coverage for a hit-and-run incident.

Quick Quiz 4.5

Highlight the answer to these questions:

1. An automobile owner/operator should only insure against risks to persons inside the vehicle.
   a. True
   b. False

2. In a standard PAP, "your covered vehicle" includes a new automobile for no more than the first thirty of ownership or until the insurer is notified.
   a. True
   b. False

3. There may be three separate liability coverage limits.
   a. True
   b. False

4. If you drive "your covered vehicle" into Mexico, your PAP coverage is effective.
   a. True
   b. False

False, True, True, False.

PART F: GENERAL PROVISIONS

There are several general provisions and conditions of the auto policy that are similar to those contained in the HO policies. One, however, deserves special attention: the PAP coverage territory.

The PAP provides coverage *only in* the United States, its territories and possessions, Puerto Rico, and Canada. When the insured travels to Mexico (where auto accidents are automatically criminal offenses), or to any other country outside the coverage territory, it is important to realize that the PAP is NOT effective. If the insured intends to drive in such a locale, the appropriate local coverages must be arranged.

LEGAL LIABILITY

The categories of liability to which clients are exposed are: torts (civil wrongs), breach of contract, and crimes (public wrongs). Liability insurance will cover certain classes of torts but not breach of contract or criminal offenses. If a court decides that an individual is liable for a civil wrong that causes injury to another, the individual will be required to make restitution usually in the form of monetary compensation.

There are three general types of torts related to liability: intentional interference, strict and absolute liability, and negligence. **Intentional interference** is, as it sounds, an intentional act committed against another that causes injury. Many of the actions that fall under intentional interference are also criminal acts and would not be covered under liability insurance. Slander and libel, however, are usually covered under personal liability insurance policies. **Slander** is defamation or harm caused by a verbal statement, and **libel** is defamation caused by a written statement.

Key Concepts

Underline/highlight the answers to these questions as you read:

1. Identify the three types of standards of care.

2. Differentiate between contributory negligence, comparative negligence, and the last clear chance rule.

Strict and absolute liability occurs as a result of law. One party is held legally liable regardless of who is responsible for the injury. Workers' compensation laws are examples of strict liability. Under workers' compensation laws the employer is liable for any injury to an employee while he or she is engaged in business activities. Even if the employee causes injury to himself, the employer will be liable unless the employer can prove the injury was due to intoxication or failure to follow orders. If workers' compensation laws provided for absolute liability, the employer would be liable even if the employee was intoxicated. Under strict liability, responsible parties have few options for defense, but under absolute liability, the responsible party has no options for defense.

If an individual causes harm to another by failing to act with appropriate care, he or she will be subject to liability due to **negligence**. In determining whether an individual has acted with appropriate care, the courts use the "prudent man" standard. The standard is met if a reasonable person confronted with the same circumstances would have performed the same acts. Direct negligence refers to acts or omissions directly attributable to an individual. An individual may also be liable for vicarious acts, which are negligent acts performed by someone else but for which the individual is held at least partially responsible. For example, in many states bartenders are vicariously liable for the negligent acts of intoxicated patrons. Liability insurance generally covers both types of negligence.

Standards of Care

Negligence is defined as the failure to act in a way that a reasonably prudent person would have acted under the circumstances. In short, negligence is imprudent to behavior. Types of liability created from negligent behavior include:

- **Strict (Absolute) Liability** - The two terms are used interchangeably. It is a liability without regard to negligence or fault. It applies to damage resulting from some extraordinarily dangerous activity or other statutorily defined activity (e.g., product liability, hazardous materials, blasting operations). Negligence does not have to be proved; however, defenses may be allowed to refute or lessen liability. Workers are indemnified for employment-connected injuries regardless of who was at fault (e.g., workers compensation). Negligence does not have to be proved on the part of the employer nor are defenses permitted by the employer to refute or lessen liability.
- **Negligence per se** - The act itself constitutes negligence, thereby relieving the burden to prove negligence (e.g., drunk driving). Burden of proof is initially borne by the injured party. Standard of proof in most civil cases is the preponderance of the evidence (more than 50%). Other concepts to consider include *res ispa loquitur* ("the act speaks for itself"). **Res ispa loquitur** is a doctrine of the law of negligence that is concerned with the circumstances and the types of accidents, that permits the use of reasonable evidence when a specific explanation of negligence is not available. For example, of a plane crashed, there is negligence. It does not have to be proven. There mere fact that a plane crashes implies negligence. Planes do not just fall out of the sky.

Damages

A tort can result in two forms of injury - bodily injury and property damage. Bodily injury may lead to medical expenses, loss of income, pain and suffering, mental anguish, and loss of consortium. The damages for bodily injury can be:
- Special damages to compensate for measurable losses.
- General damages to compensate for intangible losses (pain and suffering).
- Punitive damages - amounts assessed against the negligent party as punishment.

Property damage is usually measured by the actual monetary loss.

The **collateral source rule** holds that damages assessed against a negligent party should not be reduced simply because the injured party has other sources of recovery available such as insurance or employee benefits (health or disability insurance).

Vicarious Liability
One person may become legally liable for the torts of another (e.g., parent / child, employer where the employee is acting in the scope of employment).

Defense to Negligence
There are various defenses available to alleged negligent parties that can relieve them of legal liability in spite of negligent behavior.

Assumption of the risk - The injured party fully understood and recognized the dangers that were involved in an activity and voluntarily chose to proceed. This defense is not available in all states.

Negligence on the part of the injured party - This can be either **contributory negligence**, where there is evidence that the injured party did not look out for his own safety, or **comparative negligence**, where the amount of damage is adjusted to reflect the injured party's proportion of contribution to the cause of the injury (same with multiple defendants). Contributory negligence theories usually cause the entire action to fail, thus effecting a harsh result. Many states allow recovery for that portion of damaged not caused by the injured party (comparative negligence). The **"last clear chance" rule** may apply. This rule states that a claimant who is endangered by his own negligence may recover if the defendant has a "last clear chance" to avoid the accident and failed to do so.

PERSONAL LIABILITY UMBRELLA POLICY (PLUP)

PURPOSE
The **personal liability umbrella policy (PLUP)** is designed to provide a catastrophic layer of liability coverage on top of the individual's homeowners and automobile insurance liability coverages. A standard amount of coverage is $1 million, although higher limits may be purchased. The need for the PLUP is largely dictated by the insured's personal wealth. The more the insured has at risk, the more likely it is that a PLUP is a suitable purchase.

Key Concepts

Underline/highlight the answers to these questions as you read:

1. Describe the categories of liability, to which one may be exposed.

2. Describe the purpose of PLUP.

3. Describe some insurance needs faced by businesses.

CHARACTERISTICS
Most PLUP insurers will require the insured to maintain certain underlying limits of coverage through an HO and a PAP; and, if the insured also has other liability exposures to insure, such as watercraft liability, minimum limits of coverage will be required for those policies as well.

The PLUP provides the insured with a large amount of coverage at an affordable price. A $1 million PLUP limit might cost as little as $300 per year. The coverage provided is generally quite broad, and may even provide coverages in addition to those provided by the underlying policies. For example, the PLUP might provide personal injury coverage (for defamation of character, false arrest, etc.) even though the underlying HO policy does not. Where these additional coverages are provided, the insured is usually required to pay a **self-insured retention** (SIR) for each loss. This SIR is similar to a deductible.

PLUP coverage provides for legal defense of claims in addition to the claim itself. The cost of legal defense is not charged against the policy. Recall, however, if the insured is willing to pay the face of the policy, there is no requirement to provide legal defense.

Where both the umbrella and an underlying policy cover a loss, the umbrella does not pay any claims until the underlying coverage has exhausted its limits. From there, the umbrella picks up with no SIR imposed on the insured.

EXAMPLE 4.10

If Joe has an HO policy with a Coverage E limit of $300,000, and a $1 million PLUP, and is held liable for bodily injuries to another totaling $900,000, his HO policy will pay the first $300,000 of the claims, then the PLUP will pay the remaining $600,000.

EXCLUSIONS

PLUP forms are nonstandard, so it is difficult to generalize about what exclusions are included in each policy. Certain exclusions almost universally found in PLUPs include: damage to the insured's property; injuries sustained by the insured or a family member; injuries that were intentionally inflicted or caused by the insured; injuries to another party that should be paid under a workers compensation law; and business and professional liability incidents.

BUSINESS AND PROFESSIONAL PROPERTY AND LIABILITY INSURANCE

Similar to individuals, businesses also have insurance needs. Some of the policies used by businesses to cover property and liability include the commercial package policy, inland marine policies, the business owners policy, business liability insurance, workers compensation, business automobile, business liability umbrella policies, professional insurance, and errors and omissions.

The Insurance Services Office (ISO) has developed a commercial insurance program including a package policy (two or more coverages).

THE COMMERCIAL PACKAGE POLICY (CPP)

The commercial package policy (CPP) is both a property and a liability coverage combined into a single policy. The advantages of such a policy include lower premiums and fewer gaps

in overall coverage. Workers compensation coverage and surety coverages are not part of a CPP. A CPP policy format includes:
- a declarations page,
- a policy conditions page, and
- two or more coverage parts or forms (property, general liability, crime, boiler and machinery, inland marine, commercial auto, farm).

Each part or form of the CPP will specify:
- covered property,
- additional coverages,
- extension of coverages,
- other provisions,
- deductibles,
- coinsurance,
- valuation provisions,
- optional coverages, and
- a cause-of-loss form.

Coverages for causes of loss are basic, broad, special, or earthquake form. These forms are similar to the parallel homeowners forms. Business interruption insurance may be added. Also, a builders-risk-coverage form can be added to the CPP for buildings under construction.

INLAND MARINE POLICIES

Inland marine policies cover domestic goods in transit, property held by bailees, mobile equipment and property, property of certain dealers and means of transportation and communication. They may also be used to increase coverage limits on movables, such as furs and jewelry.

THE BUSINESS OWNER'S POLICY (BOP)

The business owner's policy is specifically designed for the needs of small-to-medium-size businesses and covers buildings and business personal property (two forms: basic and special). Basic covers listed perils, as distinguished from special, which covers all perils not excluded. The policy has a standard $250 deductible and covers business liability for bodily injury and property damage.

BUSINESS LIABILITY INSURANCE

General liability is the legal liability arising out of business activities excepting autos, motorized vehicles, aircraft, and employee (workers' compensation) injuries. Liability issues, not including exceptions mentioned, are covered by commercial general liability policies (CGL). CGL can be written either as a stand-alone policy or as a part of a commercial package policy (CPP). The usual coverage, Coverage A, is for bodily injury, property damage and legal defense, but it has significant exclusions. Coverage B is for personal and advertising injury liability. Part C covers medical payments.

WORKERS' COMPENSATION INSURANCE

Most businesses are required to carry workers' compensation insurance. The usual workers' compensation policy is a package that provides for the following coverages: workers' compensation insurance, employer liability insurance, and other state insurance. The workers' compensation insurance covers benefits provided by the insurer (state). Part two covers lawsuits by employees injured in the course of employment, but not covered by state workers' compensation law. Part three provides coverage for other listed states (business trips, etc.).

BUSINESS AUTO POLICY (BAP)

Businesses also use commercial automobile insurance policies covering both physical damage to property and liability insurance. The business auto package policy is referred to as BAP.

COMMERCIAL LIABILITY UMBRELLA POLICY

Businesses may make use of commercial liability umbrella policies for excess coverage on liability, beyond the coverage provided by the firm's basic liability policy.

MALPRACTICE INSURANCE

Most people understand malpractice insurance as liability insurance for health service providers, especially physicians and surgeons. Malpractice insurance, however, is available for all professional service providers and generally covers intentional sets as well as unintentional negligent acts committed by the insured. A typical policy will have a maximum per incident limit and an aggregate limit. The insurer is usually allowed to settle claims out of court without obtaining consent from the insured.

ERRORS AND OMISSIONS INSURANCE

Errors and omissions coverage provides protection against loss from negligent acts, errors, and omissions by the insured. Many professionals (real estate agents, insurance agents, accountants, stockbrokers, attorneys, engineers) need errors and omissions coverage for negligent acts, omissions, or failure to act within their own profession that may cause legal liability. Policies usually have large deductibles ($1,000).

Quick Quiz 4.6

Highlight the answer to these questions:

1. Courts generally use the "prudent man" standard to determine whether one acted with the appropriate amount of care, in a given situation.
   a. True
   b. False

2. PLUP forms are considered standard forms; and thus, it is easy to generalize about PLUP coverage.
   a. True
   b. False

3. Only doctors need malpractice insurance.
   a. True
   b. False

4. The commercial package policy (CPP) is business property and business liability coverage combined in one policy.
   a. True
   b. False

True, False, False, True.

A special type of errors and omissions coverage, called Directors and Officers Errors and Omissions insurance, is available for business executives. Directors and officers insurance provides protection against liability due to mismanagement. Policies usually have high deductibles and require that the insured be financially responsible for a percentage of any claims.

PRODUCTS LIABILITY INSURANCE

Businesses that manufacture products are subject to liability with respect to those products. Acts that can expose a company to product liability include:
- Manufacturing a harmful product
- Selling a defective product
- Packaging the product inappropriately
- Providing insufficient directions or warnings for use

INSURANCE CONCEPT SUMMARY FOR BUSINESSES AND PROFESSIONALS — EXHIBIT 4.5

Insurance Needs	Businesses	Professionals
Property Insurance - Buildings	CPP	CPP
Property Insurance - Personalty	CPP	CPP
General Liability Insurance	As needed	As needed
Inland Marine Coverage	If transporting goods	If transporting goods
Business Interruption Coverage	As needed	As needed
Builders Risk Insurance	If construction	If construction
Workers' Compensation	If employees	If employees
Business Automobile Policy	If autos/BAP	If autos/BAP
Commercial Liability Umbrella Policy	Excess liability coverage	Excess liability coverage
Malpractice Insurance	N/A	Yes
Errors and Omissions Insurance	N/A	Yes
Products Liability Insurance	If manufacturer	N/A

Key Terms

Actual Cash Value - The depreciated value of personal property.

Assumption of Risk - The injured party fully understood and recognized the dangers that were involved in an activity and voluntarily chose to proceed.

Collateral Source Rule - Holds that damages assessed against a negligent party should not be reduced simply because the injured party has other sources of recovery available such as insurance or employee benefits (health or disability insurance).

Collision - Auto insurance coverage that protects the insured against upset and collision damages, such as those sustained in an accident involving other vehicles, or those sustained when an auto runs off the road and into a lake.

Comparative Negligence - The amount of damage is adjusted to reflect the injured party's proportion of contribution to the cause of the injury.

Comprehensive (or Other than Collision) - Auto insurance coverage that protects the insured's auto against perils out of the insured's control, such as missiles or falling objects, fire, theft, earthquake, hail, flood, and vandalism.

Contributory Negligence - Negligence on the part of the injured party that contributes to the harm and, therefore, the injured has to bear some responsibility for the injury.

Dwelling - Residential structure covered under a homeowners insurance policy.

Endorsement - Attachment or addition to an existing insurance policy that changes the original terms.

Homeowners Insurance - A package insurance policy that provides both property and liability coverage for the insured's dwelling, other structures, personal property, and loss of use.

Intentional Interference - Intentional act committed against another that causes injury.

Last Clear Chance Rule - This rule states that a claimant who is endangered by his own negligence may recover if the defendant has a "last clear chance" to avoid the accident and failed to do so.

Libel - A written statement that causes harm to another.

Loss of Use - Under homeowners insurance coverage, loss of use is a combination of additional living expenses and loss of rental income.

Medical Payments - A no-fault, first-party insurance coverage designed to pay for bodily injuries sustained in an auto accident.

Key Terms

Negligence - Harm caused by failure to use reasonable care.

Open Perils - All-risk coverage for personal property that provides for a much broader and comprehensive protection program than named-perils coverage.

Other Structures - Small detached structures on insured's property in addition to the main house, such as garages, greenhouses, or storage buildings.

Personal Automobile Policy - Insurance policy that covers liability for injuries and damages to persons inside and outside the vehicle and covers the cost to repair/replace a damaged or stolen vehicle.

Personal Liability Umbrella Policy - Coverage designed to provide a catastrophic layer of liability coverage on top of the individual's homeowners and automobile insurance policies.

Personal Property - Valuable items owned by the insured that are covered under homeowners insurance.

Replacement Cost - The amount necessary to purchase, repair, or replace the dwelling with materials of the same or similar quality at current prices.

Res ispa loquitur - A doctrine of the law of negligence that is concerned with the circumstances and the types of accidents, which afford reasonable evidence of a specific explanation of negligence is not available.

Schedule - Attachment or addition to an existing insurance policy that lists individual items.

Self-Insured Retention - A payment similar to a deductible that an insured is usually required to pay for each loss under a personal umbrella policy.

Slander - Verbal statement that causes harm to another.

Split Limits - Three separate liability coverage limits covering bodily injury (per person and per occurrence) and property damage.

Strict and Absolute Liability - Liability resulting from law; strict liability allows for defense, absolute liability does not.

Uninsured / Underinsured Motorist - Motorist without liability coverage or whose insurer can/will not pay claim, hit-and-run driver, or motorist with insufficient liability coverage according to state law.

Vicarious Liability - One person may become legally liable for the torts of another (e.g., parent / child, employer where the employee is acting in the scope of employment).

DISCUSSION QUESTIONS

1. Explain the need for property insurance.

2. What are the basic, broad, and open-perils coverages provided by a homeowners policy?

3. Identify the various homeowners forms that are available.

4. What do Sections I and II of a homeowners policy provide?

5. What is a named-perils policy?

6. Identify and explain the various contractual options and provisions in homeowners insurance.

7. Explain why intentional acts are not usually covered by insurance.

8. What legal principle implies that property insurance policies only pay for the policy owner's insurable interest in a loss?

9. What are the ways that property insurance policies determine how losses are valued?

10. List two major general exclusions in almost all homeowners insurance policies that cover real property.

11. What are the coverages provided by a personal automobile insurance policy (PAP)?

12. Identify and explain the various contractual options and provisions in a PAP.

13. What is the need for a personal umbrella policy, and what are the umbrella's distinguishing characteristics?

14. What are three types of property and liability loss exposures facing families and businesses?

MULTIPLE-CHOICE PROBLEMS

1. Bill rents an apartment for $500 per month and has $50,000 content coverage. If he is unable to occupy his apartment due to a negligent fire caused by a neighbor, for up to how many months could he rent another apartment if the cost of the new apartment is $750 per month?

    a. 60 months.
    b. 6 months.
    c. None because negligent acts are not covered.
    d. None because content coverage does not cover reimbursement for rent.

2. Mary lives in Idaho where she carries the state-mandated minimum liability insurance on her car (15/30/10) through her personal automobile policy (PAP). She is driving through Oklahoma and has a wreck with Gerri. Oklahoma requires minimum liability insurance of 30/50/20. Gerri suffers bodily injury in an amount of $40,000 and Gerri's vehicle is damaged in an amount of $22,000. How much will Gerri collect from Mary's PAP policy?

    a. BI $40,000 and property $22,000.
    b. BI $15,000 and property $10,000.
    c. BI $30,000 and property $20,000.
    d. BI $30,000 and property $22,000.

3. Tom and Tim are brothers who frequently drive each other's cars. Their automobiles are insured as follows:

Insured	Insurance Company	Amount
Tim	ABC Co.	40/50/10
Tom	LMV Auto	100/300/25

    Tom is negligent driving Tim's car and has an accident causing bodily injury to the other party involved in the accident in the amount of $50,000. Which insurer will pay, and how much?

    a. ABC will pay $40,000 and LMV will pay $10,000.
    b. LMV will pay $50,000 and ABC will pay nothing.
    c. ABC will pay $40,000 and LMV will pay nothing.
    d. ABC will pay $25,000 and LMV will pay $25,000.

4. Under the HO-3 policy, all open-perils are covered, with some exceptions. All of the following are perils that are excluded from a HO-3 policy, except:

   a. Termite damage.
   b. Flood.
   c. Earthquake.
   d. Tornado.

5. John, who has retired to Miami, decided to purchase a condominium unit on the beach. Which of the following homeowners policies would be most appropriate for John to purchase?

   a. HO-3.
   b. HO-4.
   c. HO-5.
   d. HO-6.

6. Jennifer lives by herself and rents a one-bedroom apartment in Manhattan. Which of the following homeowners policies would be most appropriate for Jennifer to purchase?

   a. HO-3.
   b. HO-4.
   c. HO-5.
   d. HO-6.

7. Section II of a HO-3 policy provides what type of protection for the homeowner?

   a. Dwelling.
   b. Damage to other's property.
   c. Loss of use.
   d. Personal property.

8. Raymond lived in New Orleans during hurricane Katrina. His home was destroyed by wind damage and he was forced to live in a hotel for three months. Which section of his homeowners policy would reimburse him for the increased living expenses associated with the hotel stay?

   a. Dwelling.
   b. Other structures.
   c. Loss of use.
   d. Personal property.

9. Which of the following offers identical coverage for all forms of a homeowners insurance policy?

    a. Section I.
    b. Section II.
    c. No form is identical.
    d. All forms are identical.

10. Which of the following would not be considered an insured person for the purposes of Part A (Liability Coverage) for a Personal Auto Policy?

    a. You.
    b. Any family member.
    c. Any person using your covered auto with permission.
    d. Any person using your covered auto without permission.

11. Resident family members are covered for the purposes of Part A (Liability Coverage) for a Personal Auto Policy when operating all of the following except?

    a. Their auto.
    b. A rented auto.
    c. A borrowed auto.
    d. A replacement auto after 31 days.

12. Mike has the following split limits of coverage on his Personal Auto Policy of 100/300/50. Which of the following best describes Mike's coverage?

    a. $100,000 per person for bodily injury, $300,000 per occurrence for bodily injury and $50,000 for property damage.
    b. $100,000 per covered auto, $300,000 per occurrence for covered auto and $50,000 for uninsured motorist.
    c. $100,000 per person for bodily injury, $300,000 per occurrence for property damage and $50,000 for uninsured motorist.
    d. $100,000 for property damage, $300,000 per person for bodily injury and $50,000 for property damage.

13. All of the following statements are correct regarding a Personal Auto Policy Part B (Medical Payments) coverage except?

    a. Provides payment for medical expenses of an insured due to an auto accident.
    b. Provides medical payments if struck as a pedestrian.
    c. Provides payments for medical expenses for household pets if struck by the covered auto.
    d. Provides payment for medical expenses of anyone occupying the insured's covered auto.

14. Which of the following statements are correct regarding a Personal Auto Policy Part C (Uninsured Motorists) coverage except?

    a. Payment for property damage.
    b. Payment for lost wages.
    c. Payment for punitive damages.
    d. All of the above.

15. All of the following statements are correct regarding a Personal Auto Policy Part D (Coverage for Damage to Your Auto) coverage except?

    a. Collision applies when your car hits another vehicle.
    b. Comprehensive covers fire, theft, or vandalism.
    c. Collision covers damages to a borrowed or rented vehicle.
    d. Collision coverage includes contact with an animal or bird.

16. All of the following statements are correct regarding a personal liability umbrella policy except?

    a. The PLUP provides protection above and beyond the liability limits of your homeowners and automobile insurance policies.
    b. The PLUP requires the insured to carry certain underlying minimum amounts of liability for homeowners and PAP.
    c. The PLUP insurer provides legal defense to the insured.
    d. The PLUP is only appropriate for individuals with a high net worth.

Quick Quiz Explanations

Quick Quiz 4.1

1. True.
2. True.
3. False. Liability is only paid when there is legal liability, whereas medical payments to others pays claims is someone is injured, regardless of fault.

Quick Quiz 4.2

1. True.
2. False. Coverage F pays necessary medical expenses suffered by someone other than the insured or any regular resident of the household, except a domestic employee.

Quick Quiz 4.3

1. True.
2. False. In an open perils policy, the insurance company must prove that a loss not covered under the policy before it can deny payment.
3. True.
4. True.

Quick Quiz 4.4

1. True.
2. True.
3. False. Generally, the insurer has sixty (60) days after an agreement is reached regarding the amount of loss.
4. False. Generally, the insured may cancel the policy at any time by notifying the insurer.

Quick Quiz 4.5

1. False. The three major risks to insure against are for liability and injury to those inside and outside the vehicle, as well as to the vehicle itself.
2. True.
3. True.
4. False. PAP coverage is only within the U.S., and its territories and possessions.

Quick Quiz Explanations

Quick Quiz 4.6

1. True.
2. False. PLUP forms are nonstandard. It is difficult to generalize about the coverage provided and excluded.
3. False. All professional service providers face liability risks, malpractice insurance is a necessity.
4. True.

Social Security

CHAPTER 5

INTRODUCTION

Social Security benefits were never intended to provide total pre-retirement wage replacement upon retirement. Social Security was created to supplement a covered worker's pension, savings, investments, and other earnings from assets to make up an appropriate wage replacement ratio (e.g., 70 percent). Individuals who retire typically need a minimum of 70 to 80 percent of their pre-retirement income during retirement to maintain their pre-retirement standard of living.

Low wage earners receive Social Security retirement benefits approximating 60 percent of their pre-retirement income. Average wage earners receive approximately 42 percent of pre-retirement income from Social Security benefits and high wage earners receive approximately 26 percent of pre-retirement income (see Exhibit 5.1).

From a financial planning standpoint, it is important to understand Social Security law and the various benefits that are available from Social Security. This chapter provides an overview of the Social Security system and its benefits. The six major categories of benefits administered by the Social Security Administration are:
1. Retirement benefits,
2. Disability benefits,
3. Family benefits,
4. Survivors' benefits,
5. Medicare, and
6. Supplemental Security Income (SSI) benefits. SSI benefits are not funded by Social Security taxes but are funded by general funds from the Treasury.

When people think of benefits under Social Security, they are generally thinking of the retirement benefit. Full **retirement benefits** are payable at "full retirement age" (reduced benefits as early as age 62) to anyone who has obtained at least a minimum amount (40 quarters) of Social Security credits. Based on a change in Social Security law in 1983, the age when full retirement benefits are paid began to rise from age 65 in the year 2000 and increases to age 67 by the year 2027. Those workers who delay retirement beyond the full retirement age will receive a special scheduled increase (Exhibit 5.10) in their Social Security retirement benefits when they ultimately retire.

| EXHIBIT 5.1 | **AVERAGE SOCIAL SECURITY BENEFITS AS A PERCENTAGE OF PRE-RETIREMENT INCOME** |

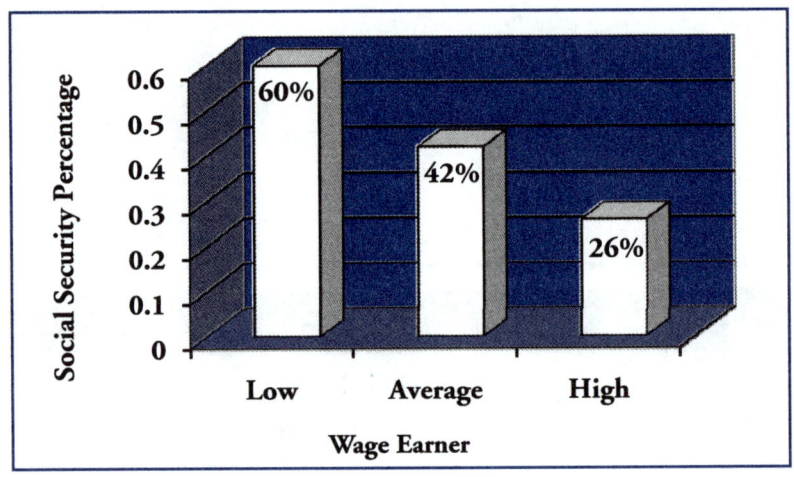

The **disability benefit** is payable at any age to workers who have sufficient credits under the Social Security system. Recipients must have a severe physical or mental impairment that is expected to prevent them from performing "substantial" work for at least a year or to result in their death. Monthly earnings of $1,000 for 2011 (if the individual is blind then the amount is increased to $1,640 per month for 2011) or more are considered substantial. The disability insurance program has built-in incentives to smooth the transition back to the workforce including continuation of benefits and health care coverage.

Key Concepts

Underline/highlight the answers to these questions as you read:

1. What are the six major categories of benefits administered by the Social Security Administration?

2. How are funds collected for Social Security?

The **family benefit** is provided to certain family members of workers eligible for retirement or disability benefits. Such family members include spouses age 62 or older, spouses under age 62 but caring for a child under age 16, unmarried children under 18, unmarried children under age 19 and full-time students, and unmarried children of any age who were disabled before age 22.

Survivors' benefits apply to certain members of the deceased worker's family if the worker earned sufficient Social Security credits. Family members entitled to survivors benefits include those listed for family benefits and may also include the worker's parents if the worker was their primary means of support. A special one-time payment of $255 may be made to the spouse or minor children upon the death of a Social Security covered worker.

Know The Numbers (2011)	
Social Security Wage Base	$106,800
Social Security Quarter of Coverage	$1,120
Social Security Bottom Bend Point	$749
Social Security Top Bend Point	$4,517
Social Security Maximum Monthly Benefit	$2,391.50
Social Security Medicare Part A Deductible Days 1-60	$1,132 per benefit period
Social Security Medicare Part A Deductible Days 61-90	$283 per day
Social Security Medicare Part A Deductible Days 91 and Over	$566 per day
Social Security Medicare Part B Deductible	$162
Social Security Skilled Nursing Care Deductible Days 21-100	$141.50 per day
Social Security Disability Monthly Earnings Limit	$1,000
Social Security Disability Monthly Earnings Limit if Blind	$1,640
Social Security Death Benefit	$255
Social Security Earnings Limitation (under full retirement age)	$14,160
Social Security Earnings Limitation (full retirement age)	$37,680

Medicare provides hospital and medical insurance. Those who have attained full retirement age or those who receive disability benefits for at least two years automatically qualify for Medicare. Others must file an application to become qualified.

Finally, Supplemental Security Income (SSI) (funded by general tax revenues and not by Social Security taxes) is another benefit that provides monthly payments to those disabled or at full retirement age who have a low income and few assets. Generally, those who receive SSI also qualify for **Medicaid**, food stamps, and other government assistance.

SOCIAL SECURITY TAXES AND CONTRIBUTIONS

Although the Social Security retirement benefits program is thought by many to be one of the most complicated and confusing programs administered by the government, the basic concept is quite simple. Employees, employers, and self-employed individuals pay Social Security taxes, known as FICA taxes, during their working years. These payments are pooled in special trust funds. Contributing workers become "covered" workers, meaning that they will fall under the Social Security umbrella of benefits after contributing for approximately 10 years (40 quarters) and will receive retirement benefits based on those contributions and the Social Security formula.

The **Federal Insurance Contributions Act (FICA)** authorized Social Security taxes, including Medicare taxes, to be deducted from paychecks. A portion of these FICA taxes pays part of the Medicare coverage. Separate and apart from Social Security taxes, general tax revenues are used to finance Supplemental Security Income, commonly referred to as "SSI." SSI is a program administered by the Social Security Administration that pays benefits to persons who have limited income and assets.

Both employers and employees pay the taxes for Social Security and Medicare. For the year 2011, an employee pays 4.2 percent of the employee's gross salary up to a limit of $106,800 for **OASDI (Old Age, Survivor, and Disability Insurance)** and the employer pays 6.2 percent. The salary limit rises annually based on annual increases in average wages. For 2011, self-employed workers pay 10.4 percent (4.2 percent + 6.2 percent) of their taxable income up to the same salary limit. The Medicare portion of the Social Security tax is 1.45 percent for both employers and employees and is 2.9 percent for self-employed workers with no limit on the amount of compensation taxed.[1] For tax years after 2011, employees pay 6.2 percent for their portion of Social Security, and self-employed persons pay a total of 15.3 percent.

EXAMPLE 5.1

If an employee earns a salary of $109,300 in 2011, the first $106,800 of the employee's salary will be subject to a tax of 5.65 (4.2 + 1.45) percent while the remaining $2,500 will be subject to a tax of only 1.45 percent. The employer pays 6.2 percent on $106,800 and 1.45 percent on $109,300.

	Taxable Amount	x Tax Rate	Total Tax
Employee - Social Security	$106,800	4.20%	$4,485.60
Employee - Medicare	$109,300	1.45%	$1,584.85
Total Tax			$6,070.45

The United States Social Security system operates on a "pay-as-you-go" basis. Social Security taxes are collected and divided among several trust funds. The federal **Old Age and Survivors Insurance ("OASI") Trust Fund** pays retirement and survivors' benefits. The OASI Trust Fund receives 5.30 percent of the FICA tax. The federal **Disability Insurance ("DI") Trust Fund** pays benefits to workers with disabilities and their families. The DI Trust Fund receives 0.90 percent of the FICA tax. OASI and DI are the two trust funds used for payment of Social Security benefits (total 6.2 percent).

---

1. For 2011 only, the employee side of OASDI is 4.2 percent instead of 6.2 percent and the self-employment percent is 13.3 percent total instead of 15.3 percent for the $106,800. The Medicare rate of 1.45 percent on both halves remains on earned income with no limit.

Quick Quiz 5.1

Highlight the answer to these questions:

1. Social Security benefits are not payable until an individual reaches full retirement age.
   a. True
   b. False

2. Social Security contributions are placed in the following trust funds: OASI, DI, and SMI.
   a. True
   b. False

False, False.

The two Medicare trust funds are the federal **Hospital Insurance ("HI") Trust Fund**, which pays for services covered under the hospital insurance provisions of Medicare (Part A), and the federal **Supplementary Medical Insurance ("SMI") Trust Fund**, which pays for services covered under the medical insurance provisions of Medicare, known as Part B and the new prescription drug provisions known as Part D.[2] The SMI Trust Fund is partially funded by the general fund of the Treasury with the remaining funding coming from monthly premiums paid by the individuals enrolled in Part B.

EXHIBIT 5.2

SOURCES OF FUNDING TO SOCIAL SECURITY TRUST FUNDS

OASI Trust Fund	5.30 percent (limited to the maximum taxable earnings)
DI Trust Fund	0.90 percent (limited to the maximum taxable earnings)
HI Trust Fund	1.45 percent (all earnings are taxed) (In 1993, the Omnibus Budget Reconciliation Act of 1993 abolished the ceiling on taxable earnings for Medicare.)
SMI Trust Fund	-0- (no FICA taxes used; funded by general federal tax revenues and monthly premiums paid by enrollees)

* *The OASI is reduced for year 2011 only by 2 percent on the employee side only.*

---

2. Medicare Prescription Drug, Improvement, and Modernization Act of 2003 (PL 108-173).

Case Study 1

The case of Veterinary Surgical Consultants, P.C. v. C.I.R., involved an owner of an S corporation who attempted to avoid FICA and FUTA taxes by declaring his remuneration as K-1 distribution of corporate net income and not W-2 wages.[1] Dr. Sadanaga performed substantial services for the S corporation, Veterinary Surgical Consultants, P.C. ("VSC"). Dr. Sadanaga worked approximately 33 hours a week for VSC. He was the only individual working for VSC. Tellingly, all of VSC's income was generated from the consulting and surgical services provided by Dr. Sadanaga. As officer and sole shareholder, Dr. Sadanaga declared all remuneration he received on a K-1 form, not on a W-2 form, thus avoiding FICA and FUTA taxes.

VSC claimed that the amounts paid to Dr. Sadanaga were distributions of its corporate net income, rather than wages, and that as an S corporation it passed its net income to Dr. Sadanaga as its sole shareholder. Not surprisingly, the Court disagreed with VSC, i.e., Dr. Sadanaga, and concluded that an S corporation cannot avoid federal FICA and FUTA employment taxes by characterizing compensation paid to its sole director and shareholder as distributions of the S corporation's net income rather than wages. The Court's analysis focused on whether payments represented remuneration for services rendered. To characterize the payments to Dr. Sadanaga as distributions of VSC's net income was "but a subterfuge for reality." The payments constituted remuneration for services performed by Dr. Sadanaga on behalf of VSC. Regardless of how an employer may choose to characterize payments made to its employees, payments representing remuneration for services rendered are subject to payroll taxes.[2] Dr. Sadanaga's reporting of the distributions as nonpassive income from an S corporation had no bearing on the Federal employment tax treatment of those wages. He was VSC's sole source of income, thereby requiring treatment as an employee.[3] In short, while an S corporation is permitted to pass through items of income in calculating its income tax liability, it may not pass through its tax liability for federal employment taxes.

---

1. Veterinary Surgical Consultants, P.C. v. C.I.R., 117 T.C. No. 14, 117 T.C. 141, 2001 WL 1242120 (U.S.Tax Ct.), Tax Ct. Rep. (CCH) 54,527, Tax Ct. Rep. Dec. (RIA) 117.14 (U.S.Tax Ct. 2001).
2. See also Spicer Accounting, Inc. v. United States, 918 F.2d 90 (9th Cir. 1990); Joseph Radtke, S.C. v. United States, 895 F.2d 1196 (7th Cir. 1990).
3. See also Spicer Accounting, Inc. v. United States, supra, at 94-95.

SOCIAL SECURITY BENEFITS – ELIGIBILITY AND CALCULATIONS

Key Concepts

Underline/highlight the answers to these questions as you read:

1. Who are covered workers with regard to Social Security?

2. Who are beneficiaries of Social Security benefits?

COVERED WORKERS AND INSURED STATUS

To qualify for retirement benefits, a worker must be "**fully insured**," which means that a worker has earned a certain number of quarters of coverage under the Social Security system. Since 1978, quarters of coverage have been determined based on annual earnings. In other words, earning a designated amount of money, regardless of when it was earned during the year, will credit the worker with a quarter of coverage for that year. In 2011, the designated amount for a quarter of coverage is $1,120. Thus, workers who earn at least $4,480 are credited with four quarters of coverage for 2011. No worker may earn more than four quarters in one year, regardless of earnings. The following list specifies the designated amounts for a quarter of coverage dating back to 1982:

DESIGNATED AMOUNTS FOR A QUARTER OF SOCIAL SECURITY COVERAGE

EXHIBIT 5.3

Year	Amount Needed to Receive a Credit for One Quarter	Year	Amount Needed to Receive a Credit for One Quarter
1982	$340	1997	$670
1983	$370	1998	$700
1984	$390	1999	$740
1985	$410	2000	$780
1986	$440	2001	$830
1987	$460	2002	$870
1988	$470	2003	$890
1989	$500	2004	$900
1990	$520	2005	$920
1991	$540	2006	$970
1992	$570	2007	$1,000
1993	$590	2008	$1,050
1994	$620	2009	$1,090
1995	$630	2010	$1,120
1996	$640	2011	$1,120

For most persons, 40 quarters of coverage (10 years of work in employment covered by Social Security) or one quarter per year from age 21 to age 62 will fully insure a worker for life. Fully insured workers are entitled to the benefits under the Social Security system. Some benefits, like survivors' benefits, are available to "currently" (although not necessarily fully) insured individuals. **"Currently" insured workers** are those individuals who have at least six quarters of coverage out of the previous 13 quarters.

EXAMPLE 5.2

In 2011, William earned $4,500 from employment subject to Social Security between January 1 and March 31. He was then unemployed for the remainder of the year. How many quarters of coverage did he earn for Social Security for 2011?

For 2011, a worker receives one quarter credit for each $1,120 in annual earnings on which Social Security taxes are withheld up to a maximum of four quarters. It is irrelevant that William earned the $4,480 all in the first quarter. William has earned four quarters.

EXAMPLE 5.3

How is a worker's insured status determined under Social Security?

It is determined by the number of quarters of coverage received. To achieve currently insured status under Social Security, a worker must have at least six quarters of coverage out of 13 calendar quarters prior to retirement, disability, or death. Any worker with 40 covered quarters is fully insured.

SOCIAL SECURITY BENEFICIARIES

Social Security benefits are paid upon retirement, disability, or death if the eligibility requirements are satisfied. The worker's spouse and children may also be eligible to receive benefits when the worker satisfies eligibility requirements. Generally, monthly Social Security benefits can be paid to:
- A disabled insured worker under age 65.
- A retired insured worker at age 62 or older.
- The spouse of a retired or disabled worker entitled to benefits who:
  - is at least 62 years old, or
  - is caring for a child who is under age 16 or disabled.
- The divorced spouse of a retired or disabled worker entitled to benefits if the divorced spouse is age 62 or older and was married to the worker for at least 10 years.
- The divorced spouse of a fully insured worker who has not yet filed a claim for benefits if both are at least age 62, were married for at least 10 years, and have been finally divorced for at least two continuous years.

- The dependent, unmarried child of a retired or disabled worker entitled to benefits or of a deceased insured worker if the child is:
  - under age 18;
  - under age 19 and a full-time elementary or secondary school student; or
  - age 18 or over but disabled (if the disability began before age 22).
- The surviving spouse (including a surviving divorced spouse) of a deceased insured worker if the widow(er) is age 60 or older.
- The disabled surviving spouse (including a surviving divorced spouse in some cases) of a deceased insured worker if the widow(er) is age 50 or older.
- The surviving spouse (including a surviving divorced spouse) of a deceased insured worker, regardless of age, if caring for an entitled child of the deceased who is either under age 16 or disabled before age 22.
- The dependent parents of a deceased insured worker at age 62 or older.

In addition to monthly survivors benefits, a lump-sum death payment of $255 is payable upon the death of an insured worker. Exhibit 5.4 provides a summary of those eligible for OASDI benefits and the percentages of the worker's primary insurance amount ("PIA") that each beneficiary will receive. The PIA is the retirement benefit that the worker would receive if he or she retires at full retirement age.

Quick Quiz 5.2

Highlight the answer to these questions:

1. "Fully insured" means that a worker has earned a certain number of quarters (generally 40) of coverage under the Social Security system.
   a. True
   b. False

2. Social Security benefits can be paid to the dependent parents of a deceased insured worker at age 62.
   a. True
   b. False

True, True.

EXAMPLE 5.4

Steve, age 38, has just died. He has been credited with the last 35 consecutive quarters of Social Security coverage since he left college. He did not work before leaving college. Which of the following persons are eligible to receive Social Security survivor benefits as a result of Steve's death?

1. Tim, Steve's 16-year-old son.
2. Grace, Steve's 18-year-old daughter.
3. Olivia, Steve's 38-year-old widow.
4. Arline, Steve's 60-year-old dependent mother.

Grace is too old; Olivia does not have a child under 16 and she is too young; and Arline is not eligible because she is too young. Thus, only Tim is eligible.

SOCIAL SECURITY BENEFITS – ELIGIBILITY AND CALCULATIONS

EXHIBIT 5.4   SUMMARY OF SOCIAL SECURITY OASDI BENEFITS (AS A PERCENTAGE OF PIA)

	Assuming Full Retirement Age of the Worker			
	Retirement	Survivorship		Disability
	Fully Insured (2)	Fully Insured (2)	Currently Insured (3)	(4)
Participant	100%	Deceased	Deceased	100%
Child Under 18 (6)	50%	75%	75%	50%
Spouse with child under 16 (7)	50%	75%	75%	50%
Spouse - Age 65 (1)	50%	100%	0%	50%
Spouse - Age 62 (1)	40%	83%	0%	40%
Spouse - Age 60 (1)	N/A	71.5%	0%	N/A
Dependent Parent (age 62)	0%	75/82.5% (5)	0%	0%

1. Includes divorced spouse if married at least 10 years (unless they have remarried). Survivorship benefits are also available to divorced spouse if remarried after age 60.
2. Fully insured is 40 quarters of coverage or one quarter for each year after age 21 but before age 62.
3. Currently insured is at least six quarters of coverage in the last 13 quarters.
4. Disability insured is based on age as follows:
   - Before age 24 - Must have 6 quarters of coverage in the last 12 quarters.
   - Age 24 through 30 - Must be covered for half of the available quarters after age 21.
   - Age 31 or older - Must be fully insured and have 20 quarters of coverage in the last 40 quarters.
5. Parent benefit is 82.5 percent for one parent and 75 percent for each parent if two parents.
6. Child under age 19 and a full-time student or of any age and disabled before age 22 also qualifies.
7. Spouse with child disabled before age 22 also qualifies.

Note: Notice that when the participant worker is alive (retirement and disability), beneficiaries who qualify for a benefit, qualify for 50% of PIA. When the participant dies, all qualified beneficiaries generally receive 75% of PIA with the exceptions being the spouse who replaces the participant at 100% and any qualified dependent parents. See note 5.

EXAMPLE 5.5

Under Social Security (OASDI), what benefits are available to the survivors of a deceased but only currently insured worker?

A $255 lump-sum death benefit, which is generally payable to the insured's spouse, and 75 percent of the worker's PIA is available to a child under 18 or to a surviving spouse with a dependent child under the age of 16.

SOCIAL SECURITY RETIREMENT BENEFITS – A CLOSER LOOK

The most well known Social Security benefit is the Retirement Benefit. Until 2000, normal retirement age, the age where full retirement benefits are available to the retiree, was 65 years. The age at which full benefits are paid began to rise in the year 2000. Exhibit 5.5 illustrates the new law, which eventually raises normal age retirement with full benefits to age 67.

AGE FULL RETIREMENT BENEFITS BEGIN (NORMAL AGE RETIREMENT)

EXHIBIT 5.5

Full Retirement Age With Full Benefits	Year Born
65 years	Before 1938
65 years, 2 months	1938
65 years, 4 months	1939
65 years, 6 months	1940
65 years, 8 months	1941
65 years, 10 months	1942
66 years	1943-1954
66 years, 2 months	1955
66 years, 4 months	1956
66 years, 6 months	1957
66 years, 8 months	1958
66 years, 10 months	1959
67 years	1960-present

People who delay receiving Social Security retirement benefits beyond full retirement age receive an increase in their benefit when they do retire. People who take early retirement, currently as early as age 62, receive an actuarially reduced monthly benefit. (Early and late retirement options are discussed later in this chapter.)

When planning for an individual, it may be appropriate to calculate the individual's expected Social Security retirement benefit or to ask the client to request a Social Security statement and consider the benefit in that individual's retirement plan. Some financial planners, however, choose not to consider the estimated retirement benefit in order to be conservative in developing a retirement plan. Others justify the exclusion of Social Security retirement benefits from retirement planning based on the belief that there will be drastic changes to the Social Security system through legislative action or through economically driven forces.

Key Concepts

Underline/highlight the answers to these questions as you read:

1. How is a person's Social Security retirement benefit calculated?

2. How does retiring early or retiring late affect Social Security retirement benefits?

THE RETIREMENT BENEFIT CALCULATION

Determining a worker's Social Security retirement benefit requires specific, detailed information pertaining to the person's age, actual earnings history that was subject to Social Security taxes, and the worker's retirement date. Social Security benefits are based on earnings averaged over most of a worker's lifetime. Actual earnings, in historical dollars, are first adjusted or "indexed" to current dollars to account for changes in average wages and inflation since the year the earnings were received. Then, the Social Security Administration calculates **average indexed monthly earnings ("AIME")** during the 35 years in which the applicant earned the most. The Social Security Administration applies a formula to these earnings and arrives at a basic benefit, which is referred to as the **primary insurance amount (PIA)**. The Social Security retirement benefit is based on the worker's PIA. The PIA determines the amount the applicant will receive at his or her full retirement age, but the dollar amount of the benefit depends on the year in which the worker retires. The PIA is indexed to the consumer price index (CPI) annually.

Figuring the Worker's Average Indexed Monthly Earnings (AIME)

To determine a worker's AIME, the worker's actual annual earnings from age 22 to 62 must be converted into current dollars by multiplying the worker's total annual earnings for each year by an indexing factor. The indexing factor is the result of dividing the national average wage for the year in which the worker attains age 60 by the national average wage for the actual year being indexed. Exhibit 5.6 provides national average wages from 1953 to 2009.

EXHIBIT 5.6 NATIONAL AVERAGE WAGE INDEXING SERIES, 1953-2009

Year	Amount	Year	Amount	Year	Amount
1953	$3,139.44	1972	$7,133.80	1991	$21,811.60
1954	$3,155.64	1973	$7,580.16	1992	$22,935.42
1955	$3,301.44	1974	$8,030.76	1993	$23,132.67
1956	$3,532.36	1975	$8,630.92	1994	$23,753.53
1957	$3,641.72	1976	$9,226.48	1995	$24,705.66
1958	$3,673.80	1977	$9,779.44	1996	$25,913.90
1959	$3,855.80	1978	$10,556.03	1997	$27,426.00
1960	$4,007.12	1979	$11,479.46	1998	$28,861.44
1961	$4,086.76	1980	$12,513.46	1999	$30,469.84
1962	$4,291.40	1981	$13,773.10	2000	$32,154.82
1963	$4,396.64	1982	$14,531.34	2001	$32,921.92
1964	$4,576.32	1983	$15,239.24	2002	$33,252.09
1965	$4,658.72	1984	$16,135.07	2003	$34,064.95
1966	$4,938.36	1985	$16,822.51	2004	$35,648.55
1967	$5,213.44	1986	$17,321.82	2005	$36,952.94
1968	$5,571.76	1987	$18,426.51	2006	$38,651.41
1969	$5,893.76	1988	$19,334.04	2007	$40,405.48
1970	$6,186.24	1989	$20,099.55	2008	$41,334.97
1971	$6,497.08	1990	$21,027.98	2009	$40,711.61

Source: Social Security Administration (www.ssa.gov)

EXAMPLE 5.6

For a worker age 62 in 2011, the indexing factor for the year 1970 is determined by dividing the national average wage for 2008 (when the worker attained age 60), which was $41,334.97, by the national average wage for 1970 (the year being indexed), which was $6,186.24, yielding a factor of 6.68175.

Year	AWI	Age 62 in 2008		Age 65 in 2008	
		Age	Factor	Age	Factor
1951	2,799	5	13.8082	8	12.1697
1952	2,973	6	12.9994	9	11.4569
1953	3,139	7	12.3116	10	10.8506
1954	3,156	8	12.2484	11	10.7949
1955	3,301	9	11.7074	12	10.3182
1956	3,532	10	10.9421	13	9.6437
1957	3,642	11	10.6135	14	9.3541
1958	3,674	12	10.5208	15	9.2724
1959	3,856	13	10.0242	16	8.8347
1960	4,007	14	9.6457	17	8.5011
1961	4,087	15	9.4577	18	8.3354
1962	4,291	16	9.0067	19	7.9380
1963	4,397	17	8.7911	20	7.7480
1964	4,576	18	8.4460	21	7.4437
1965	4,659	19	8.2966	22	7.3121
1966	4,938	20	7.8268	23	6.8980
1967	5,213	21	7.4138	24	6.5341
1968	5,572	22	6.9370	25	6.1139
1969	5,893.76	23	6.5580	26	5.7798
1970	6,186.24	24	6.2480	27	5.5066
1971	6,497.08	25	5.9490	28	5.2431
1972	7,133.80	26	5.4181	29	4.7751
1973	7,580.16	27	5.0990	30	4.4940
1974	8,030.76	28	4.8129	31	4.2418
1975	8,630.92	29	4.4782	32	3.9469
1976	9,226.48	30	4.1892	33	3.6921
1977	9,779.44	31	3.9523	34	3.4833
1978	10,556.03	32	3.6615	35	3.2271
1979	11,479.46	33	3.3670	36	2.9675
1980	12,513.46	34	3.0888	37	2.7223
1981	13,773.10	35	2.8063	38	2.4733
1982	14,531.34	36	2.6599	39	2.3442
1983	15,239.24	37	2.5363	40	2.2353
1984	16,135.07	38	2.3955	41	2.1112
1985	16,822.51	39	2.2976	42	2.0250
1986	17,321.82	40	2.2314	43	1.9666
1987	18,426.51	41	2.0976	44	1.8487
1988	19,334.04	42	1.9991	45	1.7619
1989	20,099.55	43	1.9230	46	1.6948
1990	21,027.98	44	1.8381	47	1.6200
1991	21,811.60	45	1.7721	48	1.5618
1992	22,935.42	46	1.6852	49	1.4853
1993	23,132.67	47	1.6709	50	1.4726
1994	23,753.53	48	1.6272	51	1.4341
1995	24,705.66	49	1.5645	52	1.3788
1996	25,913.90	50	1.4915	53	1.3145
1997	27,426.00	51	1.4093	54	1.2421
1998	28,861.44	52	1.3392	55	1.1803
1999	30,469.84	53	1.2685	56	1.1180
2000	32,154.82	54	1.2020	57	1.0594
2001	32,921.92	55	1.1740	58	1.0347
2002	33,252.09	56	1.1624	59	1.0244
2003	34,064.95	57	1.1346	60	1.0000
2004	35,648.55	58	1.0842	61	1.0000
2005	36,952.94	59	1.0460	62	1.0000
2006	38,651.41	60	1.0000	63	1.0000
2007	40,405.48	61	1.0000	64	1.0000
2008	41,334.97	62	1.0000	65	1.0000

Next, each year's annual earnings must be multiplied by its indexing factor to arrive at the indexed earnings for the years from age 22 to 60. Note that the indexing factor will always equal one for the years in which the worker is 60 or older. After all annual earnings are indexed, or converted to current dollar amounts, the highest 35 years of indexed earnings are added together for a total. The sum of the highest 35 years is then divided by 420 (which represents 35 years multiplied by 12 months per year). This calculation yields the average amount of monthly earnings for all indexed years, hence the name Average Indexed Monthly Earnings (AIME). Once the worker's AIME is determined, the next step in determining the worker's retirement benefit is to calculate the primary insurance amount (PIA) for the worker.

EXAMPLE 5.7

Assume you have two clients, Ronnie and Karen. Both clients retire in 2010. Ronnie retires at age 62. Karen retires at her normal (or full) retirement age. In each case, we assume Karen has covered earnings from 1968 through 2008, as shown in columns labeled "nominal earnings" and Ronnie has covered earnings from 1970 through 2008.

Indexing brings nominal earnings up to near-current wage levels. For each case, the table shows columns of earnings before and after indexing. Between these columns is a column showing the indexing factors. A factor will always equal one for the year in which the person attains age 60 and all later years. The indexing factor for a prior year Y is the result of dividing the average wage index for the year in which the person attains age 60 by the average wage index for year Y. For example, Ronnie's indexing factor for 1970 (6.6818) is the average wage for 2008 ($41,334.97) divided by the average wage for 1970 ($6,186.24).

The highest 35 years of indexed earnings are used in the benefit computation. The selected indexed amounts are bold. Below the indexed earnings are the sums for the highest 35 years of indexed earnings and the corresponding average monthly amounts of such earnings. (The average is the result of dividing the sum of the 35 highest amounts by the number of months in 35 years.) Such an average is called the "Average Indexed Monthly Earnings" (AIME).

The following chart presents Ronnie's AIME as $3,104 and Karen's AIME as $3,946.

Year	Ronnie			Karen		
	Nominal earnings	Indexing factor	Indexed earnings	Nominal earnings	Indexing factor	Indexed earnings
1970	$5,167	6.6818	**$34,525**	$5,194	5.9734	$31,026
1971	$5,525	6.3621	**$35,151**	$5,747	5.6876	$32,687
1972	$5,847	5.7942	**$33,879**	$6,262	5.1800	$32,437
1973	$6,140	5.4530	**$33,482**	$6,746	4.8750	$32,886
1974	$6,452	5.1471	$33,209	$7,253	4.6014	$33,374
1975	$7,088	4.7892	**$33,946**	$8,135	4.2815	**$34,830**
1976	$7,535	4.4800	**$33,757**	$8,815	4.0051	**$35,305**
1977	$7,988	4.2267	**$33,763**	$9,511	3.7786	**$35,939**
1978	$8,589	3.9158	**$33,633**	$10,396	3.5006	**$36,393**
1979	$9,186	3.6008	$33,077	$11,293	3.2190	**$36,353**
1980	$9,742	3.3032	$32,180	$12,151	2.9531	**$35,883**
1981	$10,521	3.0011	$31,575	$13,305	2.6830	**$35,697**
1982	$11,447	2.8445	$32,561	$14,667	2.5430	**$37,298**
1983	$12,485	2.7124	**$33,864**	$16,197	2.4249	**$39,275**
1984	$13,748	2.5618	**$35,220**	$18,051	2.2902	**$41,341**
1985	$14,513	2.4571	**$35,660**	$19,273	2.1966	**$42,336**
1986	$15,228	2.3863	**$36,338**	$20,445	2.1333	**$43,616**
1987	$16,131	2.2432	**$36,186**	$21,887	2.0054	**$43,893**
1988	$16,827	2.1379	**$35,975**	$23,063	1.9113	**$44,080**
1989	$17,335	2.0565	**$35,650**	$23,994	1.8385	**$44,113**
1990	$18,450	1.9657	**$36,267**	$25,779	1.7573	**$45,302**
1991	$19,369	1.8951	**$36,706**	$27,311	1.6942	**$46,270**
1992	$20,146	1.8022	**$36,308**	$28,659	1.6112	**$46,175**
1993	$21,087	1.7869	**$37,680**	$30,257	1.5974	**$48,334**
1994	$21,884	1.7402	**$38,082**	$31,663	1.5557	**$49,258**
1995	$23,024	1.6731	**$38,521**	$33,582	1.4957	**$50,230**
1996	$23,234	1.5951	**$37,060**	$34,155	1.4260	**$48,705**
1997	$23,869	1.5071	**$35,974**	$35,360	1.3474	**$47,643**
1998	$24,839	1.4322	**$35,574**	$37,071	1.2804	**$47,464**
1999	$26,067	1.3566	**$35,362**	$39,188	1.2128	**$47,526**
2000	$27,602	1.2855	**$35,482**	$41,790	1.1492	**$48,026**
2001	$29,061	1.2555	**$36,487**	$44,305	1.1224	**$49,730**
2002	$30,696	1.2431	**$38,158**	$47,115	1.1113	**$52,359**
2003	$32,410	1.2134	**$39,327**	$50,076	1.0848	**$54,321**
2004	$33,200	1.1595	**$38,496**	$51,629	1.0366	**$53,518**
2005	$33,551	1.1186	**$37,530**	$52,503	1.0000	**$52,503**
2006	$34,388	1.0694	**$36,776**	$54,148	1.0000	**$54,148**
2007	$36,400	1.0230	**$37,237**	$56,092	1.0000	**$56,092**
2008	$37,900	1.0000	**$37,900**	$56,408	1.0000	**$56,408**
2009	$38,113	1.0000	**$38,113**	$57,103	1.0000	**$57,103**
2010	$39,551	1.0000	**$39,551**	$59,955	1.0000	**$59,955**
		Highest-35 total	$1,303,620		Highest-35 total	$1,657,422
	Total ÷ 420 Months	AIME	$3,104		AIME	$3,946

Calculating the Worker's Primary Insurance Amount (PIA)

Generally, the PIA is the actual Social Security retirement benefit for the single retiree who retires at full retirement age. For those who retire early or late and for family or surviving beneficiaries, the PIA is not the actual amount of the benefit but the PIA is used to determine their actual benefit.

The PIA is a result of applying the AIME to the PIA formula. This benefit formula changes the dollar amounts (by CPI), but not the percentages, from year to year and depends on the worker's first year of eligibility, that is, when the worker turns 62, becomes disabled, or dies.

The PIA is the sum of three separate percentages of portions of the AIME. These portions are also known as "bend points." For the year 2011, these portions are the first $749 of AIME, the amount of AIME between $749 and $4,517, and the AIME over $4,517. The bend points for 2011 are thus $749 and $4,517. For individuals who first become eligible for retirement benefits or disability insurance benefits in 2011 or who die in 2011 before becoming eligible for benefits, their PIA will be the sum of:

> 90 percent of the first $749 of their AIME, *plus*
> 32 percent of their AIME over $749 up to $4,517, *plus*
> 15 percent of their AIME that exceeds $4,517.
> (Maximum PIA for 2011 is $2,391.50)

The sum of these three calculations is rounded down to the next lower multiple of $0.10 (if it is not already a multiple of $0.10). For calculations in subsequent years, it is useful to know how to determine a given year's bend points. Exhibit 5.7 shows the established bend points from 1980 through 2011.

EXHIBIT 5.7   BEND POINT TABLE

Dollar Amounts (bend points) in PIA Formula		
Year	First	Second
1980	$194	$1,171
1981	$211	$1,274
1982	$230	$1,388
1983	$254	$1,528
1984	$267	$1,612
1985	$280	$1,691
1986	$297	$1,790
1987	$310	$1,866
1988	$319	$1,922
1989	$339	$2,044
1990	$356	$2,145
1991	$370	$2,230
1992	$387	$2,333
1993	$401	$2,420
1994	$422	$2,545
1995	$426	$2,567
1996	$437	$2,635
1997	$455	$2,741
1998	$477	$2,875
1999	$505	$3,043
2000	$531	$3,202
2001	$561	$3,381
2002	$592	$3,567
2003	$606	$3,653
2004	$612	$3,689
2005	$627	$3,779
2006	$656	$3,955
2007	$680	$4,100
2008	$711	$4,288
2009	$744	$4,483
2010	$761	$4,586
2011	$749	$4,517

Source: Social Security Administration (www.ssa.gov)

In order to determine future years' bend points, the 1979 bend points are converted into dollars for that year. The bend points for 2011 were determined by multiplying the 1979 bend points ($180 and $1,085) by the ratio between the national average wage for 2009, which was $40,711.61, and the national average wage for 1977, which was $9,779.44, rounded to the nearest dollar. $40,711.67 divided by $9,779.44 is 4.163. When multiplying the 1979 bend points of $180 and $1,085 by 4.163, the rounded results are $749 and $4,517, the bend points for 2011. For subsequent years, the 1979 bend points should be indexed by multiplying them by the ratio for the national average wage for the year the worker attains age 60 over the national average wage for 1977.

These figures for the PIA may increase each year based on a cost of living adjustment (**COLA**) that is applied to reflect changes in the cost of living. Recent COLAs, which are based on inflation, are shown in Exhibit 5.8. The relevant law does not permit decreases that could result from negative inflation.

COST OF LIVING ADJUSTMENT (COLA) PER YEAR

EXHIBIT 5.8

Year	COLA	Year	COLA	Year	COLA
1990	5.4%	1997	2.1%	2004	2.7%
1991	3.7%	1998	1.3%	2005	4.1%
1992	3.0%	1999	2.5%	2006	3.3%
1993	2.6%	2000	3.5%	2007	2.3%
1994	2.8%	2001	2.6%	2008	5.8%
1995	2.6%	2002	1.4%	2009	0.0%
1996	2.9%	2003	2.1%	2010	0.0%

Annual COLA increases are determined in October of each year and go into effect in time so that they first appear on monthly benefit checks received in the following January. In 2011, the maximum monthly retirement benefit for retirees at full retirement age is $2,391.50, compared to $2,346 in 2010.

EXAMPLE 5.8

Recall from the previous example Ronnie retired in 2011, 2011 is the year in which he is first eligible for benefits and his AIME is $3,104. Ronnie's PIA is $1,427.70 which is calculated below.

90% x $749	$674.10
32% x ($3,104 - $749)	$753.60
15% x $0	$0.00
PIA	$1,427.70

Recall that Karen's AIME is $3,946. Since she was first eligible for benefits in 2006 (the year Karen reached age 62), the bend points for 2006 (Exhibit 5.7) must be used. In addition, her PIA must be increased by cost-of-living adjustments, or COLAs, for 2006 through 2008

(Exhibit 5.8). These COLAs are 3.3%, 2.3%, and 5.8% respectively. The resulting PIA is $1,837.10.

90% x $656	$590.40	
32% x ($3,946 - $656)	$1,052.80	
15% x (over $3,955)	$0.00	
PIA	$1,643.20	*
2006 adjustment	X 1.033	
2007 adjustment	X 1.023	
2008 adjustment	X 1.058	
Resulting PIA	**$1,837.10**	*

* = Adjusted for rounding to lower 10¢

Early and Late Retirement Options

Workers entitled to retirement benefits can currently take early retirement benefits as early as age 62. The worker will receive a reduced benefit because he or she will receive more monthly benefit payments than if the worker had waited and retired at full retirement age. The reduction to one's monthly benefit for early retirement is permanent. Conversely, a delayed or postponed retirement will permanently increase the monthly retirement benefit for a worker.

For each month of early retirement, a worker will receive a reduction in his or her monthly retirement benefit of 5/9 of one percent for up to the first 36 months. For subsequent months of early retirement, the permanent reduction percentage is 5/12 of one percent per month.

EXAMPLE 5.9

Assume Ronnie begins receiving benefits at the earliest possible age, which is age 62. Then the benefit amount for Ronnie is reduced for 48 months of retirement before Ronnie's normal retirement age, which is 66 years. The $1,427.70 PIA is thus reduced to a monthly benefit of $1,070.78.

PIA	$1,427.70
5/9 x 1% x 36 months	Less 20% reduction
5/12 x 1% x 12 months	Less 5% reduction
Monthly Benefit	$1,070.78

The benefit amount for Karen, assuming that benefits begin exactly at her normal retirement age of 65 years and 10 months, is not reduced except for rounding down to the next lower tenth of a dollar.

Although the full retirement age will increase to age 67, workers will still have the option of taking early retirement at age 62. However, the reduction percentage that is applied to the monthly retirement benefit will increase until 2027. Before 2000, those who retired at age 62 received 80 percent of their retirement benefit, but the increase in full retirement age has increased the number of months from 62 until full retirement age. For instance, in the year 2009, covered workers who retired at age 62 will receive 75 percent of their monthly retirement benefit, or 25 percent less than his or her full retirement benefit. By 2027, a covered worker retiring at age 62 (full retirement age would be 67) will receive only 70 percent of his or her monthly retirement benefit. Exhibit 5.9, which was compiled by the Social Security Administration, shows the phase-in of the Social Security full retirement age and accompanying reductions for early retirement at age 62.

SOCIAL SECURITY FULL RETIREMENT AND REDUCTIONS* BY AGE

EXHIBIT 5.9

Year of Birth	Full Retirement Age	Age 62 Reduction Months	Average Monthly Percent Reduction	Total Percent Reduction
1937 or earlier	65	36	0.555	20.00
1938	65 & 2 months	38	0.548	20.83
1939	65 & 4 months	40	0.541	21.67
1940	65 & 6 months	42	0.535	22.50
1941	65 & 8 months	44	0.530	23.33
1942	65 & 10 months	46	0.525	24.17
1943-1954	66	48	0.520	25.00
1955	66 & 2 months	50	0.516	25.84
1956	66 & 4 months	52	0.512	26.66
1957	66 & 6 months	54	0.509	27.50
1958	66 & 8 months	56	0.505	28.33
1959	66 & 10 months	58	0.502	29.17
1960 and later	67	60	0.500	30.00

*Percentage monthly and total reductions are approximate due to rounding. The actual reductions are 0.555 or 5/9 of 1 percent per month for the first 36 months and 0.416 or 5/12 of 1 percent for subsequent months.
Source: Social Security Administration (www.ssa.gov)

No matter what the full retirement age is, a worker may start receiving benefits as early as age 62 and can also retire at any time between age 62 and full retirement age. However, if a worker starts benefits at one of these early ages, the benefits are reduced a fraction of a percent for each month before the full retirement age.

EXAMPLE 5.10

Assume that Josephine, a worker born in 1939, decided to retire on her 62nd birthday. Assume that her full retirement benefit would have been $1,429.20 at age 65 and four months, her full retirement age. If she retires at age 62, what is her monthly retirement benefit?

The answer is $1,119.50 Josephine retired 40 months early. The monthly retirement benefit reduction percentage is 1/180 (5/9 x 1% = 1/180 = 0.0056) for the first 36 months (1/180 x 36 = 20 percent) and 1/240 (5/12 x 1% = 1/240 = 0.0042) for the 4 subsequent months of early retirement (1/240 x 4 = 1.6668 percent), yielding a total permanent reduction to Josephine's monthly retirement benefit of 21.6667 percent.

0.216667 percent x $1,429.20 = $309.66.

$1,429.20 - $309.66 = $1,119.50 (rounded).

EXAMPLE 5.11

What if Josephine retired at age 64 and six months? What is her permanent monthly retirement benefit (subject to COLA increases)? Note: she retired 10 months early from normal retirement age.

The answer is $1,349. 1/180 x 10 = 5.5556 percent.

5.5556 percent x $1,429.20 = $79.40.

$1,429.20 - $79.40 = $1,349.80 (rounded).

For those covered individuals who delay retirement, or when benefits are lost due to the earnings limitation, the monthly retirement benefit and the benefit paid to the surviving spouse increase each year (until age 70) as follows:

EXHIBIT 5.10 **PERCENTAGE INCREASES FOR DELAYED RETIREMENT**

Increase For Year Born	Annual Percentage Increase for Each Year Of Late Retirement	After Age
1917-1924	3.0%	65
1925-1926	3.5%	65
1927-1928	4.0%	65
1929-1930	4.5%	65
1931-1932	5.0%	65
1933-1934	5.5%	65
1935-1936	6.0%	65
1937	6.5%	65
1938	6.5%	65 and 2 months
1939	7.0%	65 and 4 months
1940	7.0%	65 and 6 months
1941	7.5%	65 and 8 months
1942	7.5%	65 and 10 months
1943 and later	8.0%	66

Note: The maximum is 132% of full benefit (8% x 4 + full benefit).
There is no compounding.

Jeanette will turn 66 in 2010 (thus she was born in 1944). She is considering taking Social Security retirement benefits at age 62, 66, or 70. Assume her monthly expected benefit is $1,000 at full retirement age, expected inflation is 4%, and her life expectancy is 90. Calculate the present value of her benefits at ages 62, 66, and 70 (A, B, or C).

EXAMPLE 5.12

Choice A – Begin Benefits at age 62.

PMT	$750	($1,000 less 25% reduction)
N	336	(90-62) x 12
i	0.3333	4/12
FV	0	
$PV_{@62}$	**$151,450.19**	

Choice B – Begin Benefits at age 66.

PMT	$1,000	Full benefit at full retirement age
N	288	(90-66) x 12
i	0.3333	4/12
FV	0	
$PV_{@66}$	$184,948.61	

Discount to age 62 for comparison.

PMT	$0	
N	4	(66-62)
i	4	
FV	$184,948.61	
$PV_{@62}$	**$158,094.84**	

Choice C – Begin Benefits at age 70.

PMT	$1,320	($1,000 plus 8% x 4 years increase)
N	240	(90-70) x 12
i	0.3333	4/12
FV	0	
$PV_{@70}$	$217,828.85	

Discount to age 62 for comparison.

PMT	$0	
N	8	(70-62)
i	4	
FV	$217,828.85	
$PV_{@62}$	**$159,165.41**	

As you can see, even though the benefit is reduced if Jeanette begins her benefit early, the PV of the total benefit at age 62 is not substantially less than if she waited to receive benefits at age 66. Similarly, if she begins her payments later, her yearly payments will be higher but the PV of the benefit at age 62 is not significantly more than if she had received benefits at age 66. The significance here is that all things being equal, the acceleration or delay of benefit generally has little impact on the PV of the benefit at age 62. However, the choice of retirement age is significant when considering the annual income and cash flow needed to maintain one's standard of living.

Although the calculations above can provide estimates of the Social Security benefits a retiring worker may receive, a financial planner should have the client obtain his entire Social Security earnings history up to the moment of retirement from the Social Security Administration to get the most accurate benefit estimate.

Reduction of Social Security Benefits

Besides early retirement, there are two other situations in which beneficiaries can have benefits reduced. The first instance is a reduction of benefits based on earnings, referred to as the **retirement earnings limitations test**. The other instance is through taxation of Social Security benefits. Both of these measures reduce one's net benefits.

A person can continue to work even though he is considered "retired" under Social Security. For a retiree who receives Social Security retirement benefits before normal retirement age, the earnings received by the beneficiary cannot exceed certain limitations without triggering a reduction in Social Security benefits. Beneficiaries can earn up to the limitation amount and receive all of their benefits, but if their earnings exceed the designated limit for the calendar year, then benefits will be reduced or eliminated. The law provides for earnings limitations of $14,160 for those under the full retirement age for 2011. The Social Security Administration reduces $1 in benefits for each $2 earned by those beneficiaries above $14,160. In the year that the retiree reaches full retirement age, $1 in benefits will be deducted for each $3 earned above the given year's limit but only for earnings before the month the retiree reaches full retirement age. For 2011, the limit for earnings in the year the retiree reaches full retirement age is $37,680. The earnings limitation increases every year as median earnings nationwide increase. Once the retiree reaches normal retirement age, benefits will not be reduced regardless of the earnings limitations.

In the event that a beneficiary, who is younger than normal retirement age, has earnings that exceed the limitation, that beneficiary's benefits will be reduced depending on his or her age. The beneficiary must file an annual report of his or her earnings to the Social Security Administration by April 15 of the year following the year worked and must provide the exact earnings for that year and an estimate for the current year. The filing of a federal tax return with the IRS does not satisfy the filing requirement with the Social Security Administration. Also, the wages count toward the earnings limitation when they are earned, not when paid, whereas income for the self-employed normally counts when paid, not earned. If other family members receive benefits based on the beneficiary's Social Security record, then the total family benefits may be affected by the beneficiary's earnings that exceed the earnings limitation. In such a case, the Social Security Administration will withhold not only the worker's benefits but will withhold those benefits payable to family members as well.

Quick Quiz 5.3

Highlight the answer to these questions:

1. Social Security benefits are based on the average of the three highest paid years for a covered worker.
   a. True
   b. False

2. Full retirement age for Social Security is decreasing because of the trend of individuals retiring early.
   a. True
   b. False

False, False.

EXAMPLE 5.13

Matthew is 64 years old and despite being retired from his occupation as an engineer, earned $20,000 in 2011 while working as a golf instructor at a local golf course. Matthew's monthly retirement benefit from Social Security is normally $1,200, which totals $14,400 for the entire year. Because Matthew exceeded the retirement earnings limitation, how much money will be reduced from Matthew's Social Security retirement benefit for 2011?

Matthew's total earnings in 2011	$20,000
Earnings limitation	($14,160)
Remainder excess	$5,840
One-half deduction	÷ 2
Benefits reduced by:	**$2,920**

The Social Security Administration will reduce Matthew's benefits for the year by $2,920. Matthew will receive $11,480 in retirement benefits ($14,400 annual retirement benefit less $2,920 reduction). Matthew's total income for 2011 will be $31,480, instead of $34,400.

EXAMPLE 5.14

Mike is 67 years old. He has a full-time job working as a masseur. This year (2011) he anticipates earning $22,000 from his job. How much, in dollars, will Mike's Social Security benefits be reduced for the earnings test?

None, because Mike is over normal retirement age.

Generally, only wages and net self-employment income count towards the retirement earnings limitation, whereas income from savings, investments, and insurance does not. The following is a nonexclusive list of sources of income that DO NOT count toward the earnings limitation:
- Pension or retirement income
- 401(k) plans and IRA withdrawals
- Dividends and interest from investments
- Capital gains
- Rental income
- Workers' compensation benefits (generally not payable after a worker has retired)
- Unemployment benefits
- Court-awarded judgments, less components of award that include lost wages
- Contest winnings

TAXATION OF SOCIAL SECURITY BENEFITS

Apart from the earnings limitation, some beneficiaries may be required to pay income tax on their Social Security benefits. For persons with substantial income in addition to Social Security benefits, up to 85 percent of their annual Social Security benefits may be subject to federal income tax. The Social Security Administration is concerned with beneficiaries' **modified adjusted gross income** (MAGI). For purposes of Social Security, MAGI is equal to the taxpayer's adjusted gross income plus tax exempt interest, including:
- interest earned on savings bonds used for higher education;
- amounts excluded from the taxpayer's income for employer-provided adoption assistance;
- amounts deducted for interest paid for educational loans;
- amounts deducted as qualified tuition expense; and
- income earned in a foreign country, a U.S. possession, or Puerto Rico, that is excluded from income.

Key Concepts

Underline/highlight the answers to these questions as you read:

1. How are Social Security benefits taxed?

2. What benefits are available from Social Security other than retirement benefits?

3. What is the maximum family benefit?

> **EXAMPLE 5.15**
>
> Last year Charlie and Eva had adjusted gross income of $40,000. They also had the following items:
>
> - Eva spent 3 months during the year in Mexico visiting her mother. While she was there, she earned $5,000 that has been excluded from their AGI.
>
> - While in Mexico, Eva fell in love with a little orphan girl. Luckily, Charlie's company has an Adoption Assistance Program. The program paid $8,000 towards the adoption and the amount was excluded from Charlie's AGI.
>
> - Charlie has been attending night school for several years and has several student loans. Last year he paid and deducted $200 in student loan interest. He also took a qualified tuition expense deduction for $600 he paid to the school.
>
> - Charlie and Eva had $900 in interest. $400 was from tax-exempt bonds and the remaining $500 was from corporate bonds.
>
> Charlie and Eva's MAGI for last year is:
>
> | | |
> |---|---:|
> | Adjusted Gross Income (AGI) | $40,000 |
> | + Foreign Income Excluded | $5,000 |
> | + Adoption Assistance Excluded | $8,000 |
> | + Student Loan Interest Deduction | $200 |
> | + Qualified Tuition Expense Deduction | $600 |
> | + Tax Exempt Bonds Interest | $400 |
> | = **Modified Adjusted Gross Income (MAGI)** | **$54,200** |
>
> Note that the $500 of corporate bond interest has already been included in Charlie and Eva's AGI.

Generally, 50 percent of Social Security benefits may be subject to federal income taxes for beneficiaries who file a federal tax return as an "individual" and have a modified adjusted gross income between $25,000 and $34,000. For those with a modified adjusted gross income plus one-half of Social Security greater than $34,000, up to 85 percent of their Social Security benefits may be subject to federal income taxation. For those beneficiaries that file a joint federal tax return and have a modified adjusted gross income with their spouse between $32,000 and $44,000, 50 percent of their Social Security benefits will be subject to federal income taxes. Finally, if beneficiaries filing a joint tax return have a modified adjusted gross income plus one-half Social Security benefits that exceeds $44,000, 85 percent of their Social Security benefits may be subject to federal income taxation.

In sum, for persons with substantial income in addition to their Social Security benefits, up to 85 percent of their annual benefits may be subject to federal income tax.

| EXHIBIT 5.11 | SOCIAL SECURITY HURDLE AMOUNTS |

	Married Filing Jointly	All Others Except MFS = 0
1st Hurdle	$32,000	$25,000
2nd Hurdle	$44,000	$34,000

If MAGI plus one half of Social Security benefits exceeds the first hurdle but not the second, the taxable amount of Social Security benefits is the lesser of:
- 50% Social Security Benefits, or
- 50% [MAGI + 0.50 (Social Security Benefits) - Hurdle 1].

EXAMPLE 5.16

A married couple has interest income of $18,000 and Social Security benefits of $20,000. What amount of their Social Security benefits must be included in their taxable income?

Lesser of:
- 0.50($20,000) = $10,000, or
- 0.50 [$18,000 + 0.50 (20,000) - 32,000] = Negative

They would have $0 inclusion due to a negative result.

EXAMPLE 5.17

A married couple has income of $30,000 and Social Security benefits of $20,000. What amount of their Social Security benefits must be included in their taxable income?

Lesser of:
- 0.50($20,000) = $10,000, or
- 0.50 [30,000 + 0.50 (20,000) - 32,000] = $4,000

They would have $4,000 of Social Security benefits included in taxable income.

If MAGI plus one-half the Social Security benefits exceeds the second hurdle, the taxable amount of Social Security benefits is the lesser of:
- 85% Social Security Benefits, or
- 85% [MAGI + 0.50 (Social Security Benefits) - Hurdle 2], plus the lesser of:
  - $6,000 for MFJ or $4,500 for all other taxpayers, or
  - The taxable amount calculated under the 50% formula and only considering Hurdle 1.

A married couple has income of $60,000 and Social Security benefits of $20,000. What amount of their Social Security benefits must be included in their taxable income?

EXAMPLE 5.18

0.85 ($20,000) = **$17,000**

0.85 [$60,000 + 0.50 ($20,000) - $44,000] = $22,100
Plus the lesser of:
- $6,000, or
- 0.50($20,000) = $10,000, or
- 0.50[$60,000+0.50($20,000)-$32,000] = $19,000

                                                 $6,000
                                                 $28,100

Therefore, **$17,000** must be included in their taxable income.

A married couple has income of $45,000 and Social Security benefits of $20,000. What amount of their Social Security benefits must be included in their taxable income?

EXAMPLE 5.19

0.85 ($20,000) = **$17,000**

0.85 [$45,000 + 0.50 ($20,000) - $44,000] = $9,350
Plus the lesser of:
- $6,000, or
- 0.50($20,000) = $10,000, or
- 0.50[$45,000+0.50($20,000)-$32,000] = $11,500

                                                 $6,000
                                                $15,350

Therefore, **$15,350** must be included in their taxable income.

EXAMPLE 5.20

Last year Michelle, a single taxpayer, received $10,400 in Social Security benefits. For the entire year, she had an adjusted gross income of $28,000. How much, if any, of her Social Security benefit is taxable?

First, determine Michelle's modified adjusted gross income. Modified adjusted gross income is the sum of adjusted gross income, nontaxable interest, and foreign-earned income. One-half of Michelle's Social Security benefits must then be added to her MAGI. For Michelle, the equation is as follows: $28,000 + [$10,400 x 0.50] = $33,200. Since Michelle's modified adjusted gross income plus one-half of her Social Security benefits is between the two base amounts for a single individual of $25,000 and $34,000, we can use the following formula to determine her taxable amount. The income tax base will be the lesser of 50% of her Social Security benefits *OR* 50% of the difference between Michelle's modified adjusted gross income plus one-half of her Social Security benefits less the base amount of $25,000. Based on this formula, Michelle will be subject to income tax on $4,100 of her Social Security benefit.

- 0.50($10,400) = $5,200
- 0.50($33,200 - $25,000) = $4,100 (the LESSER amount)

EXAMPLE 5.21

A married couple files jointly and has an adjusted gross income of $38,000, no tax-exempt interest, and $11,000 of Social Security benefits. How much, if any, of their Social Security benefits is included in gross income?

The lesser of the following:

- 0.50 ($11,000) = $5,500 or
- 0.50[$38,000+0.50($11,000)-$32,000]=0.50($11,500) = $5,750

They will include $5,500 in gross income. If the couple's adjusted gross income was $15,000 and their Social Security benefits totaled $5,000, none of the benefits would be taxable since 0.50 [$15,000 + 0.50 ($5,000) - $32,000] is negative.

Frank and Lois, married filing jointly, have tax-free municipal bond interest of $2,000. Assuming that Frank and Lois have differing AGI amounts ranging from $20,000 to $50,000, the Social Security amount includable in taxable income is shown below. Thus, if Frank and Lois have $20,000 in AGI then only $1,000 of the Social Security benefit is included (4% of the benefit is included), but if they have AGI of $50,000 then $20,400 is includable (85% of the benefit is included). Notice that once an individual is substantially over the second hurdle they can expect to include 85% of the Social Security benefit.

EXAMPLE 5.22

Preliminary AGI	$20,000	$25,000	$30,000	$35,000	$40,000	$45,000	$50,000
Tax free bond interest	$2,000	$2,000	$2,000	$2,000	$2,000	$2,000	$2,000
MAGI	$22,000	$27,000	$32,000	$37,000	$42,000	$47,000	$52,000
50% of Social Security	$12,000	$12,000	$12,000	$12,000	$12,000	$12,000	$12,000
MAGI plus 1/2 Social Security	$34,000	$39,000	$44,000	$49,000	$54,000	$59,000	$64,000
First hurdle	$32,000	$32,000	$32,000	$32,000	$32,000	$32,000	$32,000
Second hurdle	$44,000	$44,000	$44,000	$44,000	$44,000	$44,000	$44,000
Excess of income over first hurdle	$2,000	$7,000	$12,000	$17,000	$22,000	$27,000	$32,000
Excess of income over second hurdle	$0	$0	$0	$5,000	$10,000	$15,000	$20,000
1. 50% of SSB	$12,000	$12,000	$12,000				
2. 50% [MAGI + 0.50 (SSB) - Hurdle 1]	$1,000	$3,500	$6,000				
3. 85% of SSB				$20,400	$20,400	$20,400	$20,400
4. [85% [MAGI + 0.5 (SSB)- Hurdle 2]] + 6000				$10,250	$14,500	$18,750	$23,000
5. [85% [MAGI + 0.5 (SSB)- Hurdle 2]] + 50% [MAGI + 0.50 (SSB) - Hurdle 1]				$14,450	$18,700	$22,950	$27,200
6. [85% [MAGI + 0.5 (SSB)- Hurdle 2]] + 50% of SSB				$16,250	$20,500	$24,750	$29,000
Includable portion of Social Security	$1,000	$3,500	$6,000	$10,250	$14,500	$18,750	$20,400
Percent of SS Taxed	4%	15%	25%	43%	60%	78%	85%

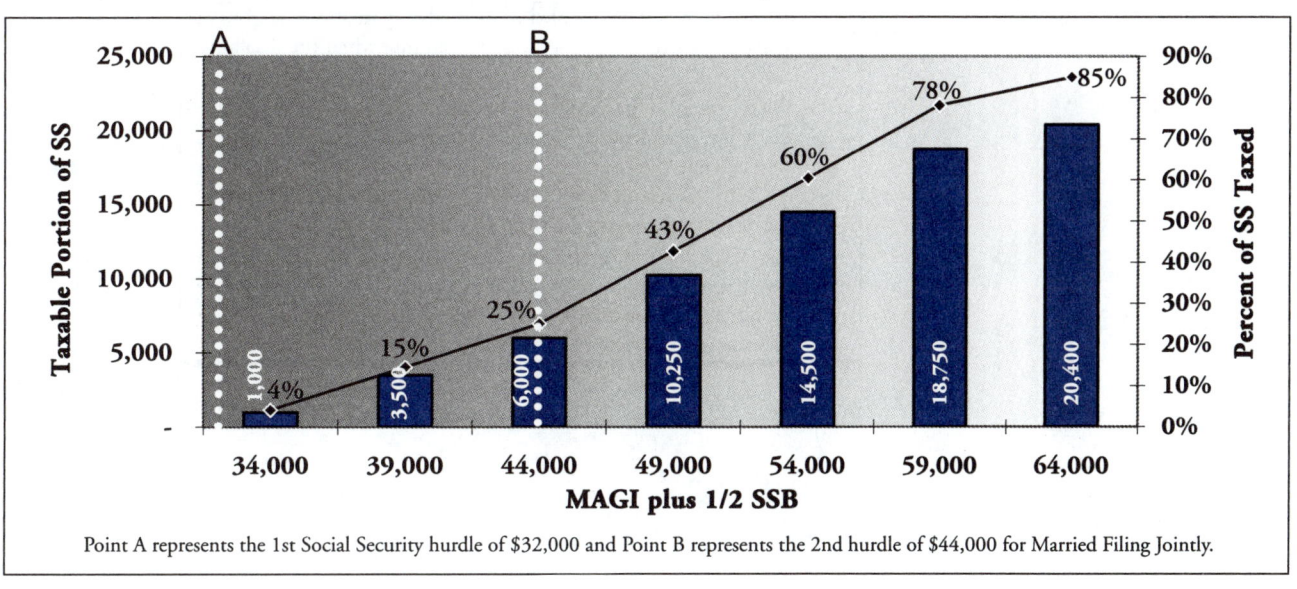

Point A represents the 1st Social Security hurdle of $32,000 and Point B represents the 2nd hurdle of $44,000 for Married Filing Jointly.

OTHER SOCIAL SECURITY BENEFITS

DISABILITY BENEFITS AND DISABILITY INSURED

Benefits are payable at any age to workers who have enough Social Security credits and who have a severe physical or mental impairment that is expected to prevent them from doing "substantial" work for a year or more or who have a condition that is expected to result in death. Workers are insured for disability if they are fully insured and, except for persons who are blind or disabled age 31 or older, have a total of at least 20 quarters of coverage during the 40-quarter period ending with the quarter in which the worker became disabled. Workers who are disabled before age 31 must have total quarters of coverage equal to one-half the calendar quarters that have elapsed since the worker reached age 21 ending in the quarter in which the worker became disabled. However, a minimum of six quarters is required.

EXHIBIT 5.12 — **WORK CREDITS FOR DISABILITY BENEFITS**

Born After 1929, Become Disabled at Age:	Number of Credits You Need:
31 through 42	20
44	22
46	24
48	26
50	28
52	30
54	32
56	34
58	36
60	38
62 or older	40

- Before age 24 - The disabled individual may qualify if they have 6 credits earned in the 3-year period ending when the disability starts.
- Age 24 to 31 - The disabled individual may qualify if they have credit for working half the time between age 21 and the time they become disabled. For example, if they become disabled at age 27, they would need credit for 3 years of work (12 credits) out of the past 6 years (between ages 21 and 27).
- Age 31 or older - In general, the disabled individual needs to have the number of work credits shown in the chart. Unless they are blind, they must have earned at least 20 of the credits in the 10 years immediately before they became disabled.

In 2011, earnings of $1,000 or more per month are considered substantial; therefore, a worker earning more than $1,000 per month would not be eligible for Social Security disability benefits. (If the individual is blind, then the amount is increased to $1,640.) The disability program includes incentives to smooth the disabled individual's transition back into the workforce, including continuation of benefits and healthcare coverage. Disability under the Social Security system is defined as an inability to engage in substantial gainful activity by reason of a physical or mental impairment expected to last at least 12 months or result in death. The impairment must be of such severity that the applicant is not only unable to do his or her previous work but cannot, considering age, education, and work experience, engage in any other kind of substantial gainful work that exists in the national economy.

FAMILY BENEFITS

If an individual is eligible for retirement or disability benefits, other members of the individual's family might receive benefits as well. Family members who may receive retirement or disability benefits include the following:
- A spouse, if the spouse is 62 years old, caring for a child under age 16, or caring for a child who was disabled before age 22.
- A child, if the child is unmarried and under age 18, under age 19 but still in school, or age 18 or older but disabled.

For those workers who are entitled to retirement or disability benefits, an ex-spouse who was married to the worker for more than 10 years could also be eligible for retirement benefits based on the worker's record.

A child's benefit stops the month before the child reaches age 18, unless the child is unmarried and is either disabled or is a full-time elementary or secondary school student. Approximately five months before the child's 18th birthday, the person receiving the child's benefits will get a form explaining how benefits can continue. A child whose benefits stop at age 18 can have them started again if the child becomes disabled before reaching age 22 or becomes a full-time elementary or secondary school student before reaching age 19. If the child continues to receive benefits after age 18 due to a disability, the child also may qualify for SSI disability benefits. When a student's 19th birthday occurs during a school term, benefits can be continued up to two months to allow completion of the school term.

SURVIVORS' BENEFITS

If a worker earned enough Social Security credits during his or her lifetime, certain members of the worker's family may be eligible for benefits when the worker dies. The family members of the deceased worker who may be entitled to survivors' benefits include:
- A widow or widower age 60, age 50 if disabled, or any age if caring for a child under age 16 or a disabled child.
- A child of the deceased worker, if the child is unmarried and under age 18, under age 19 but still in school, or age 18 or older but disabled.
- Parents of the deceased worker, if the deceased worker was their primary means of support.

A special one-time payment of $255 may be made to a deceased worker's spouse or minor children upon death. If a spouse was living with the beneficiary at the time of death, the spouse will receive a one-time payment of $255. The payment may be made to a spouse who was not living with the beneficiary at the time of death or an ex-spouse if the spouse or ex-spouse was receiving Social Security benefits based on the deceased's earnings record. If there is no surviving spouse, a child (or children) who is eligible for benefits on the deceased's work record in the month of death may claim the payment.

THE MAXIMUM FAMILY BENEFIT

When a person dies, his survivors receive a percentage of the worker's Social Security benefits ranging from 75 percent to 100 percent each. There is a limit on the amount of monthly Social Security benefits that may be paid to a family. This limit is called the **maximum family benefit** and it is determined through a formula based on the worker's PIA. While the limit varies, it is equal to roughly 150 to 180 percent of the deceased worker's PIA. If the sum of the family members' benefits exceeds the limit, the family members' benefits are proportionately reduced. For old-age and survivor family benefits, the formula computes the sum of four separate percentages of portions of the worker's PIA. For 2011, these portions are the first $957 of PIA, the amount between $957 and $1,382, the amount between $1,382 and $1,803 and the amount over $1,803. These are the bend points for the maximum family benefit formula for the year 2011, with the following percentage calculations:

Quick Quiz 5.4

Highlight the answer to these questions:

1. Up to 85% of an individual's Social Security benefits may be included in their taxable income.
   a. True
   b. False

2. Once divorced, non-working ex-spouses will not receive Social Security benefits.
   a. True
   b. False

3. The maximum family benefit establishes a limit on the benefits that can be received by one family.
   a. True
   b. False

True, False, True.

> 150 percent of the first $957 of the worker's PIA, *plus*
> 272 percent of the worker's PIA over $957 through $1,382, *plus*
> 134 percent of the worker's PIA over $1,382 through $1,803, *plus*
> 175 percent of the worker's PIA over $1,803.
> This number is rounded to the next lower $0.10.

EXAMPLE 5.23

If an individual has the maximum PIA for 2011, $2,391.50 per month, this would provide a maximum family benefit of $4,185.50 per month as shown by the calculation that follows:

$$\begin{aligned}
\$957 \times 1.50 &= \$1,435.50 \\
(\$1,382 - \$957) \times 2.72 &= 1,156.00 \\
(\$1,803 - \$1,382) \times 1.34 &= 564.14 \\
(\$2,391.50 - \$1,803) \times 1.75 &= 1,029.88 \\
&\ \$4,185.52
\end{aligned}$$

Rounded to $4,185.50

Natalie and Brian, both age 50, are married and have two children, Ashley (age 15) and Kayli (age 5). Brian is disabled and has a PIA amount equal to the maximum PIA ($2,391.50). As seen in the example above, the maximum family benefit is $4,185.50. Because Brian is disabled, Natalie, Ashley, and Kayli are each entitled to receive a benefit equal to 50% of Brian's PIA, subject to the maximum family benefit limit, because the two children are under 18 and Natalie is a spouse/caretaker of a child under 18. Without regard to the maximum family benefit, they would each receive:

EXAMPLE 5.24

Brian	$2,391.50	100% of PIA
Natalie	$1,195.75	50% of Brian's PIA
Ashley	$1,195.75	50% of Brian's PIA
Kayli	$1,195.75	50% of Brian's PIA
Total	$5,978.75	

Because the benefit exceeds the maximum family benefit, the amounts for Natalie, Ashley, and Kayli must be prorated. Therefore, they will each receive $598.00 [($4,185.50 - $2,391.50) 3].

Brian	$2,391.50	100% of PIA
Natalie	$598.00	50% of Brian's PIA subject to maximum family benefit
Ashley	$598.00	50% of Brian's PIA subject to maximum family benefit
Kayli	$598.00	50% of Brian's PIA subject to maximum family benefit
Total	$4,185.50	

Assume instead that Ashley is 19 and no longer eligible to receive benefits under Brian. The maximum family benefit would be calculated as follows:

Brian	$2,391.50	100% of PIA
Natalie	$897.00	50% of Brian's PIA subject to maximum family benefit
Ashley	$0.00	Not eligible
Kayli	$897.00	50% of Brian's PIA subject to maximum family benefit
Total	$4,185.50	

Now assume Ashley is 19 and Kayli is 17. In this case, Natalie is no longer eligible because she is not caring for a child under 16. The family benefit would be calculated as follows:

Brian	$2,391.50	100% of PIA
Natalie	$0.00	Not eligible
Ashley	$0.00	Not eligible
Kayli	$1,195.75	50% of Brian's PIA
Total	$3,587.25	

Notice that Kayli is limited to 50% of Brian's PIA, thus they do not reach the maximum family benefit.

MEDICARE BENEFITS

Key Concepts

Underline/highlight the answers to these questions as you read:

1. What benefits are provided by Medicare?

2. What benefits are provided by Supplemental Security Income?

3. How does marriage or divorce affect Social Security benefits?

Medicare is a federal health insurance plan for people who are 65 and older, whether retired or still working. People who are disabled or have permanent kidney failure can get Medicare at any age. The Health Care Financing Administration, now known as Centers for Medicare and Medicaid Services (or CMS), part of the United States Department of Health and Human Services, administers Medicare. Medicare is the nation's largest health insurance program, covering over 39 million individuals. There are three parts to Medicare: Hospital Insurance (Part A), Medical Insurance (Part B), and Prescription Drug Coverage (Part D).

Generally, individuals who are over age 65 and receive Social Security benefits automatically qualify for Medicare. Also, individuals who have received Social Security disability benefits for at least two years automatically qualify for Medicare. All other individuals must file an application for Medicare.

Part A, Hospital Insurance, is paid for by a portion of the Social Security tax. Part A helps pay for necessary medical care furnished by Medicare-certified providers, including inpatient hospital care, skilled nursing care, home health care, hospice care, and other care. The number of days that Medicare covers care in hospitals and skilled nursing facilities is measured in what is termed **benefit periods.** A benefit period begins on the first day a patient receives services in a hospital or skilled nursing facility and ends after 60 consecutive days without further skilled care. There is no limit to the number of benefit periods a beneficiary may have.

Benefit periods are identified because deductibles, coinsurance, and premiums relate to a benefit period instead of a calendar year. For instance, for coverage under Medicare under Part A, a deductible of $1,132 applies per benefit period. For the 61st through the 90th day of each benefit period, the insured individual must pay $283 a day in the form of coinsurance. Any days over 90 in a benefit period are considered lifetime reserve days. There are 60 lifetime reserve days available with coinsurance of $566 per day. Lifetime reserve days do not renew with each benefit period. It is important, therefore, to determine the number of days used in each benefit period.

MEDICARE TIME LINE

EXHIBIT 5.13

Beneficiary enters hospital

| 60 Days | 61-90 | 91-150 |
| Deductible: $1,132 per benefit period
Coinsurance: $0 | $283 per day | $566 per day
lifetime reserve |

SKILLED NURSING FACILITY TIME LINE

EXHIBIT 5.14

Beneficiary enters nursing facility

| 20 Days | 21-100 |
| Coinsurance: $0 | $141.50 per day |

Exhibit 5.15 Medicare Deductible, Coinsurance, and Premium Amounts for 2011

Hospital Insurance (Part A)

- **Deductible** - $1,132 per Benefit Period
- **Coinsurance**
  - $283 a day for the 61st through the 90th day
  - $566 a day for the 91st through the 150th day for each lifetime reserve day (total of 60 lifetime reserve days – nonrenewable)
- **Skilled Nursing Facility coinsurance** - $141.50 a day for the 21st through the 100th day per Benefit Period
- **Hospital Insurance Premium** - $450 per month (Note: This premium is paid only by individuals who are not otherwise eligible for premium-free hospital insurance and have less than 30 quarters of Medicare covered employment.)
- **Reduced Hospital Insurance Premium** - $248 (Note: For individuals having 30 to 39 quarters of coverage)
  Note: The $1,132 is 4 x $283, 2 x $566, and 8 x $141.50.

Medical Insurance (Part B)

- **Deductible** - $162 per year
- **Standard Monthly Premium** - $115.40 for new enrollees. Premium may be higher for income greater than $85,000.

Source: Social Security Administration (www.ssa.gov)

Medicare Part A helps pay for up to 90 days of inpatient hospital care during each benefit period. Covered services for inpatient hospital care include: semiprivate room and meals, operating and recovery room costs, intensive care, drugs, laboratory tests, x-rays, general nursing services, and any other necessary medical services and supplies. Convenience items such as television and telephones provided by hospitals in private rooms (unless medically necessary) are generally not covered. Medicare does not pay for custodial services for daily living activities such as eating, bathing, and getting dressed. Medicare does, however, pay for skilled nursing facility care for rehabilitation, such as recovery time after a hospital discharge. Part A may help pay for up to 100 days in a participating skilled nursing facility in each benefit period. Medicare pays all approved charges for the first 20 days relating to skilled nursing facility care, and the patient pays a coinsurance amount for days 21 through 100. Medicare may also pay the full, approved cost of covered home healthcare services, which includes part-time or intermittent skilled nursing services prescribed by a physician for treatment or rehabilitation of home bound patients. Normally, the only cost to the insured for home health care is a 20 percent coinsurance charge for medical equipment, such as wheelchairs and walkers.

Medicare Part B, Medical Insurance, is optional and a premium is charged. Part B is financed by the monthly premiums paid by those who are enrolled and out of the general revenues from the U.S. Treasury. Medicare Part B is used to pay for doctors' services; ambulance transportation; diagnostic tests; outpatient therapy services; outpatient hospital services including emergency room visits; X-rays and laboratory services; some preventative care; home healthcare services not covered by Part A; durable medical equipment and supplies; and a variety of other health services.

Medicare Part B pays for 80 percent of approved charges for most covered services. Unless an individual declines Part B medical insurance protection, the premium will automatically be deducted from their Social Security benefits. The 2011 standard premium amount is $115.40 a month. The deductible for Part B is $162 per year. The insured is responsible for paying a $162 deductible per calendar year and the remaining 20 percent of the Medicare-approved charges. Medicare Part B usually does not cover charges for prescription drugs, routine physical examinations, or services unrelated to treatment of injury or illness. Dental care, dentures, cosmetic surgery, hearing aids, and eye exams are not covered by Part B.

Various plans under Medicare are available to insureds. The original Medicare Plan is the way most individuals get their Medicare Part A and Part B benefits. This is the traditional payment-per-service arrangement where the individual insured may go to any doctor, specialist, or hospital that accepts Medicare, and Medicare pays its share after services are rendered. Medicare carriers and fiscal intermediaries are private insurance organizations that handle claims under the original Medicare Plan. Carriers handle Part B claims while fiscal intermediaries handle Part A plans. The Social Security Administration does not handle claims for Medicare payments.

Many private insurance companies sell Medicare supplemental insurance policies, such as Medigap, and Medicare SELECT. These supplemental policies help bridge the coverage gaps in the original Medicare Plan. These supplemental policies also help pay Medicare's coinsurance amounts and deductibles, as well as other out-of-pocket expenses for health care.

When a worker is first enrolled in Part B at age 65, there is a six-month open enrollment period in Medigap. During the time of open enrollment, the health status of the applicant cannot be used as a reason to refuse a Medigap policy or to charge more than other open enrollment applicants. The insurer may require a six-month waiting period for coverage of pre-existing conditions. If, however, the open enrollment period has expired, the applicant may be denied a policy based on health status or may be charged higher rates.

MEDICARE PART D SUBSIDY

Beginning January 1, 2006, new Medicare prescription drug plans became available to individuals with Medicare known as the Medicare Part D Subsidy (Part D or Medicare Prescription Drug Plan). Part D is intended to save participants money on prescription drug costs and help protect against higher drug costs in the future. Insurance companies and other private companies work with Medicare to offer these drug plans by negotiating discounts on drug prices. These plans are different from the Medicare-approved drug discount cards, which were phased out by the earlier of May 15, 2006 or when an individual's enrollment in a Medicare prescription drug plan took effect.

Medicare prescription drug plans provide insurance coverage for prescription drugs. Part D covers both brand-name and generic prescription drugs at certain pharmacies in a Part D participant's area. If an individual is enrolled in Medicare, then that individual is eligible under Part D regardless of income, assets, health status, or current prescription expenses. Like other insurance, if an individual joins, they pay a monthly premium and pay a share of the cost of their prescriptions. Although costs vary depending on the drug plan the individual chooses, the national average monthly premium for the basic standard benefit is expected to be $25, which is lower than was expected when the program was being launched in 2005 and 2006.[3]

Individuals may enroll in Part D when they first become eligible for Medicare, which is three months before the month the applicant turns age 65 until three months after the applicant turns age 65. If Medicare was available due to a disability, the applicant can join from three months before to three months after the 25th month of cash disability payments. If an individual does not enroll when they are first eligible, then that individual may be required to pay a penalty when the enrollment does occur. There are two ways to obtain Medicare prescription drug coverage. The individual can either join a Medicare prescription drug plan or join a Medicare Advantage Plan or other Medicare Health Plan that offers drug coverage. Whichever plan is chosen, Medicare drug coverage helps the participant by covering brand name and generic drugs at pharmacies.

Drug plans may vary as to what prescription drugs are covered, how much the individual must pay, and which pharmacies they can use. All drug plans will have to provide at least a standard level of coverage, which Medicare will set. The premium, deductible, co-payment/co-insurance, and coverage may vary from plan to plan. However, some plans might offer more coverage and additional drugs for a higher monthly premium. When an individual joins a drug plan, it is important for them to choose one that meets their prescription drug needs. A list of drugs that a Medicare drug plan covers is called a formulary, which includes generic drugs and brand name drugs. Most prescription drugs used by those with Medicare will be on the given plan formulary, whether it is in brand name or generic form. To insure coverage of an appropriate amount of drugs, a formulary must include at least two drugs in categories and classes of most commonly prescribed drugs to those individuals with Medicare. This helps to insure that people with varying medical conditions can get the medication or treatment that they need.

Even individuals who do not use a lot of prescription drugs should consider joining Part D because most aging people often need prescription drugs to stay healthy. For a relatively low premium, Medicare prescription drug coverage can protect the individual from unexpected drug expenses in the future.

OTHER MEDICARE HEALTH PLAN CHOICES

Medicare offers alternative methods of obtaining Medicare benefits through other health plan choices. Choices that vary by area include coordinated-care or Medicare managed care plans such as Health Maintenance Organizations (HMOs), HMOs with a point of service option, Provider Sponsored Organizations (PSOs), and Preferred Provider Organizations (PPOs). These plans involve specific groups of doctors, hospitals, and other providers who provide care to the insured as a member of the plan, like many employer-sponsored plans throughout the country. Medicare managed care plans not only provide the same services

---

3. U.S. Department of Health and Human Services, News Release, November 15, 2007.

that are covered by Part A and Part B, but most Medicare managed plans offer a variety of additional benefits like preventative care, prescription drugs, dental care, eyeglasses, and other items not covered by the original Medicare Plan. The cost of these extra benefits varies among the plans.

For those who receive Medicare and have low income and few resources, states may pay Medicare premiums and, in some cases, other out-of-pocket Medicare expenses, such as deductibles and coinsurance. The respective state decides if individuals qualify. For more general information about Medicare, the Social Security Administration's leaflet *Medicare Savings for Qualified Beneficiaries* (HCFA Publication No. 02184) is helpful, as are the websites *www.ssa.gov* and *www.medicare.gov*.

SUPPLEMENTAL SECURITY INCOME BENEFITS

Supplemental Security Income (SSI) makes monthly payments to individuals with low incomes and few assets. In order to obtain SSI benefits, an individual must be age 65, disabled, or blind. The definition of disability is satisfied when the individual is unable to engage in any substantial gainful activity due to a physical or mental problem expected to last at least a year or expected to result in death. Children as well as adults qualify for SSI disability payments. As its name implies, Supplemental Security Income supplements the beneficiary's income up to various levels depending on where the beneficiary lives. If an otherwise eligible SSI applicant lives in another's household and receives support from that person, the federal SSI benefit is reduced by one-third.

The federal government pays a basic rate. The basic monthly SSI check for 2011 is $674 per month for one person and $1,011 per month for married couples. Some states supply additional funds to qualified individuals. To ascertain the SSI benefit rates in a certain state, the financial planner or client can contact a local Social Security office in that state or visit the Social Security Administration's website. Generally, individuals who receive SSI benefits also qualify for Medicaid, food stamps, and other government assistance.

To be eligible for the monthly SSI benefit, the beneficiary must not have assets that exceed $2,000 for one person or $3,000 for married couples. This asset determination does not include the value of the home and some personal belongings, such as one car. If the potential beneficiary does not work, he or she may be eligible for SSI benefits if monthly income is less than $694 for one person and $1,031 for a couple. If the potential beneficiary works, more monthly income is allowed. SSI benefits are not paid from Social Security trust funds and are not based on past earnings of the beneficiary. Rather, SSI benefits are financed by general tax revenues and assure a minimum monthly income for needy elderly, disabled, or blind persons.

FILING FOR SOCIAL SECURITY CLAIMS

The Social Security Administration reports that many people fail to file claims with the Social Security Administration or fail to do so in a timely fashion. Individuals should file for Social Security or SSI disability benefits as soon they become too disabled to work or for survivors benefits, when a family breadwinner dies. Social Security benefits do not start automatically. Social Security will not begin payment of benefits until the beneficiary files an application. When filing for benefits, applicants must submit documents that show eligibility, such as a birth certificate for each family member applying for benefits, a marriage certificate if a spouse is applying, and the most recent W-2 forms or tax returns.

To file for benefits, obtain information, or to speak to a Social Security representative, individuals must call the Social Security Administration's toll-free number, 800-772-1213, or visit the Social Security Administration's website. The toll-free number can be used to schedule an appointment at a local Social Security office. The Social Security Administration treats all calls confidentially. Periodically, a second Social Security representative will monitor incoming and outgoing telephone calls to ensure accurate and courteous service.

OTHER ISSUES

EFFECT OF MARRIAGE OR DIVORCE ON BENEFITS

Marriage or divorce may affect one's Social Security benefits, depending on the kind of benefits received. If a worker receives retirement benefits based on his or her own earnings record, the worker's retirement benefits will continue whether married or divorced. If an individual receives benefits based on his or her spouse's record, the individual's benefits will cease upon divorce unless the individual is age 62 or older and was married longer than 10 years. Widows and widowers, whether divorced or not, will continue to receive survivors' benefits upon remarriage if the widow or widower is age 60 or older. Disabled widows and widowers, whether divorced or not, will continue to receive survivors' benefits upon remarriage if the disabled widow or widower is age 50 or older.

EXAMPLE 5.25

Larry was married at the following ages and to the following wives. Larry is now 62 years old and married to Dawn.

	Wife	Current Age	Larry's Age at Marriage	Current Marital Status	Length of Marriage
1	Alice	62	20	Single	10 years, 1 month
2	Betty	63	31	Single	10 years, 1 month
3	Claire	64	42	Single	9 years
4	Dawn	65	53	Married	9 years

Who, among the wives, may be eligible to receive Social Security retirement benefits based upon Larry's earnings if Larry is retired or not retired?

Any divorced spouse, age 62 and married to Larry for 10 years or longer, and his current wife, Dawn, if he is retired. His current spouse cannot collect if he is not retired.

If Larry is retired: Alice, Betty, and Dawn.

If Larry is not retired: Alice and Betty.

For all other forms of Social Security benefits, benefits will cease upon remarriage, except in special circumstances. When a person marries, it is presumed that at least one person in the marriage can provide adequate support. Likewise, Social Security benefits may recommence based on the previous spouse's benefits if the marriage ends.

CHANGE OF NAME

If an individual changes his or her name due to marriage, divorce, or a court order, that individual must notify the Social Security Administration of the name change so the Social Security Administration will be able to show the new name in their records and properly credit that individual for earnings. This will ensure that the individual's work history will be accurately recorded and maintained.

LEAVING THE UNITED STATES

Beneficiaries who are United States citizens may travel or live in most foreign countries without affecting their eligibility for Social Security benefits. However, there are a few countries where Social Security checks cannot be sent. These countries currently include Cuba, Cambodia, North Korea, Vietnam, and the republics that were formerly in the U.S.S.R. (except Estonia, Latvia, and Lithuania).

Beneficiaries should inform the Social Security Administration of their plans to go outside the United States for a trip that lasts 30 days or more. By providing the name of the country or countries to be visited and the expected departure and return dates, the Social Security Administration will send special reporting instructions to the beneficiaries and arrange for delivery of checks while abroad.

Quick Quiz 5.5

Highlight the answer to these questions:

1. Medicare Part A generally pays for "Places" while Part B pays for "Services."
   a. True
   b. False

2. In order to obtain Supplemental Social Security benefits, the individual must be 62, disabled, or blind.
   a. True
   b. False

3. Social Security beneficiaries who are United States citizens may live in most foreign countries without affecting their eligibility for Social Security benefits.
   a. True
   b. False

True, False, True.

EXHIBIT 5.16 2011 SOCIAL SECURITY UPDATE

Fact Sheet
SOCIAL SECURITY

2011 SOCIAL SECURITY CHANGES

o **Cost-of-Living Adjustment (COLA):**

Monthly Social Security and Supplemental Security Income (SSI) benefits will not automatically increase in 2011 as there is no increase in the Consumer Price Index (CPI-W) from the third quarter of 2008, the last year a COLA was determined, to the third quarter of 2010. Other important 2011 Social Security information is as follows:

	2010	**2011**
o **Maximum Taxable Earnings:**		
Social Security (OASDI only)	$106,800	$106,800*
Medicare (HI only)	No Limit	
o **Quarter of Coverage:**		
	$1,120	$1,120**
o **Primary Insurance Amount Bend Points:**		
First dollar amount	$761	$749
Second dollar amount	$4,586	$4,517
o **Retirement Earnings Test Exempt Amounts:**		
Under full retirement age	$14,160/yr. ($1,180/mo.)	$14,160/yr.* ($1,180/mo.)

  NOTE: One dollar in benefits will be withheld for every $2 in earnings above the limit.

The year an individual reaches full retirement age	$37,680/yr. ($3,140/mo.)	$37,680/yr.* ($3,140/mo.)

  NOTE: Applies only to earnings for months prior to attaining full retirement age. One dollar in benefits will be withheld for every $3 in earnings above the limit.

- o **Social Security Disability Thresholds:**

    Substantial Gainful Activity (SGA)

Non-Blind	$1,000/mo.	$1,000/mo.**
Blind	$1,640/mo.	$1,640/mo.*

    Trial Work Period (TWP) $ 720/mo. $ 720/mo.**

- o **SSI Federal Payment Standard:**

Individual	$674/mo.	$674/mo.*
Couple	$1,011/mo.	$1,011/mo.*

- o **SSI Student Exclusion:**

Monthly limit	$1,640	$1,640*
Annual limit	$6,600	$6,600*

* By law, these amounts will be unchanged in 2011 because there is no COLA.

**By law, these amounts will be unchanged in 2011 because there was a decrease in the national average wage index for 2009.

http://www.ssa.gov/pressoffice/factsheets/colafacts2010.pdf

Key Terms

AIME (Average Indexed Monthly Earnings) - The adjustment, or index, to a worker's historic earnings to create an equivalent current dollar value.

Benefit Periods - Begins on the first day an individual receives services as a patient in a hospital or skilled nursing facility and ends after 60 consecutive days without further skilled care.

Cost of Living Adjustment (COLA) - The cost-of-living adjustments applied to Social Security benefits.

Currently Insured Workers - A worker who has earned at least six quarters of coverage out of the previous 13 quarters for Social Security.

Disability Benefit - A Social Security benefit available to recipients who have a severe physical or mental impairment that is expected to prevent them from performing "substantial" work for at least a year or result in death. To qualify for these benefits, the recipient must have the sufficient amount of Social Security credits.

Disability Insurance (DI) Trust Fund - The trust fund that pays benefits to workers with disabilities and their families. It is funded by 0.90 percent of an individual's taxable earnings up to $106,800 (2011).

Family Benefit - A Social Security benefit available to certain family members of workers eligible for retirement or disability benefits.

FICA (Federal Insurance Contributions Act) - A law allowing Social Security taxes, including Medicare taxes, to be deducted from employee's paychecks.

Fully Insured - A worker who has earned 40 quarters of coverage under the Social Security system.

Hospital Insurance (HI) Trust Fund - The trust fund that pays for services covered under the hospital insurance provisions of Medicare (Part A). It is funded by 1.45 percent of an individual's taxable earnings (no limitation).

Maximum Family Benefit - The limit on the amount of monthly Social Security benefits that may be paid to a family.

Medicaid - Provides medical assistance for persons with low incomes and resources.

Medicare - A federal health insurance plan for those who have attained full retirement age or have been disabled whether retired or still working.

Key Terms

Modified Adjusted Gross Income (MAGI) - When calculating taxable Social Security, the sum of an individual's adjusted gross income plus tax exempt interest, including interest earned on savings bonds used for higher education; amounts excluded from the taxpayer's income for employer provided adoption assistance; amounts deducted for interest paid for educational loans; amounts deducted as qualified tuition expense; and income earned in a foreign country, a U.S. possession, or Puerto Rico that is excluded from income.

Old Age, Survivor, and Disability Insurance (OASDI) - An inclusive title given to the Social Security benefit system.

Old Age and Survivors Insurance (OASI) - The trust fund that pays retirement and survivors' benefits funded by 5.30 percent of an individual's taxable earnings up to $106,800 (2011).

PIA (Primary Insurance Amount) - The amount on which a worker's retirement benefit is based; the PIA determines the amount the applicant will receive at his or her full retirement age based on the year in which the retiree turns 62. The PIA is indexed to the Consumer Price Index (CPI) annually.

Retirement Benefit - The most familiar Social Security benefit, full retirement benefits are payable at normal retirement age and reduced benefits as early as age 62 to anyone who has obtained at least a minimum (40 quarters) amount of Social Security credits.

Retirement Earnings Limitations Test - A test that may reduce the Social Security benefit paid to an individual based on their other income.

Social Security Statement, Form SSA-7005 - A written report mailed by the Social Security Administration to all workers age 25 and over who are not yet receiving Social Security benefits that provides an estimate of the worker's eventual Social Security benefits and instructions on how to qualify for those benefits.

Supplemental Security Income (SSI) - A program administered by the Social Security Administration and funded by the general Treasury that is available to those at full retirement age or the disabled who have a low income and few assets.

Supplementary Medical Insurance (SMI) Trust Fund - The trust fund that pays for services covered under the medical insurance provisions of Medicare, known as Part B. The coverage is funded by general federal tax revenues and monthly medicare premiums paid by enrollees.

Survivors' Benefit - Social Security benefit available to surviving family members of a deceased, eligible worker.

DISCUSSION QUESTIONS

1. List and describe the six major categories of benefits administered by the Social Security Association.

2. How are Social Security funds collected?

3. Which individuals are covered workers under the Social Security system?

4. List the beneficiaries of Social Security benefits.

5. How is a person's Social Security retirement benefit calculated?

6. How does retiring early or retiring late affect the calculation of Social Security benefits?

7. How are Social Security benefits taxed?

8. What other benefits are available from Social Security other than retirement benefits?

9. Discuss the maximum family benefit.

10. What Social Security benefits does Medicare provide?

11. Describe Supplemental Security Income benefits and when they are available.

12. How does marriage or divorce affect Social Security benefits?

MULTIPLE-CHOICE PROBLEMS

1. Social Security is funded through all of the following except:

    a. Employee payroll tax.
    b. Employer payroll tax.
    c. Sales tax.
    d. Self-employment tax.

2. Brisco, now deceased, was married for 12 years. He had two dependent children, ages 10 and 12, who are cared for by their mother age 48. His mother, age 75, was his dependent and survived him. At the time of his death, he was currently but not fully insured under Social Security. His dependents are entitled to all of the following benefits except:

    a. A lump-sum death benefit of $255.
    b. A children's benefit equal to 75% of Brisco's PIA.
    c. A caretaker's benefit for the children's mother.
    d. A parent's benefit.

3. Medicare Part A provides hospital coverage. Which of the following persons is not covered under Part A?

    a. A person 62 or older and receiving railroad retirement.
    b. Disabled beneficiaries regardless of age that have received Social Security for two years.
    c. Chronic kidney patients who require dialysis or a renal transplant.
    d. A person 65 or older entitled to a monthly Social Security check.

4. Part B of Medicare is considered to be supplemental insurance and provides additional coverage to participants. Which of the following is true regarding Part B coverage?

    a. The election to participate must be made at the time the insured is eligible for Part A Medicare and at no time after.
    b. The premiums for Part B are paid monthly through withholding from Social Security benefits.
    c. Once a participant elects Part B, he must maintain the coverage until death.
    d. Coverage under Part B does not include deductibles or coinsurance.

5. A person receiving Social Security benefits under the age of 65 can receive earned income up to a maximum threshold without reducing Social Security benefits by the earnings test. Which of the following count against the earnings threshold?

   a. Dividends from stocks.
   b. Rental income.
   c. Pensions and insurance annuities.
   d. Gambling winnings.

6. It is possible for a person receiving Social Security benefits to lose eligibility (be disqualified) for those benefits. Which of the following is not considered grounds for disqualification?

   a. Marriage.
   b. Divorce.
   c. Conviction of fraud.
   d. Engaging in illegal employment.

7. Betty Sue, age 75, is a widow with no close relatives. She is very ill, unable to walk, and confined to a custodial nursing home. Which of the following programs is likely to pay benefits towards the cost of the nursing home?

   1. Medicare may pay for up to 100 days of care after a 20-day deductible.
   2. Medicaid may pay if the client has income and assets below state-mandated thresholds.

   a. 1 only.
   b. 2 only.
   c. Both 1 and 2.
   d. Neither 1 nor 2.

8. Which of the following concerning the Social Security system is correct?

   a. SSI benefits are funded by the Treasury, not Social Security taxes, as are the other benefits.
   b. The Social Security retirement benefit is payable at full retirement age with reduced benefits as early as age 59 to anyone who has obtained at least a minimum amount of Social Security benefits.
   c. The two Medicare trust funds are the federal Medical Insurance Trust Fund for Part A and the Supplementary Hospital Insurance Trust Fund for Part B of Medicare benefits.
   d. Benefits can be paid to the dependent parents of a deceased insured worker at age 59 or over.

9. Which of the following concerning the Social Security system is correct?
    a. Workers entitled to retirement benefits can currently take early retirement benefits as early as age 59.
    b. A worker who takes early retirement benefits will receive a reduced benefit because he or she will receive more monthly benefit payments as payments commence earlier than if the worker had waited and retired at full retirement age.
    c. Family members of an individual who are eligible for retirement or disability benefits include a spouse if the spouse is at least 59 years old or under 59 but caring for a child under age 16.
    d. Generally, individuals who are over the age of 59 and receive Social Security benefits automatically qualify for Medicare benefits.

10. All of the following statements concerning the Social Security system are correct except:
    a. If a worker receives retirement benefits based on his or her own earnings record, the worker's retirement benefits will continue whether married or divorced.
    b. Widows and widowers, whether divorced or not, will continue to receive survivors benefits upon remarriage if the widow or widower is age 60 or older.
    c. By providing the name of a country or countries to be visited and the expected departure and return dates, the Social Security Administration will send special reporting instructions to the beneficiaries and arrange for delivery of checks while abroad.
    d. A special one-time payment of $1,000 may be made to a deceased worker's spouse or minor children upon death.

11. All of the following statements concerning Social Security benefits are correct except:
    a. The maximum family benefit is determined through a formula based on the worker's PIA.
    b. If a worker applies for retirement or survivors benefits before his or her 65th birthday, he or she must also file a separate application for Medicare.
    c. People who are disabled or have permanent kidney failure can get Medicare at any age.
    d. The Social Security Administration is concerned with beneficiaries' combined income, which, on the 1040 federal tax return, includes adjusted gross income and nontaxable interest income.

12. All of the following statements concerning Social Security benefits are correct except:
    a. In order to obtain SSI benefits, an individual must be age 65 or older and must be disabled.
    b. The number of days that Medicare covers care in hospitals and skilled nursing facilities is measured in what is termed benefit periods.
    c. The definition of disability is that the individual is unable to engage in any substantial gainful activity due to a physical or mental problem expected to last at least a year or expected to result in death.
    d. Benefits are payable at any age to workers who have enough Social Security credits and who have a severe physical or mental impairment that is expected to prevent them from doing "substantial" work for a year or more or who have a condition that is expected to result in death.

13. Joyce and Melvin have been married for 30 years. In 2011, they received $22,000 of Social Security benefits and had $12,000 of interest income. What portion of the Social Security benefit is taxable?
    a. $0.
    b. $6,000.
    c. $10,200.
    d. $11,500.

14. Emile is single and received $28,000 of dividend income during the year. He also received $18,000 of Social Security benefits. What portion of his Social Security benefits are taxable?
    a. $0.
    b. $7,050.
    c. $9,000.
    d. $15,300.

Quick Quiz Explanations

Quick Quiz 5.1
1. False. Reduced Social Security benefits can be withdrawn as early as age 62.
2. False. Social Security contributions are placed in the following trust funds: OASI, DI, and HI. The SMI Trust Fund is not funded by Social Security contributions.

Quick Quiz 5.2
1. True.
2. True.

Quick Quiz 5.3
1. False. The Social Security retirement benefit is based on the worker's PIA. A worker's PIA is based on the worker's average indexed monthly earnings during the 35 years in which the worker earned the most.
2. False. Full retirement age for Social Security is increasing because of increasing life expectancies.

Quick Quiz 5.4
1. True.
2. False. Once divorced, a non-working ex-spouse who was married to the worker for more than ten years can still receive Social Security benefits based on the worker's record.
3. True.

Quick Quiz 5.5
1. True.
2. False. In order to obtain SSI benefits, an individual must be 65, disabled, or blind.
3. True.

Glossary

A

Accelerated Benefits Provision - Entitles a qualified insured to receive a lifetime benefit deemed nontaxable.

Activities of Daily Living (ADL) - Physical functions that an independent person performs each day, including bathing, dressing, eating, transferring, toileting, and maintaining continence.

Actual Cash Value - Represents the depreciated value of the property.

Adhesion - A take it or leave it contract.

Adverse Selection - The tendency of those that need insurance to seek it out.

Agents - Legal representatives of an insurer and act on behalf of an insurer.

AIME (Average Indexed Monthly Earnings) - The adjustment, or index, to a worker's historic earnings to create an equivalent current dollar value.

Aleatory - A type of insurance contract in which the dollar amounts exchanged are uneven.

Annual Renewable Term (ART) - Type of term insurance that permits the policyholder to purchase term insurance in subsequent years without evidence of insurability, but premiums on the policy increase each year to reflect the increasing mortality risk being undertaken by the insurer.

Annuity - Periodic payment to an individual that continues for a fixed period or for the duration of a designated life or lives

Any Occupation - Type of disability insurance policy that provides benefits to a policy owner if he or she is unable to perform the duties of any occupation.

Apparent Authority - When the third party believes, implied, or express authority exists, but no authority actually exists.

Appraised or Agreed Upon Value - Used for hard to value items and where the insured may own property that exceeds standard limits of property insurance policy.

Asset Accumulation Phase - This phase is usually from the early 20s to late 50s when additional cash flow for investing is low and debt to net worth is high.

Assignment - The process of transferring all or part of the policy's ownership rights.

Assisted Living - Senior housing that provides individual apartments, which may or may not have a kitchenette. Facilities offer 24 hour on site staff, congregate dining, and activity programs. Limited nursing services may be provided for an additional fee.

Assumption of Risk - The injured party fully understood and recognized the dangers that were involved in an activity and voluntarily chose to proceed.

Beneficiary - A person or institution legally entitled to receive benefits through a legal device, such as a will, trust or life insurance policy.

Benefit Periods - Begins on the first day an individual receives services as a patient in a hospital or skilled nursing facility and ends after 60 consecutive days without further skilled care.

Brokers - Legal representatives of an insured who act in the best interest of the insured.

Capital Earnings Approach - Method to determine life insurance needs that suggests the death benefits of a client's life insurance should equal an income stream sufficient to meet the family's needs without depleting the capital base.

Coinsurance - The amount a patient must pay for major medical care after meeting the deductible.

Collateral Source Rule - Holds that damages assessed against a negligent party should not be reduced simply because the injured party has other sources of recovery available such as insurance or employee benefits (health or disability insurance).

Collision - Auto insurance coverage that protects the insured against upset and collision damages, such as those sustained in an accident involving other vehicles, or those sustained when an auto runs off the road and into a lake.

Comparative Negligence - The amount of damage is adjusted to reflect the injured party's proportion of contribution to the cause of the injury.

Comprehensive - Auto insurance coverage that protects the insured's auto against perils out of the insured's control, such as missiles or falling objects, fire, theft, earthquake, hail, flood, and vandalism.

Concealment - When the insured is intentionally silent regarding a material fact during the application process.

Conditional - The insured must abide by all the terms and conditions of the contract if the insured intends to collect under the policy.

Conservation (Risk Management) Phase - This phase is from late 20s to early 70s, where cash flow assets and net worth have increased and debt has decreased somewhat. In addition, risk management of events like employment, disability due to illness or accident, and untimely death become a priority.

Contingent Beneficiaries - Person(s) or organization named to receive the death benefit if the primary beneficiary is not available to receive the policy proceeds.

Contributory Negligence - Negligence on the part of the injured party that contributes to the harm and, therefore, the injured has to bear some responsibility for the injury.

Co-payment - A loss-sharing arrangement whereby the insured pays a percentage of the loss in excess of the deductible.

Cost of Living Adjustment (COLA) - The cost-of-living adjustments applied to Social Security benefits.

Currently Insured Workers - A worker who has earned at least six quarters of coverage out of the previous 13 quarters for Social Security.

Custodial Care - Board, room and other personal assistance services (including assistance with activities of daily living, taking medicine and similar personal needs) that may not include a skilled nursing care component.

Declarations Section - The section of an insurance policy that describes exactly what property is being covered.

Decreasing-Term Insurance - Type of term insurance that allows the owner to pay the same premium for the insurance protection each year. The death benefit on the policy will, however, decrease each year to offset the increasing mortality cost due to the passage of time.

Deductible - The amount a patient must pay each year before the health insurance plan begins paying.

Definition Section - The section of an insurance policy that defines key words, phrases, or terms used throughout the insurance contract.

Description Section - The section of an insurance policy that describes exactly what is being insured.

Disability Benefit - A Social Security benefit available to recipients who have a severe physical or mental impairment that is expected to prevent them from performing "substantial" work for at least a year or result in death. To qualify for these benefits, the recipient must have the sufficient amount of Social Security credits.

Disability Insurance - A type of insurance that provides supplementary income in the event of an illness or accident resulting in a disability that prevents the insured from working at their regular employment.

Disability Insurance (DI) Trust Fund - The trust fund that pays benefits to workers with disabilities and their families. It is funded by 0.90 percent of an individual's taxable earnings up to $90,000 (2010).

Distribution (Gifting) Phase - This phase is from the late 40s to end of life and occurs when the individual has high additional cash flow, low debt, and high net worth.

Dwelling - Residential structure covered under a homeowners insurance policy.

Endorsement - Attachment or addition to an existing insurance policy that changes the original terms.

Estoppel - The legal process of denying a right you might otherwise be entitled to under the law.

Exclusion Section - The section of an insurance policy that will exclude certain perils, losses and property.

Express Authority - Authority given to an agent through a formal written document.

Family Benefit - A Social Security benefit available to certain family members of workers eligible for retirement or disability benefits.

FICA (Federal Insurance Contributions Act) - A law allowing Social Security taxes, including Medicare taxes, to be deducted from employee's paychecks.

Financial Risk - A loss of financial value, such as the premature death of a family's primary wage earner.

First-to-Die - Type of joint life insurance policy that covers two individuals, but the death benefit is paid upon the death of the first individual.

Flexible Spending Account (FSA) - Employer-sponsored plan that permits employees to defer pre-tax income into an account to pay for health care expenses. FSAs require the employee to either use the contributed amounts for medical expenses by the end of the year, or forfeit the unused amounts to the company.

Fully Insured - A worker who has earned 40 quarters of coverage under the Social Security system.

Fundamental Risk - A risk that can impact a large number of individuals at one time, such as an earthquake or flood.

Grace Period - A provision in most insurance policies which allows payment to be received for a certain period of time after the actual due date without a default or cancellation of the policy.

Group Health Insurance - Health plans offered to a group of individuals by an employer, association, union, or other entity.

Group Term Insurance - A type of life insurance coverage offered to a group of people (often a component of an employee benefit package) that provides benefits to the beneficiaries if the covered individual dies during the defined covered period.

Hazards - A specific condition that increases the potential or likelihood of a loss occurring.

Health Maintenance Organizations (HMOs) - A form of managed care in which participants receive all of their care from participating providers. Physicians are employed by the HMO directly, or may be physicians in private practice who have chosen to participate in the HMO network. The independent physicians are paid a fixed amount for each HMO member that uses them as a primary care physician.

Health Savings Accounts (HSA) - Employer-sponsored plan that permits employees to save for health care costs on a tax-advantaged basis. Contributions made to the HSA by the plan participant are tax-deductible as an adjustment to gross income (above the line), and distributions from the HSA to pay for medical expenses are excluded from income.

High Deductible Health Insurance Plans - Plans with a deductible of at least $1,200 for individual coverage and $2,400 for family coverage in 2011, with a maximum out of pocket stop loss amount of $5,950 for single coverage and $11,900 for family coverage in 2011.

Homeowners Insurance - A package insurance policy that provides both property and liability coverage for the insured's dwelling, other structures, personal property, and loss of use.

Hospital Insurance (HI) Trust Fund - The trust fund that pays for services covered under the hospital insurance provisions of Medicare (Part A). It is funded by 1.45 percent of an individual's taxable earnings (no limitation).

Human Life Value Approach - Method to determine life insurance needs that suggests the death benefit of a client's life insurance should equal to the economic value of the client's future earnings stream.

Implied Authority - The authority that a third party relies upon when dealing with an agent based upon the position held by the agent.

Incontestability Clause - Clause in a health insurance policy that prevents the insurer from challenging the validity of the health insurance contract after it has been in force for a specified period of time unless the insured fraudulently obtained coverage in the beginning of the policy.

Indemnity Plans - Traditional, fee-for-service health insurance that does not limit where a covered individual can get care.

Individual Major Medical Plans - Coverage purchased independently from an insurance company (not as part of a group).

Insured - Specifically named individual or institution with whom an insurance contract is made, and whose interests are protected under the policy.

Intentional Interference - Intentional act committed against another that causes injury.

Intermediate-Care Nursing Facility - A licensed facility with the primary purpose of providing health or rehabilitative services. Typically provides custodial care along with intermittent, as opposed to daily, medical care.

Joint and Survivor Annuity - An annuity based on the lives of two or more annuitants, usually husband and wife. Annuity payments are made until the last annuitant dies.

Lacking Sound Mind - The state of not having the capacity to understand the purpose and terms of the contract, therefore the contract lacks a meeting of the minds or mutual consent.

Last Clear Chance Rule - This rule states that a claimant who is endangered by his own negligence may recover if the defendant has a "last clear chance" to avoid the accident and failed to do so.

Law of Large Numbers - A principle that states the more similar events or exposures, the more likely the actual results will equal the probability expected.

Level Premium Term Insurance - Type of term insurance that charges a fixed premium each year over a specified period of years, so the premium does not increase over that period.

Level-Term Insurance - Type of term insurance that charges a fixed premium each year over a specified period of years, so the premium does not increase over that period.

Libel - Written statement that causes harm to another.

Limited-Pay Policies - Type of whole life policy with a payment schedule (typically 10 or 20 years). At the end of the payment period, the policy is considered to be paid-up, at which time no additional premium payments are due.

Long-Term Care Insurance - Coverage that pays for all or part of the cost of home health care services or care in a nursing home or assisted living facility.

Long-Term Disability - Provides coverage for specified term, until specified age, or until death.

Loss of Use - Under homeowners insurance coverage, loss of use is a combination of additional living expenses and loss of rental income.

M

Managed Care - Health-care delivery systems that integrate the financing and delivery of health care. Managed care plans feature a network of physicians, hospitals, and other providers who participate in the plan. Managed care includes HMOs, PPOs, and POS plans.

Maximum Family Benefit - The limit on the amount of monthly Social Security benefits that may be paid to a family.

Medicaid - Provides medical assistance for persons with low incomes and resources.

Medical Payments - A no-fault, first-party insurance coverage designed to pay for bodily injuries sustained in an auto accident.

Medicare - A federal health insurance plan for those who have attained full retirement age or have been disabled whether retired or still working.

Minors - In most states, a minor is under the age of 18. If a minor enters into a contract, the minor can void the contract at any time.

Modified Adjusted Gross Income (when calculating taxable Social Security) - The sum of an individual's adjusted gross income plus tax exempt interest, including interest earned on savings bonds used for higher education; amounts excluded from the taxpayer's income for employer provided adoption assistance; amounts deducted for interest paid for educational loans; amounts deducted as qualified tuition expense; and income earned in a foreign country, a U.S. possession, or Puerto Rico that is excluded from income.

Modified Endowment Contract (MEC) - A cash value life insurance policy that has been funded too quickly. Under a MEC, the death benefit payable to the beneficiary is not subject to income tax.

Modified Whole Life Policies - Type of whole life policy with lower premiums than a regular policy for an initial policy period (often 3 to 5 years), and increase to a higher level premium at the end of the initial period.

Moral Hazard - The potential loss occurring because of the moral character of the insured and the filing of a false claim with their insurance company.

Morale Hazard - The indifference to a loss created because the insured has insurance.

Mortality Risk - The risk that an individual will die within the year.

Moveable - Property capable of being moved (i.e., a car).

Mutual Consent - Common understanding and agreement between parties to a contract regarding what the contract covers and the terms of the contract.

Named Perils - Perils specifically listed in an insurance policy.

Needs Approach - Method to determine life insurance needs that suggests the death benefits of a client's life insurance should equal the cash needs that the family will require at death.

Negligence - Tort caused by acting without reasonable care.

Nonfinancial Risk - A risk that would result in a loss, other than a monetary loss.

Objective Risk - The variation of actual amount of losses that occur over a period of time compared to the expected amount of losses.

Offer and Acceptance - Consists of one party making an offer to purchase a good or service and the acceptance is when consideration is received.

Old Age, Survivor, and Disability Insurance (OASDI) - An inclusive title given to the Social Security benefit system.

Old Age and Survivors Insurance (OASI) - The trust fund that pays retirement and survivors' benefits funded by 5.30 percent of an individual's taxable earnings up to $90,000 (2011).

Open Perils - All-risk coverage for personal property that provides for a much broader and comprehensive protection program than named-perils coverage.

Ordinary (or Straight) Life - Type of whole life policy that requires the owner to pay a specified level premium every year until death (or age 100).

Other Structures - Small detached structures on insured's property in addition to the main house, such as garages, greenhouses, or storage buildings.

Own Occupation - Type of disability policy which states that if the insured is unable to perform the duties associated with his or her own occupation, the insured is deemed to be disabled and the policy will provide benefits.

Owner - Person or institution who owns the policy and can exercise the economic rights in a policy, including assignment, sale, etc. Also the person who is obligated for the payment of premiums.

P

Parol Evidence Rule - States that "what is written prevails." Oral agreements that are not reflected in the written contract are not valid.

Partial Disability Rider - Provision that provides payments less than those paid for total disability.

Particular Risk - A risk that can impact a particular individual, such as death or the inability to work because of a sickness or accident.

Perils - The immediate cause and reason for a loss occurring.

Personal Auto Policy - Insurance policy that covers liability for injuries and damages to persons inside and outside the vehicle and covers the cost to repair/replace a damaged or stolen vehicle.

Personal Liability Umbrella Policy - Coverage designed to provide a catastrophic layer of liability coverage on top of the individual's homeowners and automobile insurance policies.

Personal Property - Valuable items owned by the insured that are covered under homeowners insurance.

Physical Hazard - A physical condition that increases the likelihood of a loss occurring.

PIA (Primary Insurance Amount) - The amount on which a worker's retirement benefit is based; the PIA determines the amount the applicant will receive at his or her full retirement age based on the year in which the retiree turns 62. The PIA is indexed to the Consumer Price Index (CPI) annually.

Point of Service Plan (POS) - A form of managed care that is considered a managed care/indemnity plan hybrid, as it mixes aspects of HMOs, PPOs, and indemnity plans for greater patient choice. A primary care physician coordinates patient care, but there is more flexibility in choosing doctors and hospitals than in an HMO.

Preferred Provider Organization - A form of managed care in which participants have more flexibility in choosing physicians and other providers than in an HMO. The arrangement between insurance companies and health care providers permits participants to obtain discounted health care services from the preferred providers within the network.

Premium - The amount participants pay to belong to a health plan.

Primary Beneficiary - Person(s) or organization named to receive the death benefit upon the death of the insured.

Primary Care Physician - A physician that is designated as a participant's first point of contact with the health care system, particularly in managed care plans.

Principle of Indemnity - Asserts that an insurer will only compensate the insured to the extent the insured has suffered an actual financial loss.

Principle of Insurable Interest - Asserts that an insured must suffer a financial loss if a covered peril occurs, otherwise no insurance can be offered.

Probability of Loss - The chance that a loss will occur.

Pure Risk - The chance of loss or no loss occurring.

Rider - An attachment or addition to an existing insurance policy that changes the original terms.

Reinsurance - A means by which an insurance company transfers some or all of its risks to another insurance company.

Replacement Cost - The amount necessary to purchase, repair, or replace the dwelling with materials of the same or similar quality at current prices.

Representation - A statement made by the applicant during the insurance application process.

Residual Benefits Provision - Provision that provides continuing benefits for an insured who returns to work but suffers a loss of income due to the disability.

Res ispa loquitur - A doctrine of the law of negligence that is concerned with the circumstances and the types of accidents, which afford reasonable evidence of a specific explanation of negligence is not available.

Retirement Benefit - The most familiar Social Security benefit, full retirement benefits are payable at normal retirement age and reduced benefits as early as age 62 to anyone who has obtained at least a minimum (40 quarters) amount of Social Security credits.

Retirement Earnings Limitations Test - A test that may reduce the Social Security benefit paid to an individual based on their other income.

Risk Avoidance - A risk management technique used for any risks that are high in frequency and high in severity.

Risk Reduction - The process of reducing the likelihood of a pure risk that is high in frequency and low in severity.

Risk Retention - Accepting some or all of the potential loss exposure for risk that are low in frequency and low in severity.

Risk Transfer - The process of transferring a low frequency and high severity risk to a third party, such as an insurance company.

S

Schedule - Attachment or addition to an existing insurance policy that lists individual items.

Second-to-Die - Type of joint life insurance policy that is often used in estate planning to provide liquidity at the death of the second spouse to die. A second-to-die policy names two insureds, and pays the death benefit only when the second insured dies.

Self-Insured Retention - A payment similar to a deductible that an insured is usually required to pay for each loss under a personal umbrella policy.

Short-Term Disability - Typically has a short elimination period (5 - 30 days), the period an insured must wait before receiving benefits, and provides coverage for up to two years.

Simultaneous Death Provision - Provision in a life insurance policy for situations where the insured and the beneficiary die within a short time of one another and it is not possible to determine who died first, generally the policy death benefit is distributed as if the beneficiary had predeceased the insured.

Single Premium Policy - Type of whole life policy that requires the owner to pay a lump sum in return for insurance protection that will extend throughout the insured's lifetime. These policies require a substantial initial cash outlay, and are typically used for estate and generation-skipping transfer tax purposes.

Skilled-Nursing Care Facility - 24-hour nursing care for chronically-ill or short-term rehabilitative residents of all ages and provides the highest level of service, and combines daily medical and custodial care.

Slander - Verbal statement that causes harm to another.

Social Security Statement, Form SSA-7005 - A written report mailed by the Social Security Administration to all workers age 25 and over who are not yet receiving Social Security benefits that provides an estimate of the worker's eventual Social Security benefits and instructions on how to qualify for those benefits.

Speculative Risk - The chance of loss, no loss or a profit.

Split Definition - Type of disability policy where an insured is covered against the risk of not performing his or her own occupation for a period of time, and after that period expires, an any-occupation definition of disability is used.

Split Limits - Three separate liability coverage limits covering bodily injury (per person and per occurrence) and property damage.

SSI (Supplemental Security Income) - A program administered by the Social Security Administration and funded by the general Treasury that is available to those at full retirement age or the disabled who have a low income and few assets.

Strict and Absolute Liability - Liability resulting from law; strict liability allows for defense, absolute liability does not.

Subjective Risk - The risk an individual perceives based on their prior experiences and the severity of those experiences.

Subrogation Clause - A clause in an insurance policy that requires that the insured relinquish a claim against a negligent third party, if the insurer has already indemnified the insured.

Suicide Clause - Provision in a life insurance policy specifying that the insurance company will not pay the benefit if the insured attempts or commits suicide within a specified period from the beginning of the coverage. The clause is designed to hedge against the risk that individuals with suicidal thoughts will purchase life insurance, and shortly thereafter, commit suicide.

Supplementary Medical Insurance (SMI) Trust Fund - The trust fund that pays for services covered under the medical insurance provisions of Medicare, known as Part B. The coverage is funded by general federal tax revenues and monthly medicare premiums paid by enrollees.

Surrender Charge - A fee levied on a life insurance policyholder upon cancellation of the policy to cover the up front costs of issuing the policy in the first place.

Survivors' Benefit - Social Security benefit available to surviving family members of a deceased, eligible worker.

Survivorship Clause - Provision in a life insurance policy specifying that the death benefit will only be paid to the beneficiary if the beneficiary survives the insured by a specific number of days.

Term Insurance - Life insurance policy that states that if the premium has been paid and the insured dies during the term of the policy, the insurance company will pay the specified death benefit.

Underwriting - The process of classifying applicants into a risk pools, selecting insureds and assigning a premium.

Unilateral - There is only one promise made and it is made by the insurer to pay in the event of a loss.

Uninsured/Underinsured Motorist - Motorist without liability coverage or whose insurer can/will not pay claim, hit-and-run driver, or motorist with insufficient liability coverage according to state law.

Universal Life Insurance - Type of term insurance with a cash value accumulation feature allowing individuals to make premium contributions in excess of the term insurance premium. The excess premiums are deposited into an account with various investment options.

Variable Life Insurance - Type of life insurance policy that permits the owner of the life insurance policy to direct the investment of the policy's cash value. Variable policies typically offer a series of investment options that often include investment funds managed by the insurer and outside investment managers.

Variable Universal Life Insurance Policies (VULs) - Type of life insurance policy that combines variable and universal life insurance and gives the policyholders the option to invest as well as alter insurance coverage.

Variable Whole Life Policies - Type of life insurance that provides for a fixed premium payment and permits the cash value of the policy to be professionally managed by the insurance company or an outside investment manager.

Viatical Settlement - An arrangement in which a policyholder sells their life insurance policy to a third party.

Vicarious Liability - One person may become legally liable for the torts of another (e.g., parent / child, employer where the employee is acting in the scope of employment).

Waiver - The relinquishment a known legal right.

Warranty - A promise made by the insured that is part of the insurance contract.

Whole Life Insurance - Type of life insurance that provides guarantees from the insurer that are not found in term insurance and universal life insurance policies.

Appendix B

Index

A

Abandonment of Property 172
Accidental Losses 15
Activities of Daily Living (ADL) 138, 145
Actual Cash Value 160, 167, 168, 171
Adhesion 24
Aleatory 24
Annual Renewable Term (ART) 70
Annuities 94
Annuity 94, 96–98
    Joint and survivor annuity 97
    Pure life annuity 97
    Taxation 98
    Timing of Payments 97
    Types of 96
Annuity Payments 89–91
    Fixed Amount 89
    Fixed Period 90
    Joint and Last Survivor Income 91
    Life Income 90
Any Occupation Policies 100
Appraisal of Loss 171
Assignment of Life Insurance 88
Automobile Insurance
    See Personal Auto Policy (PAP)
Average Indexed Monthly Earnings (AIME) 214
Aviation Exclusion
    War Exclusion 89
Aviation Exclusion in Life Insurance 88

B

Bankruptcy 173
Bend Points 218
Beneficiary Designations 87

271

Contingent Beneficiary 87
Primary Beneficiary 87
Business and Professional Insurance
See Liability
Business and Professional Policies 190–193
Business Auto Policy (BAP) 192
Business Liability Insurance 191
Business Owner's Policy (BOP) 191
Commercial Liability Umbrella 192
Errors and Omissions 192
Malpractice Insurance 192
Product Liability 193
Summary of 193
Workers' Compensation 192
Business Pursuits Endorsement 170

C

Cancellation 174
Capitalized Earnings Approach 67
Cash Surrender Value 79, 80
Catastrophic Loss 16
Coinsurance 159
COLA 219
Collateral Source Rule 188
Collision
See Personal Auto Policy (PAP)
Commercial Package Policy (CPP) 190
Comparative Negligence 189
Comprehensive
See Personal Auto Policy (PAP)
Concealment 23
Conditionally Renewable Policies 132
Condominium Insurance 168
Consolidated Omnibus Budget Reconciliation Act of 1985 (COBRA) 133–135
Contributory Negligence 189
Copayment 34
Corridor Test 82
Coverage Limits
Liability Coverage 181
Currently Insured 210, 212

D

Damages 188
Decreasing-Term Insurance 71
Disability Insurance 98–104, 204
Amount of Coverage 98
Any Occupation Policies 100
Benefit Period 101
Group Disability Insurance 103
Own Occupation Policies 99
Partial Disability 101
Provisions 100
Renewability 102
Residual Benefit Provision 102
Split Definition Policies 100
Taxation 104
Term of Coverage 99
Disability Insurance (DI) Trust Fund 206

E

Earthquake Coverage 169
Endorsements 175
Business Pursuits 170
Earthquakes 169
Homeowners Insurance 168–170
Inflation Protection 169
Open Perils 168
Other 170
Personal Injury 170
Refrigerated Property Coverage 169
Replacement Cost 168
Sewer Backup Coverage 169
Watercraft 170
Errors and Omissions 192
Exclusions
Coverage E Only 166
Coverage F Only 166
Coverages E & F 163, 165
Direct Damage Coverage 186
Medical Payments 183
PAP Liability Coverage 180
Perils 157
Uninsured Motorists 184
Extended Term Insurance 80

F

Federal Insurance Contributions Act. See FICA
FICA 206
Financial Loss 11–13
Hazards 12
Perils 11
Financial Risk 4
Fire Department Service Charge 162
First-to-Die Policy 77
Flexible Spending Account (FSA) 135
Fraud 174
Fully Insured 209, 210, 212, 232

Fundamental Risk 3

G

Grace Period 84, 131
Group Health Insurance 118–121
    Basic Medical 119
    Comprehensive Major Medical 120
    Eligibility 118
    Features 119
    Major Medical 120
Group-Term Insurance 82
Guaranteed Renewable Option 126
Guaranteed Renewable Policies 132

H

Hazards 12
    Morale Hazard 13, 52
    Physical Hazard 13, 52
Health Insurance 117–138
    Grace Period 131
    Group 118–121
    Health Maintenance Organization (HMO) 128
    High Deductible Health Insurance Plans (HDHP) 137
    Incontestability Clause 131
    Indemnity Plans 127
    Individual 121–127
    Managed Care Insurance 127–130
    Noncancelable Option 126
    Point of Service Plans (POS) 129
    Preexisting Conditions 130
    Preferred Provider Organizations (PPO) 129
    Renewability 131–132
    Taxation 132
Health Maintenance Organization (HMO) 128, 240
Health Savings Accounts (HSA) 135–138
    Eligibility 136
    HDHP 137
High Deductible Health Insurance Plans (HDHP) 137
HMO. See Health Maintenance Organization
Homeowners Insurance 156–176
    All-Risk Coverage 162
    Basic Coverages 156–166
    Coinsurance 159
    Contractual Conditions 171–176
    Coverage A - Dwelling 159, 175
    Coverage B - Other Structures 160, 175
    Coverage C - Personal Property 160, 175
    Coverage D - Loss of Use 161
    Coverage E - Personal Liability 163
    Coverage F - Medical Payments to Others 164
    Damage to Trees 162
    Endorsements 168–170, 175
    Exclusions 163, 165, 166
    Fire Department Service Charge 162
    HO-2 - Broad Form 167
    HO-3 - Special Form 167
    HO-4 - Contents Broad Form (Renters) 167
    HO-5 - Comprehensive Form 168
    HO-6 - Unit Owners Form (Condominium) 168
    HO-8 - Modified Form 168
    Reasonable Repairs 162
    Section I Coverage 158–162
    Section II Coverage 162–166
    Summary of 176
    Unauthorized Use of Credit Cards 162
Homogeneous Exposures 14
Hospital Insurance (HI) Trust Fund 207
Human Life Value Approach 61–63

I

Incontestability 85
Incontestability Clause 131
Indemnity Health Insurance 127
Individual Health Insurance 121–127
    Cost 122
    Eligibility 122
    Major Medical 122
    Medical Expense 124
    Need for Coverage 121
Inflation Protection 169
Inland Marine Policy 191
Insurable Risk 14–18
    Accidental 15
    Catastrophic Loss 16
    Homogeneous Exposures 14
    Law of Large Numbers 14
    Measurable Loss 15
    Reasonable Premium 17
Insurance Contracts 18–26
    Adhesion 24
    Aleatory 24
    Conditional 25
    Personal Property 25
    Principle of Indemnity 20
    Principle of Insurable Interest 21
    Principle of Utmost Good Faith 22
    Unilateral 25
    Unique Characteristics 24–26
Intentional Interference 187

Intermediate-Care Nursing Facility 142

J

Joint and survivor annuity. See Annuity

L

Last Cleat Chance 189
Law of Large Numbers 4, 14
Level-Term Insurance 71
Liability 187–193
    Business and Professional Insurance 190–193
    Business Auto Policy (BAP) 192
    Business Liability Insurance 191
    Commercial Liability Umbrella 192
    Commercial Package Policy (CPP) 190
    Coverage 180–183
    Damages 188
    Defense to Negligence 189
    Intentional Interference 187
    Libel 187
    Malpractice Insurance 192
    Medical Payments to Others 164
    Negligence 187–189
    Personal Liability 163
    See Business and Professional Policies
    See Personal Liability Umbrella Policy (PLUP)
    Slander 187
    Split Limits 181
    Strict and Absolute 187
    Torts 187
    Vicarious 177, 188
    Vicarious Liability 189
    Workers' Compensation 192
Liability Insurance 21
Libel 187
Life Annuity Contracts 96–98
    Taxation 98
    Timing of Payments 97
    Types 96
Life Insurance 21, 58–96
    Accumulation Phase 58
    Assignment 88
    Aviation Exclusion 88
    Beneficiary Designations 87
    Capitalized Earnings Approach 67
    Conservation Phase 58
    Distribution Phase 58
    Grace Period 84
    Group-Term Insurance 82

    Human Life Value Approach 61–63
    Incontestability 85
    Misstatement of Age or Gender 85
    Modified Endowment Contracts (MECs) 82
    Mortality Risk 59
    Needs Approach 63–65
    Nonforfeiture Options 79
    Policy Loan Provisions 86
    Reinstatement 86
    Settlement Options 89–91
    Simultaneous Death Provision 88
    Suicide 86
    Survivorship Clause 87
    Taxation Of 91–96
    Term Insurance 68–73
    Universal Life Insurance 73–75
    Variable Life Insurance 80–81
    Whole Life Insurance 75–79
Life insurance
    Guaranteed renewable option 126
Long-Term Care Insurance 138–145
    Activities of Daily Living (ADL) 138, 145
    Benefit Periods 143
    Chronic Illness 145
    Intermediate-Care Nursing Facility 142
    Need for Coverage 140
    Skilled Care Facility 142
    Tax-Qualified Contracts 144
    Terminal illness 145
    Types of Coverage 142
Loss Payment 172
Loss Settlement 171–173
    Bailee 172

M

Major Medical Insurance 120, 122
Malpractice Insurance 192
Managed Care Insurance 127–130
Medical Expense Insurance 124
Medical Payments 164
Medicare 206, 207, 237, 238
    Other Medicare Health Plan Choices 240
    Part A 237
    Part B 238
    Part D 239
Medicare SELECT 239
Medigap 239
Misstatement of Age or Gender 85
Modified Adjusted Gross Income 226
Modified Endowment Contracts (MECs) 82

Corridor Test 82
Seven-Pay Test 82
Modified Whole Life Policy 76
    Modified Endowment Contract (MEC) 76
    Single Premium Policy 76
    Variable Whole Life Policies 77
Morale Hazard 13, 52
Mortality Risk 59
Mortgage Clause 172

N

Needs Approach 63–65
Negligence 187–189
    Comparative Negligence 189
    Defense to Negligence 189
    Negligence Per Se 188
    Strict (Absolute) Liability 188
Noncancelable Policies 132
Noncancelable Option 126
Nonfinancial Risk 4
Nonforfeiture Options for Life Insurance 79
    Cash Surrender Value 80
    Extended Term Insurance 80
    Reduced Paid-Up Insurance 80
Nonrenewal 174

O

Objective Risk 3
Old Age and Survivor Disability Insurance (OASDI) 206
Old Age and Survivors Insurance (OASI) 206
Open Perils 168
Optionally Renewable Policies 132
Ordinary Life Policy 75
    Whole Life Insurance 75
Own Occupation Policies 99

P

Particular Risk 4
Perils 11
    General Exclusions 157
    Intentional Acts 158
    Movement of the Ground 158
    Named perils 156
    Neglect 158
    Nuclear Hazards 158
    Open Perils 168
    Ordinance or Law 158
    Power Failure 158
    Rising Water 158
    War 158
Personal Auto Policy (PAP) 177–187
    Collision 185
    Comprehensive 185
    Coverage 180, 183, 184, 185
    Coverage Limits 181
    Dispute Resolution 185
    Eligible Autos 179
    Exclusions 180, 183, 184, 186
    Loss Payment 185
    Other than Collision 185
    Part A - Liability Coverage 180–183
    Part B - Medical Payments 183–184
    Part C - Uninsured Motorist 184
    Part D - Coverage for Damage to Your Auto 185–186
    Part E - Duties After an Accident or Loss 186
    Part F - General Provisions 187
    Policy Definitions 179
    Split Limits 181
Personal Injury
    Liability Coverage 170
Personal Liability 163
    Characteristics of 189
    Self-Insured Retention 190
Personal Liability Umbrella Policy (PLUP) 189–190
Personal Property 25, 160
Physical Hazard 13, 52
Point of Service Plans (POS) 129
Policy Loan Provisions 86
Preexisting Conditions 130
Preferred Provider Organizations (PPO) 129, 240
Premium 17
Primary Insurance Amount (PIA) 217
Principle of Indemnity 20
Principle of Insurable Interest 21
Principle of Utmost Good Faith 22
    Concealment 23
    Representation 22
    Warranty 23
Probability of Loss 4
Product Liability Insurance 193
Property Insurance 21
    Business Auto Policy (BAP) 192
    Commercial Package Policy (CPP) 190
    Inland Marine Policy 191
    Personal Property 160
    See Business and Professional Policies
    See Homeowners Insurance
    See Personal Auto Policy (PAP)
    See Personal Liability Umbrella Policy (PLUP)

Provider Sponsored Organization (PSO) 240
Pure Risk 2

R

Recovered Property 173
Reduced Paid-Up Insurance 80
Refrigerated Property Coverage 169
Reinstatement 86
Renewability 131–132
    Conditionally Renewable Policies 132
    Guaranteed Renewable Policies 132
    Non-Cancelable Policies 132
    Optionally Renewable Policies 132
Renters Insurance 167
Replacement Cost 35, 159, 160, 167, 168
Replacement Value 171
Representation 22
Retirement Earnings Limitations Test 224
Rising Water Property Damage 158
Risk
    Insurable Risk 14–18
Risk Avoidance 9
Risk Categories 2–5
    Financial Risk 4
    Fundamental Risk 3
    Law of Large Numbers 4
    Nonfinancial Risk 4
    Objective Risk 3
    Particular Risk 4
    Probability of Loss 4
    Pure Risk 2
    Speculative Risk 2
    Subjective Risk 3
Risk Management 5–11
    Evaluating Risk 7
    Evaluation of Plan 10
    Identifying Risk 6
    Implementation of Plan 10
    Risk Reduction 8
    Risk Retention 9
    Risk Transfer 8
Risk Management Process
    Risk Avoidance 9
Risk Reduction 8
Risk Retention 9
Risk Transfer 8

S

Second-to-Die Policy 77

Section I
    Conditions 171–173, 174
    Coverage 158
    Duties of the Insured 171
    Loss Settlement 171–173
Section II
    Conditions 173–174
    Coverage 162
Settlement Options 89–91
    Annuity Payments 89–91
    Interest Only 89
    Lump-Sum Payment 89
Seven-Pay Test 82
Sewer Backup Coverage 169
Simultaneous Death Provision 88
Skilled Care Facility 142
Slander 187
Social Security 203
    Average Indexed Monthly Earnings (AIME) 214
    Bend Points 219
    Beneficiaries of 210
    Benefits of 203
    COLA 219
    Currently Insured 210, 212
    Disability Benefit 204
    Disability Insured 232
    Early and Late Retirement Options 220
    Earnings Limitations Test 224
    Family Benefit 204
    Filing for 241
    Fully Insured 209, 210, 232, 246, 259
    Hurdle Amounts 228
    Maximum Family Benefit 234
    Primary Insurance Amount (PIA) 217
    Quarters of Coverage 209
    Reduction of Benefits 224
    Retirement Benefit 213, 220
        Calculation of 214
    Survivors' Benefit 204
    Taxation of Benefits 226
Social Security Administration 203
Speculative Risk 2
SSI (Supplemental Security Income) 241
Subjective Risk 3
Subrogation 174
Suicide 86
Supplemental Security Income Benefits 241
Supplementary Medical Insurance (SMI) Trust Fund 207
Surrender Charges 79
Survivorship Clause 87

T

Taxation of Life Insurance 91–96
    Death Benefit Taxation 92
    Lifetime Benefits 92
    Policy Exchanges 94
    Premium Payments 91
    Viatical Settlements 95
Term Insurance 68–73
    Annual Renewable Term (ART) 70
    Decreasing-Term Insurance 71
    Level-Term Insurance 71

U

Unauthorized Use of Credit Cards 162
Underinsured Motorist 184
Unilateral 25
Uninsured Motorist 184
    See Personal Auto Policy (PAP)
Universal Life Insurance 73–75

V

Variable Life Insurance 80–81
Variable Universal Life Insurance Policies (VULs) 81
Variable Whole Life Policies 77
Veterinary Surgical Consultants, P.C. v. C.I.R. 208
Viatical Settlements 95
Vicarious Liability 177, 188, 189
Volcanic Eruption 173

W

War Exclusion in Life Insurance 89
Warranty 23
Watercraft Coverage 170
Whole Life Insurance 75–79
    First-to-Die Policy 77
    Limited-Pay Policies 76
    Modified Whole Life Policy 76
    Policy Dividends 77
    Second-to-Die Policy 77
    Surrender Charges 79
    Taxation of 79
Workers' Compensation 192